CHANCERY BOOKS
of
CARROLL COUNTY
Maryland

Volumes 1-20
1837-1873

Abstracted by
Virginia D. Stenley

HERITAGE BOOKS
2009

HERITAGE BOOKS
AN IMPRINT OF HERITAGE BOOKS, INC.

Books, CDs, and more—Worldwide

For our listing of thousands of titles see our website
at
www.HeritageBooks.com

Published 2009 by
HERITAGE BOOKS, INC.
Publishing Division
100 Railroad Ave. #104
Westminster, Maryland 21157

Copyright © 1994, 1995 Virginia D. Stenley

Other books by the author:
Chancery Books of Carroll County, Maryland, Volumes 21-40, 1873-1889

All rights reserved. No part of this book may be reproduced or transmitted in any form or by any means, electronic or mechanical, including photocopying, recording or by any information storage and retrieval system without written permission from the author, except for the inclusion of brief quotations in a review.

International Standard Book Numbers
Paperbound: 978-1-58549-356-2
Clothbound: 978-0-7884-8083-6

Introduction

I discovered this source of genealogical information while working as a title abstractor in the Land Records of Carroll County. Since I worked around them every day I soon realized that only a handful of people knew of their existence and that they were almost always overlooked in the search for historical information.

The Equity Court of Carroll County was begun in April 1837 when the county was formed from parts of Frederick and Baltimore Counties. Several years ago these earlier Equity documents were moved to the State Archives, in Annapolis, for safekeeping. However, if an Equity case involved real estate, the proceedings were also transcribed into the Chancery Books. When having to research an old Equity case, I found it was sometimes easier to look in the Chancery Books than to search through the originals, mainly due to their deterioration. These cases deal with mortgage foreclosures, partition or sale of real estate to settle an estate, sale of real estate to satisfy creditors, divorces, etc. The Chancery Books are kept at the office of the Clerk of the Circuit Court.

This book should be used as an aid to further research. On finding something of interest, I would recommend that you go to the Clerk's Office and look at the Chancery records. They will contain many more facts than I have recorded, possibly such details as ages, health status, property plats and descriptions, neighbors, etc. If you want to examine the original documents, you may examine them at the Maryland State Archives, 350 Rowe Blvd., Annapolis, Maryland 21401. You can also make a request in advance to the Clerk of the Circuit Court, Room G8, 55 North Center St., Westminster, Maryland 21158-0190 that the records be sent there for examination.

I have noted the landmarks pertaining to the real property whenever possible, to establish the area in which the people lived. If only the land patent names were given, the Tracey Land Records can help you to pinpoint the region. This collection is located at the Historical Society of Carroll County, 210 East Main Street, Westminster, MD 21157. Individuals are assumed to have been residents of Carroll County unless otherwise noted; I have included names of slaves when surnames were given.

Virginia D. Stenley
Taneytown, Maryland
1994

Chancery Book 1, pp. 1-7   1837   Equity #1
Petition of Comfort Durbin and others. Sale of real estate.
Benjamin Durbin, of Frederick County, died 1813, testate, leaving widow Susannah Durbin, who died Dec 1836. Children: Ellen Mattingly, deceased, wife of Samuel Mattingly, mother of Charles Mattingly, Susannah Lowery, Hannah Mattingly, and Rebecca Logsden; Nancy Mattingly, deceased, wife of Henry Mattingly, mother of Dominic Mattingly, Harriet (or Honorah) Kemp, Eliza Mattingly, Benjamin Mattingly, John Mattingly, William Mattingly, and Susannah Mattingly; Comfort Durbin; Margaret Durbin; Rebecca Fowler, wife of Edward Fowler; and Catherine Durbin. Also named in Benjamin's will were grandchildren: Joseph Arnold; Margaret Arnold; Mary Arnold; Susanna Arnold; Ellenor Fowler; and Benjamin Fowler.
Property situate 2-1/2 miles from Westminster, being parts of *Iron Intention Resurveyed*, *Broad Meadow*, *Grave Yard* and *William's Luck*.

Chancery Book 1, pp. 7-15   1837   Equity #4
In the matter of the Petition of Catherine Shade, John Nace, and others. Sale of real estate.
Peter Nace, the Elder, of Baltimore County, died c. 1832, testate, leaving widow, Dellatha Nace. Children: George Nace; Mary Bachman, deceased, wife of Henry Bachman, no issue; Catherine Shade, widow of John Shade; Elizabeth Vaughan, wife of Christopher Vaughan; John Nace; Jacob Nace, deceased, father of Jacob Nace, Peter Nace, Jeremiah Nace, Noah Nace, Augustus D. Nace, Loreney Nace, Indiana Nace, and Independence Nace; Ruth Linaweaver, wife of George Linaweaver; Sarah Motter, wife of George Motter; Peter Nace; and Margaret Gittier, wife of Jacob Gittier.
Property situate 2-1/2 miles from Manchester on Baltimore Turnpike, being parts of *Everything Needful*, *Everything Needful Corrected*, *Scheaming Defeated*, *Petersburgh* and *Petersburg Resurveyed*.

Chancery Book 1, pp. 15-34   1837   Equity #6
John A. Byers and Helena Byers vs. Susan Zecharias, Susan Shaeffer, Joseph Shaeffer, and others. Sale of real estate.
George Daniel Zecharias, of Frederick County, died intestate. Children: Daniel Zecharias, deceased, father of Helena Byers (wife of John A. Byers), and Appolonia Reifsnider (wife of Jesse Reifsnider); George Zecharias, deceased, husband of Susan Zecharias, father of Susan Shaeffer (wife of Joseph Shaeffer), Savilla Zecharias, Conrad Zecharias, Jacob Zecharias, Elizabeth Zecharias, and Mary Zecharias; Rachel Troxall, wife of Jacob Troxall; Elizabeth Trimble, wife of William Trimble; and Mary Reese, wife of John Reese.
Property being parts of *Cover's Adventure*, *Zecharias Lot*, *Key's Industry* and *Resurvey on Lookabout*.

Chancery Book 1, pp. 35-43   1837   Equity #7
John Myers vs. Joseph Lantz and wife, John Formwalt, and others. Foreclosure.
Joseph Lantz, and his wife, Rachel Lantz.
Property situate in Westminster area, on Littlestown Pike, being part of *Fanny's Meadow*.

Chancery Book 1, pp. 44-53   1837   Equity #9
Frederick Town Savings Institution vs. John H. Crump. Foreclosure.
John H. Crump, and his wife, Mary Jane Crump.
Property formerly situate in Frederick County, 1-1/2 miles from Taneytown.

Chancery Book 1, pp. 53-65   1837   Equity #10
George S. Sherman vs. Thomas Kellead and J. Henry Hoppe, and others. Foreclosure.
Thomas Kellead.
Property being part of *Cleary's New Holland*.

Chancery Book 1, pp. 65-73   1838   Equity #13
In the matter of the Petition of Jacob Morelock and Susannah, his wife, next friend of David Brown and William Brown, Infants. Sale of real estate.
John Brown died intestate, leaving widow Susannah Brown, now Susannah Morelock, wife of Jacob Morelock. Children: Davious Brown; and William Brown.
Property situate 4 miles from Westminster on Cranberry Creek.

Chancery Book 1, pp. 73-87   1838   Equity #14
Henry Dell and Sarah Dell, his wife, vs. David Weaver, and others.
Sale of real estate.
Daniel Weaver died c. 1820, intestate. Children: David Weaver; Elizabeth McClellan, widow of Samuel McClellan; George Weaver; Sarah Dell, wife of Henry Dell; Ruth Weaver; and an unnamed child, deceased, w/o issue.
Property situate in and near Westminster, being parts of *The Resurvey of Bedford*, *Winter's Addition to Westminster* and *Rochester*.

Chancery Book 1, pp. 87-105   1838   Equity #16
Francis Brothers, and others vs. Elias Ogg, and others. Sale of real estate.
Joshua Brothers, of Baltimore County, died c. 26 Feb 1836, intestate. Children: Francis Brothers; Benjamin Brothers; Elias Brothers; Catherine Ogg, wife of Elias Ogg; Providence Barnes, wife of Solomon Barnes; Susan Caple, wife of William Caple of William; Ruth Houck, deceased, wife of Larkin Houck,

mother of Annastatia Houck and Joshua Houck; and William Brothers, deceased, husband of Elizabeth Brothers, and father of Nancy Brothers, Joshua Brothers, Thomas Brothers, Elizabeth Brothers, and Rebecca Brothers (all of PA).
Property formerly situate in Baltimore County, being parts of *Glendoick, Hammond Meadows* and *John Pleasant Meadow*.

Chancery Book 1, pp. 105-120   1838   Equity #19
Jacob Erb, Exr. of Peter Erb, deceased vs. Peter Erb, Jr., Abraham Erb, and others. Sale of real estate.
Peter Erb, of Frederick County, died 1836, testate. Children: Peter Erb, Jr.; Abraham Erb; Eli Erb; Eliza Koontz, wife of George Koontz; and Levi Erb.
Property situate near Taneytown-Westminster Turnpike, being part of *Molly's Fancy*.

Chancery Book 1, pp. 121-143   1838   Equity #22
Joseph Harden and Helena Harden, his wife, and others vs. Robert Welsh and others. Sale of real estate.
Mary Welsh, single woman, died 10 March 1838, intestate, probably the daughter of John Welsh, left no child, husband, brother, or sister. Heirs were descendants of her deceased brother, John Welsh, and two deceased sisters, Margaret Phillips and Catherine Manro, all who died before Mary. Margaret Phillips' children were: Thomas Phillips; and Polly Lenox, of OH, wife of John Lenox. Catherine Manro's children were: Helena Harden, wife of Joseph Harden; James Manro, of OH, husband of Sarah Manro; Squire Manro, of OH; Thomas Manro, of OH; David Manro, of OH; and Sarah Chambers, deceased, mother of Helena Chambers and Mary Chambers (both of MO). John Welsh's children were: Ferdinand Welsh; William Welsh; Mary Ann Welsh; Maria Waters, wife of Jacob Waters; Ann E. Bond, wife of Benjamin Bond; Jane Welsh; Robert Welsh; Lydia Welsh; and John Welsh, deceased, husband of Susanna, father of Sarah Elizabeth Welsh (of VA).
Property formerly situate in Baltimore County, 1 mile from Eldersburgh, and 19 miles from Baltimore, north of Liberty Road, being part of *Arabia Petria Enlarged*.

Chancery Book 1, pp. 144-162   1838   Equity #23
Onellana Owings and Thomas B. Owings vs. Thornton Poole and Rachel R. Poole, his wife, and others. Sale of real estate.
Dr. Thomas B. Owings died Oct 1835, intestate, leaving widow Cordelia Owings. Children: Onellana Owings; Thomas B. Owings; Rachel R. Poole, wife of Thornton Poole; Celius W. Owings; and Cordelia E. Owings.

Properties situate in Carroll And Frederick counties. Some near Liberty, New Market, Ridgeville and Franklinville. Being parts of *Resurvey on Gilboa, Caleb's Delight Enlarged, Bite Him Softly, Peter's Garden Enlarged, Paris Range* and *Shivers Integrity*.

Chancery Book 1, pp. 162-176   1838   Equity #24
Amos Hooker and Lloyd Hooker vs. James S. Hooker, Amos Hooker, and others. Sale of real estate.
Jacob Hooker died c. 1818, testate, leaving widow, Mary Hooker, who died 16 June 1838. Children: Jesse Hooker, deceased, father of James S. Hooker (of Baltimore County); Amos Hooker; Lloyd Hooker; Susanne Hooker, deceased, died testate; John Hooker, deceased father of Amos Hooker (of Baltimore County); Elizabeth Peddicord, wife of Humphrey Peddicord, mother of Mary Ann Peddicord; Charlotte Brown, deceased, wife of Joel Brown, mother of Hester Ann Brown (of OH), Margaret Brown (of OH), Joel Brown (of OH), and Rachel Brown (of OH).
Property situate on Baltimore-Westminster Road, being parts of *Long Meadow, Stephen's Folly Resurveyed, Simon's Delight, Blindfold* and *Flaggs Meadow*.

Chancery Book 1, pp. 177-199   1838   Equity #25
Peter Geiger, John Roop, of Joseph, and Joseph Englar, of David vs. Sarah Smeltzer and others. Sale of real estate to satisfy creditors.
George Smeltzer died, leaving widow, Sarah Smeltzer. Children: Josiah Pearce Smeltzer; Isaac Washington Smeltzer; and Carolina Louisana Smeltzer.
Property situate 1-1/4 miles from New Windsor, being parts of *Stevenson's Lot, Resurvey on Good Will* and *Stevenson's Garden*.

Chancery Book 1, pp. 200-204   1838   Equity #26
John Worthington vs. Samuel Jordan.   Foreclosure
Samuel Jordan.
Property being parts of *Caledonia Since Resurvey* and *Edinburgh*.

Chancery Book 1, pp. 205-211   1838   Equity #27
Bill of William B. Gwinn vs. James Getty and Catherine Getty, his wife, and others. Sale of real estate
Mary Crouse, heir of Jacob Good, died intestate. Children: William B. Gwinn; Catherine Getty, wife of James Getty; Washington Gwinn; Ellen M. Gwinn; Mary E. Gwinn; and John Gwinn.
Properties were situate in or near Taneytown, some on Emmittsburg and Gettysburg roads, various lots on the present West Baltimore and York streets, and town lots #3 through #24, being part of *Brother's Agreement*.

Chancery Book 1, pp. 212-218   1839   Equity #34
Petition of William Lampert, next friend of George Lampert and Andrew I. Lampert, Infants. Sale of real estate.
Michael Lampert died, leaving children: George Lampert and Andrew I. Lampert. Brother was William Lampert.
Property situate 2 miles from Westminster.

Chancery Book 1, pp. 218-228   1839   Equity #41
Chancery Book 2, pp. 72-74
Basil Hayden vs. John Hayden, and others. Sale of real estate.
William Hayden, of Baltimore County, died 15 May 1832, testate, leaving widow, Catherine Hayden, since deceased. Children: Basil Hayden; John Hayden; Eleanor Logsden, wife of Joseph Logsden; Catherine Corban, deceased, wife of William Corban; Anna Durbin, wife of Daniel Durbin; Dennis Hayden; James Hayden; Richard Hayden, deceased, father of William Hayden, Agatha Wolf (wife of Abigal Wolf), and Richard Hayden; Ambrose Hayden, deceased, father of Theresa Ann Hayden; and William Hayden.
Properties situate near Westminster, being parts of *Glendoick* and *Friendship Completed*.

Chancery Book 1, pp. 229-237   1839   Equity #38
Stephen Keys and William Sullivan vs. David Keys and others. Sale of real estate to satisfy creditors.
Elizabeth Keys died intestate, leaving brother, David Keys, and his son, Samuel Keys.
Property situate 4 miles from Westminster on Littlestown Turnpike, being part of *Honor Delight*.

Chancery Book 1, pp. 237-245   1839   Equity #42
Frederick Ritter, and others vs. Heirs at Law of John Ritter, Jr. Sale of real estate.
John Ritter, of Baltimore County, died. Children: Frederick Ritter; Michael Ritter; Lewis Ritter; Catherine Humburg, wife of George Humburg; Mary Crumrin, wife of Daniel Crumrin; Barbara Hinkle, wife of George Hinkle; Jacob Ritter, husband of Polly Ritter; John Ritter, deceased, of OH, husband of Mary Ann Ritter, and father of 5 minor children, names unknown.
Property situate c. 3 miles from Manchester on Westminster-Manchester Road.

Chancery Book 1, pp. 245-258   1840   Equity #48
Thomas E. Stocksdale and wife, and others vs. Cornelius Stocksdale, and others. Sale of real estate.

Edmund H. Stocksdale, of Baltimore County, died c. 13 May 1836, intestate. Children: Thomas E. Stocksdale, husband of Eliza Stocksdale; Solomon Stocksdale, husband of Dolly Stocksdale; Edmund H. Stocksdale; Sarah Whalen, deceased, mother of Thomas Fisher (husband of Sophia Fisher), Catherine Canouff (wife of William Canouff), Ann Rebecca Whalen, and Martha Whalen; Rebecca Gosnell, wife of Jesse Gosnell; Cornelius H. Stocksdale, of KY, formerly of Philadelphia PA, husband of Mathilda Stocksdale; and Nathan Stocksdale, deceased, father of Julia H. Stocksdale (of Philadelphia, PA). Edmund had deceased brother, Nathan Stocksdale.

Property situate in Freedom District, near Westminster-Washington Road, c. 8 miles from Westminster, being parts of *Caledonia* and *Edinburgh*.

Chancery Book 1, pp. 258-265   1839   Equity #45
Robert Crawford and Eve Crawford, his wife, and others vs. Sarah Humbert. Sale of real estate.
Catharine Humbert died April 1838, intestate, unmarried, and w/o issue. Brothers and sisters were: Eve Crawford, wife of Robert Crawford; Magdalena Fisher, wife of Jacob Fisher; Aaron Humbert, deceased, father of John Humbert, Peter Humbert, George Humbert, Mary Shealer (wife of Anthony Shealer), Michael Humbert, Catherine Humbert, Aaron Humbert, Daniel Humbert, and Sarah Humbert; Michael Humbert, deceased, father of Sarah Tunious (wife of Charles Tunious); and Frederick Humbert, deceased, father of Henry Humbert, Susanna Humbert and Mary Harrison (wife of Benjamin Harrison).
Location of property not given.

Chancery Book 1, pp. 265-271   1840   Equity #54
David Kiler, Exr. of Simon Kiler vs. Jacob Greenholtz.   Foreclosure Jacob Greenholtz.
Property being parts of *York Company Defense* and *Rich Meadow*.

Chancery Book 1, pp. 271-285   1838   Equity #30
James Connor and Hannah L. Conner, his wife, and others vs. John Harris, Henrietta Harris, and others.   Sale of real estate.
John Harris died testate. Children: William Harris, deceased, father of Mary J. Harris (of Boston MA), Hannah L. Conner (of Westmoreland County PA, wife of James Conner), Ann E. Hart (of Frederick County, wife of William A. Hart), Maria Wharfe Harris (of Westmoreland County PA), John Harris (of Westmoreland County PA), Henrietta Harris (of Westmoreland County PA), Eliza J. Harris (of Westmoreland County PA), and Louisa C. Harris (of Westmoreland County PA); Nancy Harris; Judah Biggoth; and Susanna Liver.
Property situate near Monocacy River, being part of *Harrisburgh*.

Chancery Book 1, pp. 286-297 1841 Equity #63
Joshua Green, Thomas Green, and others vs. James Givens and wife, and others. Sale of real estate.
Shadrack Green, of Baltimore County, died testate, leaving wife, Rachel Green. Children: Joshua Green; Thomas Green; Rachel Green, wife of Joshua B. Green; Ann Bosley, wife of Joshua Bosley; Matilda Miles, wife of Abraham Miles; Elizabeth Givens, of KY, wife of James Givens; Airey Ann Givens, of KY, wife of Moses Givens; Sarah Sparks, deceased, wife of Laban Sparks, mother of Mathilda Sparks, Cecilia Sparks, and Airetta Sparks; and Temperance Mays, deceased, wife of John Mays, Sr., mother of Elizabeth Miller (wife of Robert Miller), Rachel Miller (wife of Stephen Miller), John Mays, Jr., and Thomas Mays.
Property situate 2 miles south of Manchester, being part of *Everything Needful Corrected.*

Chancery Book 1, pp. 297-308 1840 Equity #56
David A. Snider vs. Mary Magdalena Snider, and others. Sale of real estate.
George Snider died 4 Feb 1839, leaving widow, Susannah Snider. Children: David A. Snider; Mary Magdalene Snider; William Snider; Catherine Snider; George Washington Snider; and Daniel Snider.
Property situate 5 miles from Westminster on Westminster-Manchester Road, being parts of *Richards Lot, Addition to Richards Lot, Iron Intention, Stansbury's Prospect* and *John Fancy Enlarged.*

Chancery Book 2, pp. 1-20 1839 Equity #46
John Gross vs. Jacob Shearer, Admr., and others. Sale of real estate to satisfy creditors.
Henry Gross died intestate, leaving only brothers and sisters: Elizabeth Shearer, wife of Jacob Shearer; Catherine Sentz, deceased, wife of Philip Sentz, mother of Mary Sentz and Rachel Sentz (all of Pittsburgh PA); Mary M. Miller, wife of Jacob Miller; and half brother, John Gross.
Property formerly situate in Baltimore County, being part of *Walker's Paradise Resurveyed.*

Chancery Book 2, pp. 20-29 1839 Equity #35
James Smith and Ann Eliza Smith, his wife vs. George Price, and others. Sale of real estate.
Richard Coale, of Frederick County, died 22 July 1834, testate, leaving grandchildren (children of George Price): Ann Eliza Smith, wife of James Smith; George Price; Catharine Price; and James Price.
Property situate midway between Taneytown and Middleburg.

Chancery Book 2, pp. 30-52   1840   Equity #52
Ann Roberts vs. William Poole, and others.   Sale of real estate to satisfy creditors.
William Poole died c. Oct 1839, intestate. Children: William Poole, Jr.; Thomas Poole; John Poole, of TN; Ann Zimmerman, widow of Jacob Zimmerman; Mary Neff, widow of Samuel Neff; Frances Poole; Thomsey Danner, wife of John Danner; Ellen Poole; Margaret Poole; Dennis Poole, deceased, died Oct 1840, c. 12 years old; and Charles Poole.
Various properties situate in or near New Windsor.

Chancery Book 2, pp. 52-60   1840   Equity #57
Joshua Vaughn, and others vs. Caleb Vaughn, and others.   Sale of real estate.
Richard Vaughn died. Children: Caleb Vaughn, out of state; Thomas Vaughn, out of state; Tabitha Strong, out of state, wife of Charles Strong; Joshua Vaughn, of Frederick County; Mary Vaughn, of Frederick County MD; Ruth Sharer, of Frederick County, wife of Jacob Sharer; Elizabeth Anders, of Frederick County, wife of Henry Anders; Rebecca Shue, out of state; and Amelia Parks, out of state.
Property being part of *Richards Hunting Ground*.

Chancery Book 2, pp. 60-72   1842   Equity #90
Petition of Basil Perry Brown for the division of the real estate of William Brown, late of Carroll County, dec.   Division of real estate into lots.
William Brown died c. March 1838, intestate, leaving widow, Ann W. Brown. Children: Thomas C. Brown; William A. T. Brown; Benjamin F. Brown; Jamima E. Brown; Lucinda R. I. Brown; Rebecca M. W. Brown; Mary Ann Brown; Susanna D. Brown; Ann Virginia Brown; and Basil Perry Brown.
Property being parts of *Brown's Free and Independent Prospect, Victory, Fine Soil Forrest, Hunter's Chance* and *Deaver's Forrest*.

Chancery Book 2, pp. 74-82   1841   Equity #76
Petition of Susannah Shaffer, Elizabeth Shaffer, and others.   Sale of real estate.
John Reichart, Sr., died testate, leaving widow, Elizabeth Reichart, who died Feb 1841. Children: Susannah Shaffer, widow of Benjamin Shaffer; Elizabeth Shaffer, widow of Andrew Shaffer; Magadalina Keeffer, deceased, wife of John Keeffer, mother of Daniel Keeffer, Judy Hammond (widow of Phillip Hammond), Susannah Keeffer, Elizabeth Keeffer, and Ferdinand Keeffer; Amelia Albaugh, deceased, wife of Abraham Albaugh, mother of John Albaugh, Zachariah Albaugh, Lydia Miller (wife of Amon Miller), and Abraham Albaugh; and John Reichart.
Property consisted of 7 lots.

Chancery Book 2, pp. 83-93 1840 Equity #60
Magdalena Bushman vs. Adam Tailor and Elizabeth Tailor, his wife, and others. Sale of real estate.
Henry Miller died intestate, without issue, wife or brothers. His sisters were: Magdalena Bushman, of Adams County PA, widow of Andrew Bushman; and Catherine Bushman, deceased, wife of Jacob Bushman, mother of Elizabeth Tailor (of Bedford County PA, wife of Adam Tailor), Mary Bushman (of OH), Henry Bushman (of Adams County PA), Susannah Tailor (of Bedford County PA, wife of Jacob Tailor), John Bushman (of Allegheny County PA), Rachel Barkley (of Adams County PA, wife of Frederick Barkley), Jacob Bushman (of OH), Fanny Kauffman (of Franklin County PA, wife of David Kauffman), and Margaret Bushman (of OH).
Property near PA line in Myers District, being parts of *Ohio* and *Shriver's Bottom*.

Chancery Book 2, pp. 94-100 1842 Equity #101
Chancery Book 3, pp. 240-245
John Colhoon, Ann Philips Colhoon, and others vs. Edward Ireland.
Chancery Book 5, pp. 382-385
Edward Ireland, Jr., and Elizabeth H. Ireland, his wife vs. Jesse Hollingsworth. Changes to Trust.
John Colhoon and his wife, Ann Philips Colhoon (nee Hollingsworth). She died 19 Jan 1845. Children: Benjamin C. Colhoon, died intestate, unmarried and w/o issue; Elizabeth H. Ireland, wife of Edward Ireland, Jr.; and Mary C. Colhoon, died as infant, intestate, and w/o issue.
Property being parts of *John's Choice, Forest Level, Hammonds Fine Soil Forest* and *Owens Outland Plains*.

Chancery Book 2, pp. 100-112 1843 Equity #111
Daniel Batson vs. The heirs of John Wampler, deceased. Completion of sale.
John Wampler, of Frederick County, died 27 July 1831, intestate, leaving widow, Elizabeth Wampler. Children: Samuel Wampler; Catherine Wampler; Sarah Ann Kuhn, wife of John Kuhn; Lydia Kelly, wife of John A. Kelly; Henry H. Wampler; James S. Wampler; George E. Wampler; Maria L. Wampler; William A. Wampler; and Emily Jane Wampler.
Property formerly situate in Baltimore County, being parts of *Bucks Range Resurveyed, Cambridge* and *Peter's Discovery Enlarged*.

Chancery Book 2, pp. 112-127   1841   Equity #66
William Crumrine and Lydia Crumrine, his wife, and others vs. Lewis Kroh, and others. Sale of real estate.
John Weaver died, leaving widow, Catherine Weaver. Children: Lydia Crumrine, wife of William Crumrine; Catherine Sellers, wife of John Sellers; Mary Morelock, wife of Michael Morelock, Jr.; Susanah Morelock, wife of Jacob Morelock; Julia Ann Kroh, wife of John Kroh; Elizabeth Kroh, of OH, wife of Lewis Kroh; John Weaver, of OH; Barbara Sellman, of OH, wife of Beall Sellman; Samuel Weaver, of OH; Anne Weaver, an idiot; and George Weaver, deceased, w/o issue.
Properties situate in or near Manchester, some on Bachman's Valley Road. Being parts of *United Friendship, Cornwall's Desire, Wells Care, Lippy's Addition, Klinck's Beginning, Prospect, German Church, Old Fort* and *Worms*.

Chancery Book 2, pp. 127-149   1841   Equity #65
Elizabeth Kautz, George Warehame and Conrad Warehame, Excrs. of Henry Warehame, deceased, vs. Nancy Kautz, Joshua Kautz and Henry Kautz, Admrs. of Michael Kautz. Sale of real estate to satisfy creditors.
Michael Kautz, of Baltimore County, died c. 1836, intestate, leaving widow, Nancy Kautz, and only child, Joshua Kautz.
Property formerly situate in Baltimore County, being parts of *Richard's Lot, Addition to Richard's Lot, Walker's Paradise* and *Small Bit*.

Chancery Book 2, pp. 150-159   1841   Equity #81
George Connand, Martin Danner, Exrs. of Andrew Cramer vs. John Fowble, of Jacob. Foreclosure.
John Fowble, of Jacob, of Baltimore County.
Property situate in or near Hampstead, being part of *Petersburg Resurveyed*.

Chancery Book 2, pp. 160-172   1841   Equity #78
John Logsdon, and others vs. Prudence Logsdon and Mary Ellen Logsdon. Sale of real estate.
John Logsdon, Sr., died 1826, intestate. Children: John Logsdon, of New Castle DE; Anna Logsdon, of Frederick County; William Logsdon, of New Orleans LA; Honor Logsdon, of Frederick County; Prudence A. Logsdon, of Baltimore City; Mary Ellen Logsdon, of Frederick County; and James Logsdon, deceased, w/o issue.
Property formerly situate in Frederick County, being part of *Bond's Meadow Enlarged*.

Chancery Book 2, pp. 172-198   1842   Equity #102
Jacob Bixler, John Bixler, and others vs. Mary Ann Bowman. Sale of real estate.

Jacob Bixler (probably son of Jacob Bixler, Sr., and Elizabeth Bixler, his wife) died c. Aug 1842, intestate, leaving widow, Barbara Bixler. Children: Jacob Bixler; John Bixler; Sarah Fink, wife of Solomon Fink; Catharine Bailey, wife of Daniel Bailey; Rachel Foreman, wife of John Foreman; Barbara Shaffer, wife of Jesse Shaffer; Magdalena Bowman, deceased, wife of George Bowman, mother of Mary Ann Bowman; and Elizabeth Fisher, widow of George Fisher. Property formerly situate in Baltimore County, near Manchester, being parts of *Everything Needful Corrected*, *Wells Care Enlarged* and *Batchelors Prospect*.

Chancery Book 2, pp. 198-212 1842 Equity #108
Jacob Brungart, and others vs. George Brungart, and others. Sale of real estate.
John Brungart (or Brunicord) died 1842, intestate, leaving widow, Barbara Brungart. Had only one child who died at birth. Brothers and sisters: Jacob Brungart, of York County PA; Mary Brungart, of York County PA; George Brungart, of Columbiana County OH; Elizabeth Bangue, of Adams County PA, wife of George Bangue; Catharine Condo, of Columbiana County OH, wife of George Condo; and Margaret Newcomer, deceased, wife of John Newcomer, of OH, mother of Sarah Fuhrman (of Clark County OH, wife of Frederick Fuhrman), Margaret Rohrbaugh (of York County PA, wife of Solomon Rohrbaugh), and Mary Ann Newcomer, of York County PA.
Property formerly situate in Baltimore County, in Manchester District, c. 4-1/2 miles from Manchester on Manchester-York Road, being parts of *Mattingan* and *Stoney Point*.

Chancery Book 2, pp. 213-235 1843 Equity #113
Francis Haines vs. John Yingling and wife, and others. Sale of real estate.
Christian Yingling, of Baltimore County, died c. Oct 1824, testate, leaving widow, Molly Yingling, who died c. Jan 1843. Children: John Yingling, husband of Magdalena Snyder Yingling; George Yingling, husband of Sarah Hinkle Yingling; Jacob Yingling, husband of Catherine Snyder Yingling; David Yingling, husband of Lydia Shaffer Yingling; Polly Yingling, unmarried, deceased, intestate, mother of Catherine Yingling Richart (widow of David Richart); Rachel Snyder, wife of Michael Snyder; and Susanna Utz, out of state, wife of Michael Utz.
Property formerly situate in Baltimore County, in Manchester District, c. 4 miles from Manchester and 1-1/2 miles from Bachman's Mills, being parts of *Iron Intention* and *John's Pleasure*.

Chancery Book 2, pp. 235-253 1841 Equity #62
Elizabeth Brothers vs. Thomas Miller and Elias Brothers.
Claim of widow's dower.

Joshua Brothers died c. Feb 1836, leaving widow, Elizabeth Brothers.
Property formerly situate in Baltimore County, being parts of *Glendoick* and *Hammond's Choice*.

Chancery Book 2, pp. 253-275   1841   Equity #67
Chancery Book 2, pp. 551-552
Nicholas H. Brown, and others vs. George Brown, and others.   Sale of real estate.
Nicholas Hall Brown died testate, leaving widow, Ruth Brown, who died 21 Mar 1841. Children: Belinda Barnes, wife of William Barnes; William Stansbury Brown; Nicholas Hall Brown; Nelson Brown; Ruth Brown; Susan Brown; George Brown; Elizabeth Ann Price, wife of Thomas Price; Andrew Jackson Brown; Charles Westley Brown; and Charity Brown.
Property situate near Westminster, being parts of *Brown's Plague, Fanny's Meadow, Addition to Good Run Resurveyed on Dairy, York Company Defense* and *Rochester*.

Chancery Book 2, pp. 276-308   1842   Equity #99
Chancery Book 3, pp. 256-258
James Crocket, and others vs. William Rudisel and Thomas Rudisel, Exrs., and others. Sale of real estate to satisfy creditors.
Ludwick Rudisel died c. July 1842, testate, leaving widow, Nancy Rudisel. Children: William Rudisel; Thomas Rudisel; Tobias Rudisel; Alice Motter, wife of Lewis Motter; Sarah Grabil, of Frederick County, wife of Peter Grabil; Anna Rudisel; and Margaret Rudisel.
Properties situate in and near Taneytown, being parts of *Resurvey on Brother's Agreement* and *New York*.

Chancery Book 2, pp. 308-321   1842   Equity #104
Henry Elder and Ann Elder, his wife, and others vs. Catherine Elder, and others. Sale of real estate.
Catherine Elder, died 1836. Children: Monacai Clabaugh, wife of James Clabaugh; Henry Elder, of Baltimore County, husband of Ann Elder; Lucy Hand (or Hahn), of PA, wife of Harry Hand; Hilary Elder, deceased, father (with first wife) of Francis Elder (of Baltimore), Elizabeth Elder (of Baltimore), and Catherine Shaw (of Baltimore, wife of Erasmus Shaw), and father (with second wife and widow, Catherine Elder) of Mary Ann Elder, Susan Elder, Eleanora Elder, Margaret Elder, and Lucy Ann Elder (all of Baltimore); and Catherine Elder, of Emmittsburg, Frederick County.
Property situate in Taneytown, known as Lot 32.

Chancery Book 2, pp. 322-336 1842 Equity #106
Reuben Conaway, and others vs. Amelia Conaway, and others. Sale of real estate.
Charles W. Conaway, son of John Conaway and his wife, Amelia Conaway, died Nov 1840, intestate, leaving widow, Sarah Ann Conaway, w/o issue. Brothers and sisters: Reuben Conaway; Cornelius Conaway, of OH; Hail Columbus Conaway, of IN; Louisa Shipley, wife of Grove Shipley; Cordelia Shipley, wife of John F. Shipley; John O. Conaway, deceased, father of Amelia P. Conaway, of IN, Louisa C. Conaway, of OH, and John W. Conaway, of OH; and Lloyd N. Conaway, deceased, father of Louisa N. Conaway, of OH.
Property formerly situate in Baltimore County, being parts of *Monzie* and *Dorsey's Industry.*

Chancery Book 2, pp. 337-347 1840 Equity #58
John Santz, and others vs. Adam Santz, and others. Sale of real estate.
Peter Santz (or Sense), of Baltimore County, died 10 Aug 1820, intestate, leaving widow, Catherine Santz. Children: Andrew Santz, deceased, husband of Salone (or Sarah) Santz; George Santz, husband of Mary Santz; Mary Renoull, wife of Jacob Renoull; Catherine Zimmerman, wife of Frederick Zimmerman; Margaret Miller, wife of Henry Miller; Susanna Shaffer, wife of John R. Shaffer; Adam Santz, of OH, husband of Mary Santz; John Santz, of OH, husband of Mary Santz; David Santz, of OH, husband of Eliza Santz; and Susan Wink, wife of George Wink.
Property formerly situate in Baltimore County, being parts of *Iron Intention, Molly's Delight, Christopher's Lot,* and *Winfall.*

Chancery Book 2, pp. 347-369 1842 Equity #98
Martha Curry vs. Theadore Curry, and others. Sale of real estate.
William Curry died c. 1830, intestate, leaving widow, Martha Curry. Children: Theadore Curry; Francis Curry; and Martha G. Curry.
Property situtate in or near Uniontown.

Chancery Book 2, pp. 370-382 1843 Equity #112
George Erbaugh, and others vs. Margaret Erbaugh, and others. Sale of real estate.
John Erbaugh died 1842, intestate, leaving widow, Margaret Erbaugh. Children: Henry Erbaugh, of OH; Jacob Erbaugh, of OH; Peter Erbaugh, of OH; John Erbaugh, of OH; Mary Keith, of OH, wife of Kinsey Keith; George Erbaugh; William Erbaugh; Conrad Erbaugh; and Elizabeth Erbaugh.
Property formerly situtate in Baltimore County, being part of *Sarah's Pleasure.*

Chancery Book 2, pp. 383-389 1843 Equity #125
John Robertson vs. Jacob Grove and James Hook. Sale of real estate to satisfy creditors.
James Hook.
Property being part of *Rochester*.

Chancery Book 2, pp. 390-427 1842 Equity #87
David Stouffer and Elizabeth Chew vs. Jacob Stouffer, Hannah Cover, and others. Sale of real estate.
Christian Stouffer, of Frederick County, died 1815, testate, leaving widow, Catherine Stouffer, who died 25 Dec 1841. Children: David Stouffer; Jacob Stouffer, of OH; Henry Stouffer, deceased, died c. 1820, intestate, husband of Ann Stouffer, father of Matilda Steiner (of Baltimore City, wife of James Steiner), Amelia Barbour (of Westmoreland County PA, wife of James Barbour), Rachel McKain (of Baltimore City, widow of Alexander McKain), Josiah Stouffer (of Galena, IL), Leah Ames (of Baltimore City, wife of Joseph Ames) Miranda Cropsey (of Brooklyn NY, wife of Francis J. Cropsey) and Louisa F. Stouffer (of Baltimore City; Hannah Cover, of Frederick County, widow of David Cover; John Stouffer, deceased, died Nov 1840, testate; Elizabeth Chew, wife of William H. Chew; and Catherine Rittenhouse, deceased, wife of Mathias Rittenhouse, deceased, mother of Henry Rittenhouse (of OH), Jesse Rittenhouse (of OH), Samuel Rittenhouse (of OH), Christian Rittenhouse (of OH), Joseph Rittenhouse (of OH), Daniel Rittenhouse (of PA), Mathias Rittenhouse (of PA), and Hannah Rittenhouse (of PA).
Property situate near Uniontown, being part of *Orchard*.

Chancery Book 2, pp. 428-444 1842 Equity #107
John Orendorff vs. Isaac Shriver, Joshua Smith and Lebbeus Heddington. Sale of real estate to satisy creditors.
James O. Heddington died w/o issue, was son of Lebbeus Heddington, of OH.
Property situate in Westminster, on Westminster-Taneytown Road, being part of *Fanny's Meadow*.

Chancery Book 2, pp. 445-464 1843 Equity #110
Barbara Ocker vs. Josiah Ocker, and others. Sale of real estate.
Jacob Ocker died 1842, leaving widow, Barbara Fleagle Ocker. Children: Josiah Ocker; Henrietta Ocker, of Frederick County; Ann Elisa Ocker, of Frederick County; Thomas Ocker, of Frederick County; Samuel Ocker; Jacob Ocker; and John Henry Ocker.
Property being parts of *Escape, Terra Rubra, Disappointment* and *Waddle's Delight*.

Chancery Book 2, pp. 465-484 1842 Equity #94
David Evans vs. Joshua Evans and wife, and others. Sale of real estate to satisfy creditors.
Charles Washington Franklin, son of Charles Franklin, died c. 1842, intestate, unmarried, and w/o issue. Brothers and sisters: James Franklin, husband of Eliza Franklin; Joshua Franklin, husband of Elizabeth Franklin; Resin Franklin, husband of Amaretta Franklin; Elizabeth Wilt, wife of Jacob Wilt; Anna Barnes, wife of James A. Barnes; Amelia Pickett, widow; John Franklin, deceased, father of Helen M. E. V. Franklin.
Property situate 1 mile southeast of Franklinville.

Chancery Book 2, pp. 485-524 1842 Equity #103
Joseph Ebaugh, John Sykes, and Jonas Deal vs. Peter Reister, Henry Seabrooks and Catherine Sykes, and others. Sale of real estate to satisfy creditors.
Nathaniel Sykes died 1841, intestate, leaving widow, Catherine Sykes. Children: William Sykes; John T. Sykes; Lewis Sykes; and George Sykes.
Property situate in Hampstead, being part of *Transylvania*.

Chancery Book 2, pp. 525-539 1838 Equity #15
Thomas Weakley, and others vs. Enoch Loveall, and others. Sale of real estate.
Luther Loveall, of Baltimore County, died testate, leaving widow, Rebecca Loveall, who died c. 1834. Children: Rachel Sense, wife of Peter Sense; Enoch Loveall, father of Greensbury Loveall and Solomon Loveall; Nancy Weakley, wife of Thomas Weakley; John Loveall; Stephen Loveall; Charity Loveall; and Sarah James.
One property formerly situate in Baltimore County and other property situate on Fink's Fork, VA.

Chancery Book 2, pp. 540-550 1843 Equity #116
Petition of Helena Byers, next friend, and others. Sale of real estate.
John A. Byers died 19 June 1842, intestate, leaving widow Helena Byers. Children: William G. Byers; Susannah Byers; Daniel Byers; Elizabeth Byers; and John F. Byers.
Property situate on Littlestown Turnpike, being part of *Kelly's Range*.

Chancery Book 2, pp. 553-579 1843 Equity #114
Ephraim Brown vs. William Sullivan, Margaret O'Hara, and others. Sale of real estate to satisfy creditors.
Lydia Sullivan died Mar 1843, intestate, w/o issue. Brother and sisters: Margaret O'Hara, of MS; Mary Todd, of OH; Honor Hednor, of PA; Sarah Cornell, of PA; Catherine Copenhaver, deceased, children unknown, residence unknown;

and Henry Brown, deceased, father of Ephraim Brown, James Brown (of OH), Elijah Brown (of OH), and Jane Brown (of OH).
Property situate in Westminster, being part of *Fanny's Meadow*.

Chancery Book 2, pp. 581-591 1844 Equity #136
Isabella Jordan and Robert H. Jordan vs. William R. Jordan, and others. Sale of real estate.
William N. Jordan, of Baltimore County, died c. 1826, testate, leaving widow, who died soon after husband. Children: Zacheriah Jordan, deceased, died Oct 1843, unmarried, intestate; Robert H. Jordan; and Edward Jordan, deceased, father of Isabella Jordan, William Robert Jordan, Lovelace Jordan, and Edward Jordan.
Property formerly situate in Baltimore County, being parts of *Buckingham's Good Will, Stevenson's Manor, The Indian Town, Mount Safety, Nathan's Desire* and *Chance*.

Chancery Book 3, pp. 1-29 1842 Equity #105
Beal Buckingham, and others vs. Ephraim Buckingham, and wife. Sale of real estate.
Richard Condon, died c. 1839, intestate. Children: Rachel Buckingham, wife of Beal Buckingham; Amelia Buckingham, wife of Ephraim Buckingham; Harriet McClain, wife of William McClain; Thomas Condon, deceased, died c. Nov 1842, leaving widow, deceased, father of Corrilla Conaway (of OH, wife of Hale C. Conaway), Elizabeth Barnes (wife of Alfred Barnes), Rachel E. Buckingham (wife of Nimrod Buckingham), Richard W. Condon, Prudence Amelia Condon, Mary Jane Condon, Levi Z. Condon, Ellen Condon, and Thomas Condon; Cordelia Franklin, wife of Thomas Franklin; Richard U. Condon; and Arey Condon.
Property formerly situate in Baltimore County, on Liberty Road, being parts of *Eppington Forest* and *The Last Resurvey on Sheredines Range*.

Chancery Book 3, pp. 30-39 1843 Equity #115
Conrad Kealbaugh, and others vs. Catherine Baublits, and others. Sale of real estate.
Christian Kealbaugh (or Kelbaugh) died 20 May 1835, intestate. Children: Conrad Kealbaugh; John Kealbaugh; Jacob Kealbaugh; Mary Albon, wife of Henry Albon; Elizabeth Hines, wife of Anthony Hines; Catherine Baublits, deceased, wife of Michael Baublits, mother of Jacob Baublits, Ephraim Baublits, Catherine Baublits, Henry Baublits, Samuel Baublits, Rachel Baublits, and Michael Baublits; and William Kealbaugh.
Property formerly situate in Baltimore County, near Town of Hampstead.

Chancery Book 3, pp. 40-57 1844 Equity #137
Azariah Fuller and Adedzelah Ford vs. Ann Rebecca Fuller, and others. Sale of real estate.
Angelico Fuller died c. 1841, widow of Nicholas Fuller, who died c. 1834. Children: Ann Rebecca Fuller; Oliver P. Fuller; Emily Fuller; Mary Elizabeth Fuller; Leander Fuller, of Baltimore County; Adedzelah (or Adazillah) Ford, wife of Isaac Ford; and Azariah Fuller.
Property formerly situate in Baltimore County, near road from Cockey's Mill to Westminster and also on Turnpike Road from Westminster to Reisterstown, being parts of *Hooker's Meadow Enlarged* and *Bells Venture*.

Chancery Book 3, pp. 58-71 1843 Equity #123
Elijah Woolery vs. Lenhart Rosenberger. Foreclosure.
Lenhart Rosenberger, formerly of Baltimore City.
Property formerly situate in Baltimore County, adjacent to Baltimore-Westminster Turnpike, 4 miles below Westminster, being part of *Bucks Park*.

Chancery Book 3, pp. 72-85 1844 Equity #130
Chancery Book 3, pp. 246-248
Petition of Lovelace M. Gorsuch and Nathan I. Gorsuch. Sale of real estate.
Obediah Buckingham died c. 1839, testate, leaving widow, who died c. 1844. Children: Nicholas Buckingham; Owen F. Buckingham; Obediah Buckingham; George H. Buckingham; Appulla Hayden, wife of Basil Hayden; Catherine Gardner, wife of Nimrod Gardner; Ruth Gardner, wife of Freeborn Gardner; Benjamin Buckingham, deceased, father of Nancy Buckingham, Mary Ann Barnes (wife of James Barnes), Nora Jane Buckingham, Margaret Ruth Buckingham, and Benjamin W. Buckingham; Elias Buckingham, deceased, father of William B. Buckingham, Lucinda Buckingham, and Silas Buckingham; Ann Gorsuch, deceased, wife of Nathan Gorsuch, deceased, mother of Lovelace M. Gorsuch and Nathan I. Gorsuch; and Laban Buckingham, deceased, father of Leonard Buckingham, Julian Oliver (wife of James Oliver), Rebecca Oliver (wife of Thomas Oliver), Westly Buckingham, and George W. Buckingham.
Property being parts of *Buckinghams Good Will*, *Buckinghams Venture* and *Edinburgh*.

Chancery Book 3, pp. 86-118 1843 Equity #119
John Fisher and Jacob Reese vs. Jacob Sherman Shriver and Elizabeth Shriver, his wife. Dispute.
Jacob Sherman, of Frederick County, died 1822, testate, leaving widow Elizabeth Sherman, who died 10 June 1842. Children: Eve Shriver, mother of William Waggoner Shriver, Jacob Sherman Shriver (b. 1805, m. his wife, Eliza

H. Shriver, of Wheeling, Ohio County VA, in 1826), and Elizabeth Shriver. Jacob's brother, Conrad Sherman had son, George S. Sherman.

Property situate in and adjoining Westminster, being parts of *Timber Ridge, Resurvey on Timber Ridge, Resurvey on Bedford, Bond's Meadow Enlarged* and *White's Level.*

Chancery Book 3, pp.119-131 1843 Equity #117
Christian Royer and Jesse Royer vs. Levi Evans, Sarah Warfield, and others. Foreclosure.

Peter Royer died 10 July 1842, testate, leaving widow, Ann Royer. Children: Catherine Wampler, wife of Philip Wampler; Christian Royer; Jesse Royer; Mary Merring, wife of Jacob Merring; Ann Waybright, wife of John Waybright; Louisa Englar, wife of David Englar; and Jehu Royer.

Property situate near intersection of Main Street and Liberty Road, being part of *Winter's Addition to Westminster.*

Chancery Book 3, pp. 132-139 1844 Equity #149
Petition of Samuel Bennett and Mary Bennett, his wife, Isabella Wilson, Robert Wilson, and others. Sale of real estate.

William Ewing died 9 Aug 1844, testate. Nieces and nephews: Rebecca Dunn, of Baltimore, wife of William Dunn; Nancy Watt, of Donegal County, Ireland, wife of Robert Watt; William Wilson, deceased, husband of Jane Wilson, of Baltimore MD, father of Mary Jane Wilson and Robert Wilson; Elizabeth Wilson; Mary Wilson Bennett, wife of Samuel Bennett; Jane Buchanan, wife of John Buchanan; Isabella Wilson; Robert Wilson; and Martha Wilson.

Property location not given.

Chancery Book 3, pp. 140-172 1843 Equity #124
Richard W. Condon, Alfred Barnes and Elizabeth Barnes, his wife, vs. Abraham Wampler, Samuel Wampler and other heirs of John Wampler, deceased, Prudence A. Condon, and others. Partition and sale of real estate to satisfy creditors.

Thomas Condon died 1842 intestate. Children: Richard W. Condon; Elizabeth Ann Barnes, wife of Alfred Barnes; Rachel E. Buckingham, wife of Nimrod Buckingham; Corrilla Ann Conaway, wife of Hale C. Conaway; Prudence A. Condon; Mary Jane Condon; Levi Z. Condon; Eliza E. Condon; and Thomas E. Condon.

Property owned by Thomas Condon was situate formerly in Baltimore County, being part of *Dorsey's Industry.* He was buying other land, formerly situate in Baltimore County, being parts of *Dorsey's Industry, John's Industry, Mary's Victory, Pleasant Valley, Porters Pleasant Level, Porter's Treble Purchase* and *Lawrences Pleasant Valley.*

The latter property was owned by Abraham Wampler and the heirs of John Wampler, deceased. They were: Samuel Wampler; Catherine Wampler; Sarah A. Kuhn, wife of John Kuhn; Lydia Kelly, wife of John A. Kelly; Henry H. Wampler; Maria L. Wampler; James L. Wampler; George E. Wampler; William A. Wampler; and Emily Jane Wampler.

Chancery Book 3, pp. 173-188   1844   Equity #142
Jacob Fisher and Elisha D. Payne vs. Cornelius L. Poulson and Samuel Evans, Admr. Sale of real estate to satisfy creditors.
Lee Poulson died c. June 1843, intestate, leaving widow, Mary Ann Poulson, and only child, Cornelius S. Poulson.
Property formerly situate in Frederick County, on Little Pipe Creek, being parts of *Poulson's Chance, Resurvey on Poulson's Chance, York Company Defense* and *Resurvey on Stoney Batter*.

Chancery Book 3, pp. 189-204   1844   Equity #148
Peter Snyder, Jr., vs. Ephraim Benzel, John Benzel, and others, and Abraham Zentz, Admr. Sale of real estate to satisfy creditors.
Jacob Benzel died 2 Sep 1842, intestate, leaving widow, Ann Mary Benzel. Children: Ephraim Benzel; John Benzel; Elizabeth Benzel; Emeline Benzel; Catharine Benzel; William Benzel; and David Benzel.
Property formerly situate in Frederick County, being part of *Owing's Second Chance*.

Chancery Book 3, pp. 205-217   1845   Equity #157
Petition of Henry Crawmer and Helpher Crawmer. Sale of real estate.
Peter Long, late of York County PA, died 1823, testate, leaving widow, Margaret Long, who died Jan 1845. Estates were to go to his and her brothers and sisters. His siblings were: Ludwick Long, deceased; Conrad Long, deceased; George Long, deceased; Elizabeth Young, deceased, wife of David Young, of Frederick County; Molly Zile, deceased, wife of Conrad Zile, of Baltimore County; Anna Mary Helm, deceased, wife of Francis Helm, of OH; and Catherine Buse, deceased, wife of Peter Buse, of VA. Her siblings were: Christiana Neidig Crawmer, deceased, wife of Philip Crawmer, of Frederick County; Sophia N. Crawmer, deceased, wife of Helpher Crawmer, of York County PA; Barbara N. Firefrock, deceased, wife of Andrew Firefrock, of York County PA; Catherine N. Shoe, deceased, wife of Zachariah Shoe; Rosina N. Rites, of York County PA, widow of Frederick Rites, Sr.; and Anna Mary Dearhoff, widow of Henry Dearhoff.
Property formerly situate in Frederick County, in Franklin District, 1-1/2 miles south of Franklinville, near Buffalo Road, being part of *Bite Him Softly*.

Chancery Book 3, pp. 218-239 1841 Equity 86
John P. McCormick, Admr. of James McCormick, Jr., deceased, vs. Rezin Brown. Foreclosure.
James McCormick, Jr., late of Baltimore County and Washington, D.C., died 1841, leaving widow, Elizabeth McCormick.
Property formerly situate in Baltimore County, about 7 miles from Westminster, being parts of *Bells Recovery* and *Hale's Venture*.

Chancery Book 3, pp. 249-255 1845 Equity #160
Petition of Catherine Shue, Abraham Haines, Mary Baile, and others. Sale of real estate.
John Haines, of Frederick County, died Jan 1828, testate, leaving widow, Mary Haines, who died Mar 1845. Children: Catherine Shue, deceased, wife of David Shue; Abraham Haines; Sarah Cullimore, wife of David Cullimore; Mary Baile, deceased, wife of Michael Baile, deceased; John Haines; Susanah Benzer, wife of John Benzer; Michael Haines, deceased, w/o issue; Matilda Benzer; Joel Lewis Haines, deceased, w/o issue; and Lydia Bigham, wife of Joseph Bigham. Property being part of *Leigh Castle*.

Chancery Book 3, pp. 259-272 1845 Equity #155
Petition of George Zepp, and wife. Sale of real estate.
George Utz died c. 1841, testate, leaving widow, Magdalena Utz. Children: John Utz; Frederick Utz; David Utz, deceased, died c. 1846; George Utz; Sarah Utz; Rachel Utz; Elizabeth Face, widow of Frederick Face; Catherine Zepp, wife of George Zepp; and Magdalena Arter, wife of Philip Arter.
Property formerly situtate in Baltimore County, 2-1/2 miles from Manchester, 2-1/2 miles from Bachman's Mills and 1/4 mile from Hanover-Baltimore Turnpike, being part of *Utz's Inheritance*.

Chancery Book 3, pp. 273-289 1842 Equity #93
Rachel H. Shipley vs. Ruth Shipley, and others. Sale of real estate.
William Shipley of Robert, died 10 Nov 1836, intestate, leaving widow, Ruth Shipley. Children: Robert H. Shipley; Ruth E. Shipley; Juliana B. H. Shipley; Cornelius H. Shipley; Henry H. Shipley; Charles H. Shipley; and Francis L. Shipley (all of Baltimore County).
Property formerly situate in Baltimore County, 2 miles E. of Franklinville, 5 miles from Woodbine Depot, being parts of *John's Industry, Dorsey's Industry, Dorsey's Claim, Lawrences Pleasant Vallies, Marys Victory* and *Evans Search*.

Chancery Book 3, pp. 290-303 1844 Equity #134
Philip Zentz and Rachel Zentz, his wife, James Coutter and Polly Coutter, his wife vs. John Gross and others. Sale of real estate.

John Gross, of Baltimore County, died before 1830, intestate. Children: Catherine Zentz, deceased, died c. 1836, wife of Philip Zentz, mother of Rachel Zentz (of Alleghany County MD, wife of Philip Zentz), and Polly Coutter (of Alleghany County MD, wife of James Coutter); John Gross, Jr.; Henry Gross, deceased, died c. 1835-36, intestate; Elizabeth Sharrer, wife of Jacob Sharrer; and Mary Miller, wife of Jacob Miller.
Property being parts of *Pleasant Hills* and *Everything Needful Corrected.*

Chancery Book 3, pp. 304-332   1844   Equity #146
Petition of Samuel Baumgardner and Barbara Baumgardner, his wife. Sale of real estate.
Paul Koons died c. 1815, testate, leaving widow, Mary Ann Koons, who died 1844. Children: Barbara Baumgardner, wife of Samuel Baumgardner; Peter Koons, deceased; Andrew Koons; Paul Koons; Salley McGuigan, wife of James McGuigan; Catherine Black; Lenah Baumgardner; Elizabeth Adelsperger; and Margaret Baumgardner; and his step-daughter, Mary Null.
Property, formerly situate in Frederick County (probably around Taneytown area).

Chancery Book 3, pp. 333-343   1845   Equity #156
Samuel Fink, Elizabeth Fink, and others vs. Catherine Fink. Sale of real estate.
Adam Fink, of Baltimore County, died 1831, testate. Children: Catherine Fink; Sarah Fink, deceased, died Apr 1843, intestate; Samuel Fink, of Baltimore City; Elizabeth Fink, of Baltimore City; Theresa Henry, of PA, wife of Joseph Henry; and Mary Shoemaker, deceased, wife of Jacob Shoemaker, mother of John Shoemaker (of Baltimore City), Samuel Shoemaker (of Baltimore City), and Elizabeth Shoemaker (of PA).
Property formerly situate in Baltimore County, being parts of *Hookers Meadow* and *Flagg's Meadow.*

Chancery Book 3, pp. 344-370   1845   Equity #159
Henry E. Beltz vs. Andrew Dewees, Mary Sharrer and David Sharrer, her husband, and Jacob Frankforter, Admr. Sale of real estate to satisfy creditors.
Mary Stever died Jan 1843, testate, leaving granchildren: Andrew Dewees; and his sister, Mary Sharrer, wife of David Sharrer.
Property situate in Town of Manchester.

Chancery Book 3, pp. 371-379   1845   Equity #163
Barbara Hoover vs. Adam Hoover. Sale of real estate to satisfy creditors.
Adam Hoover, a lunatic, and his wife, Barbara Hoover, and only child, Daniel Hoover.
Property situate in Town of Hampstead on Turnpike.

Chancery Book 3, pp. 380-395 1845 Equity #170
Petition of John Lammott, Jacob Lammott, and others. Sale of real estate.
Henry Lammott died Feb 1845, testate. Children: Rachel Knote; Samuel Lammott, deceased, died Oct 1845, father of Sarah Lammott and Josephine Lammott; Catherine Hoover, wife of Daniel Hoover; John Lammont; Elizabeth Birely, wife of Thomas Birely, mother (by first husband) of John T. Gill, Rose A. Gill, and Jane K. Algire (wife of George Algire); Sarah I. Bucken, wife of Henry Z. Bucken; Jacob Lammott; and Julia Ann Wells, wife of Thomas Wells.
Properties situate in Hampstead and in the Manchester District, near Kroh's Mill, being parts of *Kentucky, We Found the Beginning, Transylvania, White Oak Bottom* and *Alltogether*.

Chancery Book 3, pp. 396-413 1845 Equity #176
Jacob Mathias and Joshua Smith, Exrs. of Peter Shoemaker, deceased vs. Hezekiah Crout, Basil Root, and John A. Kelly. Sale of real estate to satisfy creditors.
Peter Shoemaker, of Frederick County, died testate. Children: Susanna Rinehart, deceased; Mary Martin, deceased, mother of Barbara Martin; Sarah Barnhart; and Elizabeth Sprinkle.
Also mentions family of negro slaves to be freed: John Sater; his wife, Anna Sater; and their children: Sarah Sater; Samuel Sater; Elizabeth Sater; Mariah Sater; and John Sater.
Properties situate in Westminster on Westminster-Littlestown Road and also on Westminster-Taneytown Road, midway between Westminster and Taneytown, being parts of *Lookabout, Father's Choice* and *Fanny's Meadow*.

Chancery Book 3, pp. 414-444 1846 Equity #180
John Baile, Admr. of Amos Markey, deceased vs. George Ohler, Daniel Sell, and others. Attempt to collect on debt.
Amos Markey, deceased, of Preble County OH, had obtained judgment against George Ohler in 1844. Left widow, Jane Markey, and children: John Henry Markey; Christian Markey; Susannah Markey; Amos Markey; Nathaniel Markey; Joseph Markey; and Samuel Markey (all of OH).
Property, sold to Daniel Sell by Sheriff prior to complaint, was situate near Keys School House, being parts of *Terra Rubra Resurveyed, Dealeys Delight* and *Boot*.

Chancery Book 3, pp. 445-458 1846 Equity #184
Elizabeth Owings vs. Leonard Jarvis, and others. Right of Dower
Richard Owings died 9 Apr 1845, leaving widow, Elizabeth Owings.
Property formerly situate in Baltimore County, being parts of *Stinchcombs Reserve, Rich Meadows* and *Rochester*.

Chancery Book 3, pp. 459-472 1846 Equity #185
Ephraim Wilson, and others vs. C. W. Webster, and others. Sale of real estate to satisfy creditors.
Henry Gushara died 1845, intestate, leaving widow, Pamela Gushara, and only child, Mary Ann Stultz (wife of Abraham Stultz).
Property being part of *Retirement Corrected*.

Chancery Book 3, pp. 472-479 1845 Equity #161
James Heird vs. John Geselman. Sale of real estate to satisfy creditors.
John Geselman.
Property situate near PA line.

Chancery Book 3, pp. 480-489 1846 Equity #181
Ruth Price vs. Caleb Lane. Foreclosure.
Caleb Lane.
Property situate in Hampstead District, on Baltimore-Manchester Turnpike, 1/2 mile from Hampstead, being parts of *Petersburg Resurveyed*, *Eastern Branch Resurveyed* and *Fowble's Lot*.

Chancery Book 3, pp. 490-503 1846 Equity #191
John W. Davis, and others vs. George Davis and Jonathan Davis. Sale of real estate.
Jonathan C. Davis died 4 Jan 1842, intestate, husband of Mary Davis. Children: John W. Davis, husband of Mary Jane Davis; Ann Marie Davis; Aaron Davis; Joseph Davis; William Davis; Jonathan Davis; and George Davis.
Property formerly situate in Frederick County on Big Pipe Creek, c. 1 miles from Middleburgh and 4 miles from Taneytown, being parts of *Buck Lodge* and *Lower Slipe*.

Chancery Book 3, pp. 504-520 1845 Equity #166
Andrew Lohr vs. Catherine Lohr, Margaret J. Lohr, and David B. Earhart. Sale of real estate to satisfy creditors.
Levi Lohr died 1844, leaving widow, Catherine Lohr, and only child, Margaret Josephine Lohr.
Property situate in District 3, being part of *Resurvey on Ten Tracts*.

Chancery Book 3, pp. 521-525 1847 Equity #225
Eliza O. Dorsey vs. Ferdinand Dorsey.   Divorce.
Eliza O. Dorsey and Ferdinand Dorsey were married 13 Jan 1835 in Baltimore County, now Carroll County. Husband abandoned her on 5 Jan 1841, left state, then settled in Frederick County.

No real property mentioned.

Chancery Book 3, pp. 526-530   1847   Equity #222
Ruth Litty vs. Robert Litty.   Divorce.
Ruth Litty and Robert Litty were married 22 May 1841. Husband abandoned her on 11 Aug 1843 and left state.
No real property mentioned.

Chancery Book 4, pp. 1-11   1846   Equity #183
Joseph Utz, and others, by their next friend and guardian, Elizabeth Utz vs. Henry Tasto and Sally Tasto, his wife, and others.   Sale of real estate.
Peter Utz died Nov 1839, leaving widow, Elizabeth Utz. Children: Joseph Utz; Eliza Utz; Elizabeth Utz; Sally Tasto, wife of Henry Tasto; Mary Geiman, wife of John Geiman; David Utz; Peter Utz; Rebecca Utz; Lydia Utz; and Daniel Utz.
Properties situate in Manchester District, near Hanover Turnpike, north of Manchester, being parts of *Utz's Inheritance* and *Reister's Last Shift*.

Chancery Book 4, pp. 12-42   1845   Equity #174
John Jones vs. Elizabeth Brown and Joseph Shaeffer, Admrs., and others.   Sale of real estate to satisfy creditors.
Nicholas H. Brown, son of Ruth Brown, died Mar 1845, intestate, leaving widow, Elizabeth Brown, and no issue. Brothers and sisters: Belinda Barnes, out of state, wife of William Barnes; William S. Brown; Nelson Brown; Ruth Fletter, wife of Jacob Fletter; Susan Myerly, wife of Jacob Myerly; George Brown; Elizabeth Price, wife of Thomas Price (he lives out of state); Andrew J. Brown; Charles W. Brown; and Charity Brown.
Property situate in 4th District, near Sandymount Meeting House, 5 miles below Westminster, being parts of *Elizabeth's Fancy*, *Perth* and *Costly*.

Chancery Book 4, pp. 43-61   1846   Equity #186
The Bank of Westminster and John Fisher vs. William Krause, Admr. of Jacob Krause, and others.   Foreclosure.
Jacob Krause (or Crouse) died c. Jan 1846, intestate. Children: William Krause; John Krause; Lydia Wampler, wife of Lewis Wampler; Catherine Fowler, wife of Benjamin Fowler; Rachel Sheets, wife of George Sheets; Eliza Krause; and James Krause, deceased, father of Jesse W. Krause (of PA), and James L. Krause, (of PA).
Properties formerly situate in Baltimore County, being parts of *Bonds Meadow Enlarged* and Lot 81 of *Addition of The Town of Westminster*.

Chancery Book 4, pp. 62-67 1847 Equity #215
Petition of John Bowman and Sarah Ann Switzer, by William Stansbury, her guardian and next friend. Sale of real estate.
Peter Arbaugh died testate, leaving widow Mary Arbaugh, who died c. 1846. Mentions John Bowman and Sarah Ann Switzer, but relationship is not established.
Property location is not established, but was site of tavern house.

Chancery Book 4, pp. 68-98 1844 Equity #143
Jonas Deal vs. Mary Gittinger, wife of Jacob Gittinger, Jr., and others. Sale of real estate.
John Deal, of Baltimore County, died c. 1815-1820, intestate, leaving widow, Rachel Deal (nee Powder), who later married Samuel Hooker of Baltimore County and became known as Rachel Hooker. Children: Mary Gittinger, of OH or IN, wife of Jacob Gittinger; Sarah Harry, of OH or IN, widow of Tobias Harry; David P. Deal, deceased, died 1841, intestate, no issue, widow, Catherine Deal, who later married and became known as Catherine Shue, of PA; and Jonas Deal.
Property situate part in Baltimore County and part in Carroll County on west side of Baltimore-Hanover Turnpike, being parts of *Manheime Town*, *Hooker's Meadow Resurveyed* and *Jerusalem*.

Chancery Book 4, pp. 100-109 1847 Equity #214
George Everhart, Jr. vs. Daniel Bollinger. Foreclosure.
Daniel Bollinger.
Properties situate 3 miles from Manchester on York Road, being parts of *Ill Neighborhood* and *Level Ground*.

Chancery Book 4, pp. 110-117 1847 Equity #218
Elizabeth Zimmerman vs. Henry B. Jones. Foreclosure.
Henry B. Jones, formerly of York County PA.
Property formerly situate in Baltimore County, c. 5 miles from Manchester, 1 mile from Clinefelter's Mill, being parts of *Bite the Biter* and *Inclosure*.

Chancery Book 4, pp. 118-125 1847 Equity #221
George Zepp vs. Frederick Utz. Sale of real estate to satisfy creditors.
Frederick Utz, a lunatic, and his wife, Polly Utz, a sister of George Zepp.
Property situate 5 miles from Manchester.

Chancery Book 4, pp. 126-143   1846   Equity #199
Chancery Book 11, pp. 44-51
Petition of David Heath and Sarah Ann Heath, his wife, next friend of Mary Virginia Franklin. Sale of real estate.
John Franklin died c. 1839, intestate, leaving widow, Sarah Ann Franklin, who later married David Heath and became known as Sarah Ann Heath. Child: Mary Virginia Franklin, of Baltimore City. Brothers: Joshua Franklin; Rezin Franklin; and Jesse W. Franklin.
Properties situate on north side of Baltimore-Libertytown Road, near Frederick County line, in Franklinville, being parts of *Halls Range, This or Nothing* and *Resurvey on Smith's Lot.*

Chancery Book 4, pp. 144-164   1847   Equity #211
John Angel, George Kephart, Sarah Kephart and Hannah Kephart vs. Eliza Angel, James Crouse, and others. Sale of real estate to satisfy creditors.
Michael Angel (or Engle) died 15 Sep 1846, intestate, leaving widow, Eliza Angel. Children: Abraham Angel; Emily Stonesifer, wife of Uriah Stonesifer; Mary Angel; Thomas Angel; and Ephriam Angel.
Property being parts of *Resurvey on Brothers Agreement* and *Brick Mills*.

Chancery Book 4, pp. 165-181   1847   Equity #217
Petition of Maria Rosensteel. Sale of real estate.
Thomas Adams, son of Magdelena Adams, of Frederick County, died c. 1825, leaving widow, Mary Adams, who died in Dec 1846, near Emmittsburg, Frederick County. Children: Maria Rosensteel, widow of Charles Rosensteel, mother of Mary Rosensteel; and Elizabeth Steigers, deceased, wife of George Steigers, deceased, mother of Susannah Hughes (wife of Patrick Hughes), Margaret Steigers, Barbara Steigers, Eliza Sneeringer (wife of Samuel G. Sneeringer), John Steigers, and Mary Nankivil (wife of John Nankivil). Brother-in-law was John Dougherty.
Properties formerly situate in Frederick County, being parts of *Millers Chance, Resurvey on Owings Chance, Resurvey on the Pines* and *The Addition to the Pines.*

Chancery Book 4, pp. 182-199   1847   Equity #224
Michael Fringer vs. Susan Fringer, John Thomson, Admr. of George Fringer, deceased, and others. Sale of real estate to satisfy creditors.
George Fringer died Oct 1846, intestate, leaving widow, Susan Fringer. Children: Alice Fringer; George Fringer; Nicholas Fringer; Michael Fringer; Jacob Fringer; Washington Fringer; and Ephraim Fringer.
Property was situate on Taneytown-Gettysburg road, being part of *Resurvey on Brothers Agreement.*

Chancery Book 4, pp. 200-217 1847 Equity #226
Thomas Conaway and Catherine A. Bennett vs. Obediah Buckingham, Admr. of Thomas V. Buckingham, and others. Sale of real estate to satisfy creditors.
Thomas V. Buckingham died 4 May 1846, intestate, leaving widow, Maranda Buckingham, and only child, Eleanor E. Buckingham.
Property being Lot #3 of the division of real estate of the late Obadiah Buckingham; location not established.

Chancery Book 4, pp. 218-241 1845 Equity #152
Levi Devilbiss vs. William G. Shipley. Foreclosure.
William G. Shipley.
Property situate in Woodbine on Baltimore and Ohio Railroad, being part of *Bunker's Hill Fortified*.

Chancery Book 4, pp. 242-257 1846 Equity #188
David Foutz vs. Samuel Rhodes, Lydia Bare, and others. Sale of real estate to satisfy creditors.
Samuel Bare died c. Jan 1845, intestate, leaving widow, Lydia Bare. Children: Susanna Bare; Maria Bare; Lydia Bare; David Bare; Daniel Bare; Samuel Bare; and Elizabeth Bare.
Property being part of *The Resurvey on Lookabout*.

Chancery Book 4, pp. 259-279 1847 Equity #210
George Duderer, and others vs. Conrad Duderer, and others. Sale of real estate.
John Duderer (or Dutterer) died Jan 1847, intestate. Children: George Duderer; Conrad Duderer, out-of-state; Andrew Duderer, of Frederick County; Henry Duderer; Mary Bowersox, wife of Daniel Bowersox; Lydia Troxel, wife of John Troxel; and Margaret Byers, deceased, wife of Michael Byers, mother of Noah A. Byers, Joseph Byers, Joshua Byers, Elizabeth C. Byers, John G. Byers, George M. Byers, David H. Byers, Jacob Byers, Margaret Byers, Francina Byers, and Caroline Byers.
Properties formerly situate in Frederick County, in 3rd District, Silver Run Valley, 1 miles from Silver Run Church on Baltimore Turnpike, 10 miles from Westminster, being parts of *Ohio, Youngblood's Choice, High Germany, Lemon's Choice* and *Dyer's Mill Forest*.

Chancery Book 4, pp. 281-311 1846 Equity #190
Sarah Aikin and Decatur Levering vs. John Heiner, Daniel Engle and Philip Greenwood. Dispute.
John Heiner, formerly of Carroll County, now IN.

Property situate on Big Pipe Creek, being parts of *Retirement Corrected* and *Bedford*.

Chancery Book 4, pp. 312-336   1846   Equity #204
Petition of Moses R. Lawson, Sarah A. Lawson and Ruth Litty. Sale of real estate.
Moses Lawson died Jan 1846, testate, leaving widow, Elizabeth Lawson. Children: Thomas Lawson; Moses R. Lawson; Sarah Lawson, of Adams County, PA; Ruth Litty, wife of Robert Litty; Jacob Lawson; John Lawson; and Edward Lawson.
Property situate 1/2 mile from Manchester on Manchester-Westminster Road, being part of *Dey's Adventure*.

Chancery Book 4, pp. 337-365   1845   Equity #154
Violette E. Barnes, next friend of Archibald Barnes vs. Sally Elizabeth Barnes. Sale of real estate to satisfy creditors.
Archibald Barnes, of Baltimore County, died before 1843, testate.
Brother: Thomas Barnes, who died June 1843, testate, leaving widow, Violette E. Barnes, of Baltimore County (later married Wilson L. Soper and became Violette E. Soper, and moved to Montgomery County MD), father of Archibald Barnes and Sally Elizabeth Barnes. Sister: Arey Barnes. Nephew: Alfred Barnes. Niece: Louisa Buckingham.
Property formerly situate in Baltimore County, on Liberty Road, being parts of *Eppington Forest, John's Industry, Lawrence's Pleasant Valley* and *Dodson's Tent*.

Chancery Book 4, pp. 366-386   1846   Equity #195
Henry Shoemaker, and others vs. Hester Shoemaker, and others. Sale of real estate.
George Shoemaker, of Frederick County, died c. 1819-20, intestate, leaving widow, Hester Shoemaker. Children: Henry Shoemaker; Henrietta Heiner, wife of William Heiner; Barney Shoemaker; Joseph Shoemaker; Thomas Shoemaker, of PA; George Shoemaker; Samuel Shoemaker, deceased, w/o issue; William Shoemaker; and John Shoemaker.
Property being part of *Brother's Agreement*.

Chancery Book 4, pp. 387-408   1846   Equity #206
George Everhart and Daniel Weaver vs. George Crouse, Admr. of George E. Weaver, deceased, and others. Sale of real estate to satisfy creditors.
George E. Weaver died June 1846. Brothers and sisters: Elizabeth Crouse, wife of George Crouse; Daniel Weaver, of Baltimore County; William Weaver, of VA; Philip Weaver, of PA; Lydia Brown, of Baltimore County, wife of George

W. Brown; Sarah Frankforter, wife of Jacob Frankforter; Mary Myerly, wife of Elias Myerly; Rebecca Ann Motter, wife of Henry Motter; Greenburg Weaver, of OH; and David Weaver, deceased, father of Mary Elizabeth Weaver (of OH), and David Weaver (of OH).
Properties situate about 1 mile from Manchester, adjacent to or south of road to Westminster, being parts of *Stoney Ridge, Everything Needful Corrected* and *Old Fort.*

Chancery Book 4, pp. 409-429 1846 Equity #207
George Everhart and Elizabeth Shaffer vs. Henry Shaffer, and others. Sale of real estate to satisfy creditors.
John Shaffer died May 1845, intestate, leaving widow, Margaret Shaffer. Children: Henry Shaffer; Nicholas Shaffer; William Shaffer; Emanuel Shaffer, out-of-state; James Shaffer, of Baltimore City; Mary Uhl, of Baltimore City, wife of Louie Uhl; Samuel Shaffer; and Ellen Shaffer.
Property situate in Manchester District, being part of *Ohio.*

Chancery Book 4, pp. 430-441 1847 Equity #219
Jesse Spangler, and others vs. John Spangler. Sale of real estate.
Jonas Spangler, of PA, died c. Aug 1846, intestate, leaving widow, Elizabeth Spangler, of Adams County PA. Children: Jesse Spangler; Jonas Spangler; Lydia Rathfon, wife of John Rathfon; John Spangler, of PA; Jacob Spangler, of PA; Barbara Ann Spangler, of PA; Isabella Spangler, of PA; and Joseph Spangler, deceased, father of Lydia Spangler (of PA), David Spangler (of PA), and Joseph Spangler (of PA).
Property situate part in MD, and part in PA, being part of *Exchange.*

Chancery Book 4, pp. 442-453 1848 Equity #234
William Frizzle and Catharine Frizzle, his wife vs. Mary A. Baile, and others. Sale of real estate.
Michael Baile, son of Peter Baile, died Sept 1834, intestate, leaving widow, Mary A. Baile. Children: Catharine Frizzle, wife of William Frizzle; Reuben Baile; and Susanna Baile. Brothers and sisters: John Baile; William Baile; Ludwick Baile; Abraham Baile; David Baile; Catherine Prugh; Elizabeth Cook; Sally Lindsay, deceased, wife of John Lindsay; Mary Greenwood; and Sophia Baile.
Property formerly situate in Frederick County.

Chancery Book 4, pp. 454-466 1848 Equity #237
John Williams, and others vs. James Williams. Sale of real estate.
Benjamin Williams died c. 1817 in Baltimore County, intestate, leaving widow who died in May 1847. Children: John Williams; Thomas Williams, of Baltimore City; Elizabeth Byers, wife of David Byers; Prudence Kelly, of OH, wife of

William Kelly; Lovelace Williams, of OH; Absolum Williams, of OH; James Williams; Sarah Heddington, deceased (1844), wife of Laban Heddington, mother of Thompson P. Heddington, Jesse Heddington, Julia A. Stone (wife of James Stone), Eliza A. Porter (wife of Harry Porter), Martin Van Buren Heddington, Jarrett Heddington, Oliver Heddington, Andrew Jackson Heddington, Murray Barrow Heddington, Margaret Heddington and Sarah Heddington (all of OH); and Nathan Williams, deceased, w/o issue.

Property formerly situtate in Baltimore County, being part of *Peach Brandy Forest*.

Chancery Book 4, pp. 467-477   1848   Equity #242
William H. Engleman vs. Julia Ann Engleman, and others.   Sale of real estate.
John Engleman, Jr., died Mar 1841, intestate, leaving widow, Julian Engleman. Children: William H. Engleman;   Mary Engleman;   Palmer Engleman; Emaline Engleman;   Varden Engleman, of Baltimore City;   Elizabeth Engleman; and Harriett Engleman.

Property formerly situate in Frederick County, being part of *Second Resurvey on Brierwoods*.

Chancery Book 4, pp. 478-500   1847   Equity #228
Mary Ann Baightel, mother and next friend of Emmet Baightel vs. Joshua Metcalf, Exc. of Samuel Baightel, deceased, and others.   Sale of real estate.
Samuel Baightel (or Bechtel) died 12 Dec 1846, testate, a miller, leaving widow, Mary Ann Baightel.   Children: Emmet Baightel;   Uriah Baightel;   Jonas Baightel;   Noah Baightel; and Isaiah Baightel.

Property formerly situate in Frederick County, on Little Pipe Creek, 4 miles west of Westminster, southeast of Uniontown, 2 miles east of New Windsor, being parts of *Cornwell, Addition to Cornwell* and *Resurvey on Mill Lot*.

Chancery Book 4, pp. 501-510   1848   Equity #243
Joseph Winters vs. Richard Brown and Susan Brown, his wife.   Foreclosure.
Richard Brown and his wife, Susan Brown.
Property being part of *Molly's Fancy*.

Chancery Book 4, pp. 511-521   1848   Equity #246
Hanson T. Bartholow vs. Thomas Bartholow and Cornelia Bartholow, his wife. Foreclosure.
Thomas Bartholow and his wife, Cornelia Bartholow.
Property being part of *Stepney's Causeway*.

Chancery Book 5, pp. 1-29   1848   Equity #235
Charles Reck, and others, vs. Henry Reck, and others.
Sale of real estate and to satisfy creditors.

Adam Reck, of Frederick County, died 1829, testate, leaving widow, Catherine Reck. Children: Henry Reck; John Reck, deceased, died May 1840, intestate, husband of Ann Reck, deceased (died in 1847), father of Charles Reck, Mary Hiteshew (wife of Ephraim Hiteshew), Catharine Reck, Hester Ann Reck, and Elias Reck; and Mary Crabs.
Property formerly situate in Frederick County, being part of *Retirement Corrected*. Another property was situate in Germany Township, Adams County, PA, being part of *Sideling Hill*.

Chancery Book 5, pp. 31-64   1847   Equity #227
Jesse Hann vs. Anna Copenhaver, Cornelius Baust, Admr. of William Copenhaver, and others.   Sale of real estate to satisfy creditors.
William Copenhaver died 16 May 1847, intestate, leaving widow, Anna Copenhaver. Children: Mathias Copenhaver; Elizabeth Copenhaver; Catherine Copenhaver; Barbara Angel, wife of Abraham Angel; Rebecca Copenhaver; John Copenhaver; Susannah Copenhaver; and William Copenhaver.
Properties formerly situate in Frederick County, being part of *Durbin's Mistake*.

Chancery Book 5, pp. 65-117   1841   Equity #61
David Banker, Peter Banker, and others vs. David Leister and wife, and others Sale of real estate to satisfy creditors.
Peter Banker, Sr., died 26 June 1840, intestate, leaving widow, Elizabeth Banker. Children: David Banker; Peter Banker, Jr.; Ephraim L. Banker; William Banker; Abdiel Banker; Catherine Sentz, wife of Joseph Sentz; Lydia Banker; Rachel Yoost, wife of John Yoost of William; Barbara Sholl, wife of Peter Sholl; Hannah Brown, wife of Peter Brown, Jr.; Sabilla Banker; and Elizabeth Cashman, of Adams County PA, wife of John Cashman.
Peter's widow, Elizabeth, was the daughter of Daniel Stonesifer and his wife, Maria Elizabeth Stonesifer. Their other children were: Hannah Stonesifer, who had a daughter Catherine Stonesifer; Jacob Stonesifer; Peter Stonesifer; Abraham Stonesifer; Henry Stonesifer; Isaac Stonesifer; Daniel Stonesifer; Barbara Stonesifer; Lovice Wymert, wife of Peter Wymert; Christina Stonesifer; Martin Stonesifer, deceased, father of John Stonesifer, Polly Leister (wife of David Leister), Henry Stonesifer, and Rachel Stonesifer; and John Stonesifer, deceased. There was also mentioned a granddaughter, Barbara Routzon, who was wife of Henry Routzon.
Property formerly situate in Frederick County, being part of *High Germany*.

Chancery Book 5, pp. 118-136   1847   Equity #230
John Sykes vs. Margaret Lammott and Michael Sullivan, Admr. of Samuel Lammott, deceased, and others.   Sale of real estate to satisfy creditors.
Samuel Lammott died 1845, intestate, leaving widow, Margaret Lammott. Children: Sarah Lammott; and Josephine Lammott.

Property situate in Hampstead, being part of *Transylvania*.

Chancery Book 5, pp.137-148 1847 Equity #232
William Whalen vs. Matilda Philips and Basil T. Philips. Sale of real estate.
John Phillips, of Baltimore County, died 1829, testate. Children: John T. Phillips, deceased, testate; Lemuel McAlister Phillips, deceased; Harriet Phillips; Eliza Phillips; Julian Phillips; Matilda Phillips; and Susan Phillips.
Property being part of *Wilmot's Wilderness*.

Chancery Book 5, pp. 151-169 1848 Equity #240
Levi Heiner, Samuel Heiner, and others vs. William Heiner. Sale of real estate and to satisfy creditors.
Henry Heiner died 1847, intestate. His wife, Hannah Heiner, predeceased him. Children: Levi Heiner; Samuel Heiner; Elizabeth Garner, wife of John Garner; Susannah Baker, wife of Jacob Baker; Catherine Heiner; Emily Heiner; William Heiner; and Mary Earhart, deceased, wife of Daniel Earhart, mother of Edward Earhart, Priscilla R. Earhart, Horatio Earhart, Martha E. Earhart, and Mary Earhart.
Property situate about 1 mile from Crabs Mill on Big Pipe Creek, 2 miles from George Kephart's Mill, 3 miles from Uniontown, 10 miles from Westminster, being parts of *Bedford, Resurvey on Retirement* and *Retirement Corrected*.

Chancery Book 5, pp. 171-196 1848 Equity #251
Ann Roberts and Mary Eckard vs. Jesse Eckard, and others.
Chancery Book 5, pp. 511-512
In the matter of the Petition of Jacob Eckard. Sale of real estate to satisfy creditors.
George Eckard died 8 April 1848, near Uniontown, intestate. His wife, Rebecca Eckard, died 5-6 years before him. Children: Jesse Eckard, of Frederick County; Sarah Ann Eckard; Susanna Jane Eckard; Mary Eckard; William Eckard; Jacob Eckard, of Frederick County; Henry Eckard; and Thomas Eckard.
Property being part of *Meadow Branch, The Branch Enlarged, Horn's Meadows* and *Ashburners Disappointment*.

Chancery Book 5, pp. 197-209 1849 Equity #258
John S. Shriver, Thomas Shriver, et al. vs. Olivia Brengle,
Elizabeth Brengle, Catherine B. Steiger, et al. Sale of real estate.
Andrew Shriver died Sept 1847, intestate. Children: Catherine Brengle, deceased, mother of Olivia Brengle (of Frederick County), and Elizabeth Brengle (of Frederick County); Ann Maria Steiger, deceased, mother of Catherine B. Steiger, Benjamin T. Steiger, Emma Maria Steiger, and Augustus F. Steiger; John S. Shriver; Thomas Shriver; Joseph Shriver; Andrew K. Shriver;

William Shriver; Eliza Brengle, wife of Lawrence T. Brengle; Rebecca Renshaw, deceased, mother of Ann Maria Zimmerman (wife of Benjamin F. Zimmerman), and John Alexander Renshaw; James Shriver, deceased, father of Samuel S. Shriver, and Eliza Jane McLane (wife of George McLane); and Matilda Spangler, deceased, mother of Augustus G. Spangler, William H. Spangler, Alexander R. Spangler, Andrew M. Spangler, Benjamin F. Spangler, Josephine M. Spangler, and Margaret M. Spangler.
Property being parts of *The Mill Lot, Hill Spring, Carolina, Addition to Carolina, Ground Oak Hill, Ground Oak Thicket, Ohio* and *Leonard's Lot.*

Chancery Book 5, pp. 211-250   1846   Equity #189
Stephen Gorsuch vs. Petitia Gorsuch, Admr. of Nathan Gorsuch, deceased, and William P. Gorsuch, and others. Sale of real estate to satisfy creditors.
Nathan Gorsuch died 11 Nov 1840, intestate, leaving widow, Petitia Gorsuch. Children: William P. Gorsuch; Elizabeth Ann Gorsuch; and John Thomas Gorsuch.
Properties formerly situate in Baltimore County, in Freedom District, near and adjoining Baltimore and Ohio Railroad, 2 miles east of Sykesville, being parts of *Dorsey's Interest, Forrest's Venture, Dorsey's Neglect, Turkey Thicket* and *Hunter's Chance.*

Chancery Book 5, pp. 251-266   1848   Equity #253
Petition of Mary Zepp, as mother and next friend of Catherine Zepp, and others. Sale of real estate.
David Zepp died Dec 1847, intestate, leaving widow, Mary Zepp. Children: Catharine Zepp; Abdiel Zepp; Henry Zepp; Elizabeth Zepp; Ann Maria Zepp; George Zepp; and Noah Zepp, deceased, w/o issue.
Properties being part of *Henry Ebaugh's Resurvey.*

Chancery Book 5, pp. 266-287   1849   Equity #270
Samuel A. Haines vs. Thomas Fowble, M. Julian Fowble, his wife, and others. Sale of real estate to satisfy creditors.
Jacob Haines died Aug 1847, intestate. Children: Samuel A. Haines; M. Julian Fowble of Baltimore City, wife of Thomas Fowble; Margarette C. Haines; Ellen M. Haines; John T. Haines; Mary E. Haines; and William H. Haines.
Property formerly situate in Baltimore County with part in Frederick County, being part of *Resurvey on Father's Gift.*

Chancery Book 5, pp. 288-303   1849   Equity #267
Abraham Harner and Barbara Harner, his wife, and others vs. Eliza Ohler, John Ohler, and others. Sale of real estate.

George Adam Ohler died after 1838, testate. Children: Thomas Ohler; Frederick Ohler; James Ohler; Mary Harps, wife of Michael Harps; Barbara Knox, wife of Col. William Knox; Elizabeth Smith; Catherine Crabbs, deceased, wife of Frederick Crabbs; George Ohler; and Abraham Ohler, deceased, died Feb 1849, husband of Margaret Ohler, father to Barbara Harner (wife of Abraham Harner), Mary Brown (of PA, wife of Barney Brown), Eliza Ohler, John Ohler, Jacob Ohler, James Ohler, and Gassaway Ohler.

Property formerly situate in Frederick County, being part of *Addition to Brook's Discovery on the Rich Lands*.

Chancery Book 5, pp. 304-314   1848   Equity #257
William Otter and Elizabeth Otter, his wife vs. Elizabeth Latham and Joseph Latham. Sale of real estate.

Joseph Latham, of Frederick County, died 1823, intestate, leaving widow, since deceased. Children: Elizabeth Otter, wife of William Otter; and Joseph Latham, deceased, died 1844, husband of Louisa Latham, father to Elizabeth Latham, and Joseph Latham (all of Emmittsburg, Frederick County).

Property situate formerly in Frederick County, in Taneytown, being known as Lot 11.

Chancery Book 5, pp. 315-343   1848   Equity #250
William Horner, Jr., James L. Horner, and others vs. George Bramwell and Amanda Bramwell, his wife, Charles W. Horner, and others. Sale of real estate.

William Horner, Sr., died Aug 1847, leaving widow, Elizabeth Horner. Children: Amanda Bramwell, wife of George Bramwell; Franklin T. Horner; Charles W. Horner; Lavina J. Wagner, of Baltimore County, wife of Edward Wagner; Eaton G. Horner, of Baltimore City; John A. Horner, of Baltimore City; George W. Horner; Elizabeth Barrick, of Frederick County, wife of John Barrick; William Horner, Jr., of Baltimore City; James L. Horner, of Fayetteville PA; Eli R. Horner, of Fayetteville PA; Alexander H. Horner, of Fayetteville PA; David Horner, of Knox County OH; Mary Auld, of Dark County OH, wife of James Auld; and Matilda Heagy, deceased, wife of Andrew Heagy, deceased, mother of Hannah M. Heagy, William Heagy, Margaret E. Heagy, and Andrew Heagy (all of OH).

Properties situate on Westminster-Baltimore road, in or near town of Finksburg, being parts of *Hooker's Meadow* and *Porter's Desire*. One was commonly called the *tavern property*.

Chancery Book 5, pp. 344-365   1849   Equity #259
Magdalana Snyder, widow, and others vs. Daniel Snyder, and others. Sale of real estate.

Christian Snyder died 27 Feb 1842, testate, leaving widow, Magdalana Snyder. Children: Jacob Snyder; Michael Snyder; Henry Snyder; Magdalena Yingling,

wife of John Yingling; Barbara Vitter, wife of Samuel Vitter; Catherine Yingling, wife of Jacob Yingling; Leah Glase, wife of Henry Glase; Rachael Keller, wife of Philip Keller; George Snyder, deceased, father of David A. Snyder, Mary Snyder, George W. Snyder, Catherine Snyder (of Baltimore City), and Daniel Snyder; Elizabeth Rodkey, deceased, wife of John Rodkey, deceased, mother of Mary Rodkey, Elizabeth Rodkey, John Rodkey, Catherine Rodkey, Daniel Rodkey, Esther Rodkey, George Rodkey, Jonathan Rodkey, Michael Rodkey, and Leah Rodkey (all of OH); and Anna Maria Whiteleather, deceased, wife of Andrew Whiteleather, of PA, mother of David Whiteleather, Martin Whiteleather, Rebecca Whiteleather (of Baltimore City), and Jacob Whiteleather (of PA).
Property location not established.

Chancery Book 5, pp. 365-382 1847 Equity #229
George Warner, Exr. of Henry Kontz, deceased vs. George Wentz. Foreclosure.
George Wentz.
Property being part of *Overpronn* and *Everybodys Land*.

Chancery Book 5, pp. 386-409 1849 Equity #269
Levi T. Bennett, and others vs. Ephraim Cook and Ruth Cook, his wife, and others. Sale of real estate.
Gideon Mitchell died Feb 1849, intestate. Children: Elizabeth Buckingham, of Frederick County, widow of Benjamin Buckingham; Charlotte Prugh, of OH, wife of Peter Prugh; Ruth Cook, wife of Ephraim Cook; Rebecca Bartholow, deceased, wife of Thomas Bartholow, mother of Hanson F. Bartholow, Matilda Gorsuch (wife of Thomas Gorsuch), and Margaret A. R. Bartholow (of Baltimore City); and Polly Bennett, deceased, wife of Benjamin Bennett, deceased, mother of Levi T. Bennett, Rebecca Zepp (wife of Solomon Zepp), Ruth E. Bennett, and Larkin Bennett, deceased (father of Adaline Bennett, Mary E. Bennett, Eli T. Bennett, and Larkin Samuel Bennett).
Properties formerly situate in Baltimore County, being parts of *Chestnut Ridge, Shadrack's Last Shift, Lawrences Pleasant Hills, Marys Victory* and *Peach Brandy Forrest*.

Chancery Book 5, pp. 410-435 1848 Equity #254
Daniel Geiser vs. Barbara Whitmyer, and others. Sale of property to satisfy creditors.
Simon Whitmyer died c. Aug 1848, intestate, leaving widow, Barbara Whitmyer. Children: Elizabeth Crouse, wife of David Crouse; Catharine Zepp, wife of Peter Zepp; Mary Sell, wife of Jacob Sell; Rebecca Whitmyer; Lydia Whitmyer; and Daniel Whitmyer, deceased, died 1 Sept 1848, intestate, husband of Lydia

Whitmyer, father of Mary Elizabeth Whitmyer, Sarah Ellen Whitmyer, and William Ezra Whitmyer.

Property formerly situate in Frederick County, being parts of *Resurvey on Friendship, Clary, Resurvey on Lookabout, Empty Cupboard, Runnymede* and *Peace and Goodwill.*

Chancery Book 5, pp. 435-450 1849 Equity #272
Jacob Morelock, next friend of David Ezra Morelock, and others vs. David Ezra Morelock, and others. Sale of real estate.
Joseph Morelock, son of Michael Morelock, Sr., died Feb 1847, intestate. Children: David Ezra Morelock; Jeremiah Andrew Morelock; Mary Ann Rebecca Morelock; Dennis Abraham Morelock; Uriah James Morelock; Elizabeth Amy Morelock; and Louisa Morelock, deceased, w/o issue. Brother was Jacob Morelock.
Property formerly situate in Frederick County, on Little Pipe Creek, 3 miles south of Westminster, being parts of *Stocksdale's Hill, Resurvey on the Addition to Stocksdale's Hill, Good Fellowship* and *Resurvey on Good Fellowship.*

Chancery Book 5, pp. 450-453 1849 Equity #284
(ten page nos. repeated)
John S. Shriver, et al. vs. Olivia Brengle, et al. Sale of real estate.
Andrew Shriver died 1847. Children: John S. Shriver; Thomas Shriver; Joseph Shriver; Andrew K. Shriver; William Shriver; Eliza Brengle, wife of Lawrence Brengle; Rebecca Renshaw, deceased, mother of Ann Maria Zimmerman (wife of Benjamin F. Zimmerman), and John Alexander Renshaw; James Shriver, deceased, father of Samuel S. Shriver, and Eliza Jane McLane (wife of George McLane); Matilda Spangler, deceased, mother of William H. Spangler, Alexander R. Spangler, Andrew M. Spangler, Benjamin F. Spangler, Josephine M. Spangler, and Margaret M. Spangler; Catherine Brengle, deceased, mother of Olivia Brengle, and Elizabeth Brengle (both of Frederick County); and Maria Steiger, mother of Catherine B. Steiger, Benjamin F. Steiger, Anna Maria Steiger, and Augustus F. Steiger (all of Washington, D. C.).
Property formerly situate in Frederick County, 2 miles south of Union Mills.

Chancery Book 5, pp. 454-462 1849 Equity #266
Daniel Engle vs. Charles Owens and Sarah Owens, his wife. Foreclosure.
Charles Owens and Sarah Owens, his wife.
Property situate c. 1-1/2 miles south of New Liberty Road, being part of *Batchelor's Refuge Resurveyed.*

Chancery Book 5, pp. 463-475 1849 Equity #280
Isaac Hull, and others vs. Hezekiah Hull and Rebecca Hull. Sale of real estate.

Peter Hull died May 1848, intestate, leaving widow, Fanny Hull. Children: Isaac Hull; William Hull; David Hull; Maria Ann Margaret Cover, wife of Samuel Cover; Savilla Maus, wife of John Maus, Jr.; Hezekiah Hull; and Rebecca Hull. Properties situate in Myers District, near PA line, being part of *Ohio*.

Chancery Book 5, pp. 476-488 1849 Equity #274
Petition of John Marker, and others. Sale of real estate and to satisfy creditors. John Marker, of Frederick County, died c. 1824, testate, leaving widow, Susannah Marker, deceased, died March 1849. Children: Margaret Byers, wife of Peter Byers; John Marker; Jacob Marker; Elizabeth Frock, deceased, wife of Peter Frock; Barbara Hiltebridle, wife of Jacob Hiltebridle; Mary Young, wife of Jacob Young; David Marker; Rachel Wantz, widow of Valentine Wantz; and Catherine Stonesifer, deceased, formerly known as Catherine Frock, widow of Michael Frock Jr., deceased (died c. 1839), then became wife of Jacob Stonesifer.
Property formerly situate in Frederick County, being part of *Keefer's Range*.

Chancery Book 5, pp. 489-510 1849 Equity #271
Nicholas Ogg, Samuel I. Jordan, and others vs. Nathan Gorsuch and Corrilla Gorsuch, his wife, and others. Sale of real estate.
George Ogg died c. 1770, testate, leaving widow Hellen Ogg. Children: Rachel Ogg; Benjamin Ogg; George Ogg, deceased, died 13 Nov 1847, intestate, no widow, father of George Ogg, John Ogg, Sarah Shockney (of IN, wife of Charles Shockney), Moses Ogg (of OH), Nicholas Ogg, Hellen Jordan, deceased (wife of William Jordan, mother of Corrilla Gorsuch [wife of Nathan Gorsuch], Hezekiah Jordan, Hanson P. Jordan, Samuel I. Jordan, Mary Jordan, James W. Jordan, Elias Jordan, and George W. Jordan), Rachel Wade, deceased (wife of Larkin Wade, mother of Emanuel Wade, Ann Biden [wife of John Biden], Rachel Wade, and Benedict Wade [all of Baltimore County]), Ann Criswell, deceased (wife of Elijah Criswell, mother of Barbara Arnold [of Baltimore County, wife of James Arnold], Mary Arnold [wife of John Arnold], Catherine Arnold [wife of Caleb Arnold], George C. Criswell, and Elijah Criswell), William Ogg, deceased (father to William Ogg, James Ogg, Susan Ogg, Henrietta Ogg, Laben Ogg, and Richard Ogg, [all of OH]), and Catherine Shipley, deceased (wife of Lloyd Shipley, mother of John R. Shipley, George W. Shipley, and Mary A. Buckingham [wife of Elisha Buckingham]); William Hamilton Ogg; and Mary Ogg.
Properties formerly situate in Baltimore County, 6 miles from Westminster near Nicodemus Road, being parts of *Caledonia, George's Lot, Curgaforgus, Fort Royal* and *Grey's Meadow*.

Chancery Book 5, pp. 513-521 1849 Equity #263
In the matter of the Petition of Elias K. Ebaugh. Sale of real estate to satisfy creditors.
Elizabeth Ebaugh, lunatic. Children: Elias K. Ebaugh; Conrad Ebaugh; George Ebaugh; Henry Ebaugh; John K. Ebaugh; David Ebaugh; Adam Ebaugh; Andrew Ebaugh; Catherine Sharrer; Elizabeth Brown; Mary Yingling; Susan Gorsuch; and Jacob Ebaugh, deceased, father of Joseph Ebaugh, Benjamin Ebaugh, Jacob Ebaugh, William Ebaugh, Jesse Ebaugh, Amos Ebaugh, Elisha Ebaugh, and Henry Ebaugh.
Properties situate in Hampstead, at intersection of Turnpike Road and Middletown Road, parts of *Transylvania* and *Petersburgh*.

Chancery Book 5, pp. 523-540 1848 Equity #238
Daniel Engle, Guardian and next friend of Susannah Polk Ingles vs. Hanson T. Ingles, John Ingles, and others. Sale of real estate.
John Ingles died c. 1826, testate. Children: Lacy Thomas, mother of Samuel Thomas, Joseph Thomas and Jane Thomas; Ellenor Powell; John Ingels; and Thomas Ingels, deceased, died 1844, intestate, husband of Margaret Ingles (she became Margaret Harp when she later married James Harp), father of Hanson T. Ingles, John Ingles, Rachel Ingles, deceased (died c. 1846, unmarried, mother of Susannah Polk Ingles), and Jane Ingles, deceased (died c. 1846, w/o issue).
Properties formerly situate in Frederick County and Baltimore County, being parts of *Pork Hall, Brother's Inheritance, Mulberry Bottom, Leigh Castle* and *Caledonia*.

Chancery Book 5, pp. 541-552 1848 Equity #256
Andrew Fitez, Mary Fitez, his wife, and others vs. Hiram Fogle and Elizabeth Fogle, his wife. Sale of real estate.
George Whitmore died April 1848, leaving widow Mary Whitmore, who later married and became Mary Fitez, wife of Andrew Fitez. Children: Sarah Hahn, wife of William Hahn; Jacob Whitmore; William Whitmore; Benjamin Whitmore; Greenberry Whitmore; and Elizabeth Fogle, wife of Hiram Fogle.
Property being part of *Terra Rubra*.

Chancery Book 5, pp. 553-561 1849 Equity #278
Frederick Winters vs. Mary Winters.
Divorce.
Frederick Winters married Mary Creager, widow of the late George Creager, daughter of Jacob Appler in the Town of New Windsor by Rev. Jonathan Forrest. She left in 1846. No issue.
Property formerly situate in Frederick County.

Chancery Book 5, pp. 562-578 1849 Equity #287
Yoder Masemer, and others vs. Mary M. Dressler, widow, and others. Sale of real estate to satisfy creditors.
John Dressler died May 1847, intestate, leaving widow, Mary Magdelina Dressler, of York County, PA. Children: Anna Mary Dressler; and George Dressler; both of York County, PA.
Property being parts of *Venus's Arbour* and *Dehoof's Pleasure*.

Chancery Book 6, pp. 1-22 1849 Equity #289
Catherine Crumbacker vs. Sarah Ecker, and others. Sale of real estate to satisfy creditors.
John Ecker, of Frederick County, died c. 1836, testate, leaving widow, Hannah Ecker. Children: Jacob Ecker, deceased, died 25 Mar 1849, intestate, husband of Sarah Ecker, father of Peter Ecker, Harrison Ecker, William Ecker, Mary Catherine Ecker, and John Ecker; David Ecker; Samuel Ecker; William Ecker; Jonas Ecker; and Deborah Ecker.
Property situate 1 mile south of New Windsor.

Chancery Book 6, pp. 23-35 1849 Equity #288
Hugh Gelston vs. William T. R. Saffell. Foreclosure.
William T. R. Saffell and Mary Ann Saffell, his wife.
Property being parts of *Sally's Chance Resurvey, Pool's Desire, Warfield's Forest* and *Richard's Third Chance*.

Chancery Book 6, pp. 36-48 1850 Equity #310
Jacob Otto and Catherine Otto, his wife vs. Jacob Keefer, and others. Sale of real estate.
Henry Keefer and his wife, Sarah Keefer. Children: Thomas Keefer, deceased, died June 1850, intestate, no issue; Jacob Keefer; Elizabeth Ann Hann, wife of Phillip Hann; Susanna Hann, wife of Phillip W. Hann; and Catherine Otto, wife of Jacob Otto.
Properties formerly situate in Frederick County, being parts of *Maidens Point* and *Brook's Discovery on the Rich Lands*.

Chancery Book 6, pp. 49-62 1850 Equity #296
Otho Flemming and wife vs. Mary E. Davis, et al. Sale of real estate.
Thomas Davis, of Zachariah, died 25 Feb 1850, intestate, his wife having died several years prior. Children: Elizabeth A. Flemming, of Howard District, Anne Arundel County MD, wife of Otho Flemming; Mary E. Davis; Susan J. Davis, of Anne Arundel County MD; Amelia C. Davis; Silas W. Davis, of Anne Arundel County MD; and Thomas Davis, of Anne Arundel County MD.
Property being parts of *Hampton Court* and *Chases Forrest*.

Chancery Book 6, pp. 63-77 1850 Equity #306
Petition of Robert J. Jameson and wife. Sale of real estate.
George Pusey, Jr., died June 1850, testate, his wife, Sarah Pusey having died earlier. Children: Thomas Pusey; Catherine Jameson, wife of Robert J. Jameson; Elizabeth Kagel, wife of John C. Kagel; and Margaret A. Stevens, wife of Clemson Stevens, mother of Sarah Stevens.
Property situate in McKinstry's Mills on Sam's Creek. Other property located in Town of New Market, Frederick County.

Chancery Book 6, pp. 78-91 1850 Equity #308
Petition of John Thomson and wife. Sale of real estate.
Nicholas Fringer died 12 July 1840, testate, leaving widow, Margaret Fringer, who died 12 Aug 1850. Children: George Fringer, deceased, father of Alice Fringer, George Fringer, Nicholas Fringer, Michael Fringer, Jacob Fringer, Worthington Fringer, and Ephraim Fringer; Jacob Fringer, deceased, father of Theodore Fringer, Elmira Fringer, and Harman Fringer; Nicholas Fringer; Louisa Thomson, wife of John Thomson; Michael Fringer; and Mary Null, deceased, wife of Abraham Null, mother to Mary Jane Kesselring (wife of Samuel Kesselring), Sarah Yingling (wife of Edward Yingling), Lovice Kuhn (wife of John Kuhn), George Null, Margaret Null, Lydia Null, Rebecca Null, and Henry Null.
Property was known as Lot 43 in Taneytown.

Chancery Book 6, pp. 92-107 1850 Equity #305
Josiah P. Smeltzer, and others vs. Sarah Smeltzer, and others. Sale of real estate.
George Smeltzer died c. 1836, intestate, leaving widow Sarah Smeltzer, of Frederick County. Children: Josiah P. Smeltzer, of Frederick County; Isaac W. Smeltzer, deceased, died 1850, husband of Rachel Smeltzer, father of Solomon S. Smeltzer; Caroline L. Rhodes, of Frederick County, wife of Henry C. Rhodes.
Property formerly situate in Frederick County, being parts of *Resurvey on Good Will* and *Stevenson's Garden*.

Chancery Book 6, pp. 108-136 1849 Equity #285
Samuel G. Davis, and others vs. Catherine M. Davis. Sale of real estate.
Samuel Davis and his wife, Hanna G. Davis, both died intestate. Children: Samuel G. Davis; Hanna A. Davis; Rachel Davis; Lucy Ann Sim, wife of Dr. Thomas Sim; and Catherine Mary Davis.
Properties formerly situate in both Baltimore County and Frederick County, being parts of *Hampton Court*, *Resurvey on Gilboa* and *Resurvey on Long Trusted*.

Chancery Book 6, pp. 137-171 1849 Equity #268
Petition of Eurith Barnes, next friend of Esther Ann Barnes and Julia Ann Rebecca Barnes. Sale of real estate and to satisfy creditors.
Aquilla G. Barnes died 13 Feb 1849, intestate, leaving widow, Eurith Barnes. Children: Esther Ann Barnes; and Julia Ann Rebecca Barnes.
Properties being parts of *Flaggs Meadow* and *Parrish's Chance*.

Chancery Book 6, pp, 172-196 1850 Equity #303
Petition of James Hesson and Catherine Hesson, his wife, next friend of Levi Haifleigh and Catherine A. Haifleigh. Sale of real estate.
George Haifleigh died 1841, intestate, leaving widow, Catherine Haifleigh, who became Catherine Hesson when she later married James Hesson. Children: Levi Haifleigh; and Catherine A. Haifleigh.
Property formerly situate in Frederick County, being parts of *Glade Springs*, *Molly's Fancy*, and *Lookabout*.

Chancery Book 6, pp. 197-230 1849 Equity #273
Jacob Frankforter, next friend, and others vs. Francis Gross, Abraham Wampler, Trustee, and others. Sale of real estate.
John Gross, Jr., son of John Gross, died May 1846, intestate, leaving widow, Mary Gross, who became Mary Shaeffer when she later married Jacob Shaeffer. Children: Francis Gross; John Gross; Lydia Gross; Mary Gross; and William Gross. Jacob Frankforter was the children's uncle.
Property being part of *Pleasant Hills*.

Chancery Book 6, pp. 231-280 1849 Equity #264
Catherine Dorsey, and others vs. Samuel T. Dorsey, and others. Sale of real estate.
Benjamin Dorsey, (son of Benjamin Dorsey, of Baltimore County, who died 1829), and his wife, Rachel Dorsey. Children: Samuel T. Dorsey; Isabella H. Dorsey; Susan J. Dorsey; Hannah E. Dorsey; and Joshua Dorsey.
Property being parts of *Brother's Discovery*, *Dorsey's Thicket*, *Kindall's Delight*, *John's Chance* and *Bagdad*.

Chancery Book 6, pp. 282-317 1850 Equity #299
Joshua Wisner, next friend vs. Henry Simpers, and others. Sale of real estate.
Henry Zouck, of Baltimore County, died 1843, testate, leaving widow, Barbary Zouck. Children: Barbary Armacost; John Zouck; George Zouck; Catherine Storms; Elizabeth Armacost; and Mary Wisner, died 20 Apr 1849, wife of Joshua Wisner, mother to Henry Simpers, and Mary Ann Simpers (both by first

husband, Benjamin Simpers, deceased), Barbara Wisner, Joshua Wisner, Jr., Andrew Wisner, Sarah Jane Wisner, and Richard Wisner.
Property formerly situate in Frederick County, being parts of *Ohio* and *Three Springs*.

Chancery Book 6, pp. 319-340   1851   Equity #319
John Frock and James Airing vs. Sarah Frock, et als. Sale of real estate to satisfy creditors.
Jacob Frock died 29 Nov 1848, intestate. Children: Sarah Frock; Isaah Frock; Jacob Frock; John Frock; Mary Frock; and Elizabeth Frock, of Frederick County.
Property formerly situate in Frederick County, being parts of *Hersch's Second Purchase* and *Resurvey on Mackey's Choice*.

Chancery Book 6, pp. 342-368   1850   Equity #311
Samuel Angel vs. John W. Weant, Michael Sluss, Admr. of Jacob Weant. Sale of real estate to satisfy creditors.
Jacob Weant died July 1850, intestate, leaving only child and heir, John Washington Weant.
Property being part of *Cliffs*.

Chancery Book 6, pp. 369-388   1850   Equity #315
Petition of Elizabeth R. Rinehart, Susan C. Rinehart, and others. Sale of real estate.
Peter S. Rinehart died 23 Dec 1847, intestate, leaving widow, Maria Rinehart. Children: Elizabeth R. Rinehart; Susan C. Rinehart; Martha J. Rinehart; Margaret Rinehart; Sarah A. Rinehart; Rachael A. Rinehart; and Ann M. Rinehart.
Property being parts of *Clary, Ohio, Resurvey on Friendship, Resurvey on Three Springs* and *Runnymede Enlarged*.

Chancery Book 6, pp. 389-407   1851   Equity #323
Petition of John Rinehart, Peter Masonheimer, Adam W. Feeser and wife. Sale of real estate.
Magdalena Rinehart died testate. She was grandmother of Catherine Susan Feeser, wife of Adam W. Feeser, mother of Eliza A. Feeser, Sarah A. Feeser, Susan Feeser, Mary E. Feeser, and John Feeser.
Property formerly situate in Frederick County, commonly known as the *Lingenfelter's Place*.

Chancery Book 6, pp. 309-334   1850   Equity #302
(pages should be numbered 409-434)

Fanny Hull, in her own right and as next friend of Hezekiah Hull, Rebecca Hull, and others vs. Isaac Hull and William H. Hull. Sale of real estate.
Peter Hull died May 1848, leaving widow, Fanny Hull. Children: Hezekiah Hull; Rebecca Hull; Maria Ann Margaret Cover, wife of Samuel Cover; Savilla Maus, wife of John Maus, Jr.; David Hull; Isaac Hull; and William H. Hull.
Property formerly situate in Frederick County, being parts of *Unity, Lemon's Choice, The First Trapezinm* and *The Second Trapezinm.*

Chancery Book 6, pp. 436-466   1851   Equity #332
James W. Lantz, and others vs. Sarah Lantz, and others. Sale of real estate.
John Lantz died 3 Feb 1851, intestate, leaving widow, Sarah Lantz. Children: James W. Lantz; William L. Lantz; Louisa A. Otto, wife of Peter Otto; Elizabeth A. Lantz; John T. Lantz; and Theodore A. Lantz.
Properties formerly situate in Frederick County, being parts of *Batchelor's Prospect, Wagoner's Fancy, Recovery Unexpected, Resurvey on Brierwood, Resurvey on Black Oak Hill, Etzler's Contentment, Bethel* and *Neighborhood Contention.*

Chancery Book 6, pp. 470-520   1851   Equity #320
Abraham Null, et al. vs. William H. Null, et al. Sale of real estate.
Michael Null, Jr., died 11 Dec 1850, intestate, leaving widow, Elizabeth Null. Children: Abraham Null; Jacob Null; Samuel Null; Susannah Fringer, widow of George Fringer; Rebecca Snider, wife of Jacob Snider; Mary Hess, deceased, mother of Abraham N. Hess; John Null, deceased, died 1849, father of John H. Null (of Frederick County), Margaret E. Null (of OH), William H. Null, Emily J. Null, and Mary E. Null.
Michael's widow, Elizabeth, was the daughter of Frederick Black, of Frederick County, who died in 1826, leaving widow, Rebecca Black. Their other children were: Ulrick Black; Adam Black; John Black; Frederick Black; Magdalena Black, deceased; Mary Lightner, deceased, mother of Mary Lightner and Joseph Lightner; Mary Derr; Rebecca (or Margaret) Hawk, wife of George Hawk; and Joseph Black.
Properties formerly situate in Frederick County, some situate on Piney Creek and some on Piney Creek Road and Taneytown-York Road, being parts of *Brooks Discovery on the Rich Lands, Resurvey on Brother's Agreement* and *Fredericksburgh.*

Chancery Book 6, pp. 521-537   1850   Equity #300
Solomon Hipsley, et al. vs. Joshua Shipley. Sale of real estate.
John Hipsley died March 1850, intestate. Children: Solomon Hipsley; Ellen Hobb, wife of Gustavious Hobb; Elizabeth Ware, widow of John Ware; Nancy Shipley, wife of Peter Shipley; and Joshua Hipsley.

Property formerly situate in Baltimore County, in Freedom District, being parts of *Additional Progress, Progress* and *Dorsey's Delama.*

Chancery Book 6, pp. 539-556   1851   Equity #335
Abraham Short and Mary Ann Short, et al. vs. Margaret Boyers.   Sale of real estate.
Peter Boyers died March 1851, leaving widow, Margaret Boyers. Children: Mary Ann Short, wife of Abraham Short; John Boyers; Elizabeth Boyers; Henry Boyers; Susan Boyers; David Boyers; and Peter Boyers.
Property formerly situate in Frederick County, being parts of *Lookabout, Father's Advice* and *Addition to Molley's Fancy.*

Chancery Book 7, pp. 1-26   1851   Equity #331
Elisha J. Cook vs. Rachel Haines.   Sale of real estate to satisfy creditors.
Eli Haines, son of Joseph Haines, died c. Oct 1850 intestate, leaving widow, Rachel Haines. Children: William Henry Haines; Joel Haines; and Augusta Ann Haines. Brothers and sister were: Samuel Haines; Elizabeth Hibberd, wife of Silas Hibberd; Nathan Haines; Job Haines; Isaac Haines; and Reuben Haines.
Property formerly situate in Frederick County, being parts of *Stevenson's Garden* and *Cornwell.*

Chancery Book 7, pp. 29-60   1850   Equity #301
John Hiner, et als. vs. Harrison B. Hiner, et als.   Sale of real estate.
Peter Hiner, of Frederick County, died c. 1828, intestate, leaving widow, Elizabeth Hiner. Children: John Hiner; Eliza Hartzell, of PA, wife of Samuel Hartzell; Ann Hiner; Catherine Haugh, wife of William Haugh; Jesse Hiner, deceased, died c. 1848, intestate, husband of Sophia Hiner, father of Harrison B. Hiner and Mary Hiner (all of IN); and Susanna Hartzell, of Adams County, PA, widow of John Hartzell, deceased (died Aug 1849).
Property formerly situate in Frederick County, along Big Pipe Creek, being part of *Retirement Corrected.*

Chancery Book 7, pp. 63-93   1850   Equity #304
Francis Warner, et al. vs. Magdalena Warner, et al.   Sale of real estate.
Jacob Warner died Feb 1850, intestate, leaving widow, Magdalena Warner. Children: Francis Warner; Mary Warner; Samuel E. Warner, of PA; Rachel Warner; and Sarah Warner.
Property formerly situate in Baltimore County, being parts of *Peter Trashel's Management, What You Please, Addition to Curpoy* and *Eight Sisters.*

Chancery Book 7, pp. 94-129   1849   Equity #290
Joseph Kopp and Henry Motter vs. Joseph Parker, Admr., Lysander Kopp, et als.   Sale of real estate to satisfy creditors.
Joshua F. Kopp died Dec 1846, intestate, leaving widow, Sarah Kopp. Children: Lysander Kopp; Alfred Kopp; Theodore Kopp; Francis Thomas Kopp; Julia Frances Kopp; and Sarah Kopp.
Properties being parts of *The German Church, Everything Needful Corrected* and *Stoney Point.*

Chancery Book 7, pp. 131-145   1848   Equity #245
Abijah Young, Hardress Young, and others vs. John S. Young, and others.   Sale of real estate.
Benjamin Young, of Baltimore County, died 13 Aug 1828, intestate. Children: Elhanan Young, deceased, died c. 1836, father of Eliza Ann Johnson (wife of Jeremiah Johnson), John S. Young, Samuel Young, and Thomas E. Young; Respeah Young, deceased, unmarried and w/o issue; Abijah Young; Hardress Young; Manoah Young; and Micajah Young.
Property formerly situate in Baltimore County, being part of *Windsor Forest.*

Chancery Book 7, pp. 147-195   1849   Equity #261
Elisha D. Payne vs. Nancy Wagus, and others.   Sale of real estate to satisfy creditors.
William Wagus died 27 Mar 1848, testate, leaving widow, Nancy Wagus. Children: Mary Criswell, wife of Elijah Criswell, mother of William Wagus Criswell; Rachel Roach, wife of Caleb Roach; John Wagus, of OH; Richard Wagus, of IN; and Ann Pennington, deceased, died c. 1840, wife of Obid Pennington, mother of Owen Pennington.
Property situate on Deer Park Road, being part of *Peach Brandy Forest.*

Chancery Book 7, pp. 197-230   1850   Equity #318
James Crockett vs. Rebecca Royer, Uriah Royer, and others.   Sale of real estate to satisfy creditors.
Emanuel Royer died 11 July 1850, intestate, leaving widow, Rebecca Royer. Children: Uriah Royer; Jacob B. Royer; Sarah I. Royer; Susan A. Royer; Joseph D. Royer; Samuel Royer; and Jesse Royer.
Property formerly situate in Frederick County, being part of *Addition to Brook's Discovery on the Rich Lands.*

Chancery Book 7, pp. 232-268   1851   Equity #324
Samuel McKinstry vs. Joseph Missler, and others.   Sale of real estate to satisfy creditors.

David Missler died 1851, intestate, leaving no widow, and no issue. Father was John Missler, late of Frederick County, from whom David inherited his land. Brothers and sister: Joseph Missler, of OH; William Missler, deceased, father of Reuben Missler, Elin Slick (wife of David Slick), Ann Missler, John Missler, Mahlon Missler, Barbara Arnold (wife of John Arnold), Grenelda Missler (all of OH), and Benjamin Missler (of IL); Mary Farquhar, deceased, mother of John H. Farquhar, Elinora Haines (wife of John Haines), William L. Farquhar (all of IN), and George A. Farquhar (of Baltimore City); and John Missler, deceased, father of Ulrick Missler, John T. Missler, Margaret Caylor (wife of Levi Caylor), Elinora Missler, and Martha Missler.
Property formerly situate in Frederick County.

Chancery Book 7, pp. 270-315   1847   Equity #233
Benjamin Mathias, and others vs. Joseph Mathias, and others.   Sale of real estate.
Mary Mathias died 23 Aug 1847, intestate. Children: Benjamin Mathias; Daniel Mathias; Leah Mathias, also known as Leah Hoppe; Rachel Rumler, wife of Perry Rumler; Polly Little, wife of George Lewis Little; Rebecca Hull, wife of Eli Hull; Joseph Mathias; John Mathias, of Baltimore City; and Reuben Mathias, deceased, father of Leander Mathias, and Silvester Mathias.
Property situate in Westminster.

Chancery Book 7, pp. 317-344   1850   Equity #314
Joshua Souder vs. Eliza C. Myers, Admrx. of Samuel Myers, and others. Sale of real estate to satisfy creditors.
Samuel Myers died 10 Sept 1850, intestate, leaving widow, Eliza C. Myers. Children: Charles F. Myers; John D. Myers; Ann Eliza Myers; and Samuel J. Myers.
Property being part of *Good Intent*.

Chancery Book 7, pp. 346-366   1850   Equity #295
William Haugh, et al. vs. Samuel Diffendall, and wife.   Sale of real estate.
Paul Haugh, Jr., died 5 Mar 1847, intestate. Children: William Haugh; Ann E. Haugh; Mary A. Slick, widow of James Slick, deceased, (died 1844); David Haugh; John Haugh; Margaret Diffendall, wife of Samuel Diffendall; and Elijah Haugh, died 3 Feb 1849, intestate, unmarried and w/o issue.
Property formerly situate in Frederick County, being parts of *Bedford* and *Logsdon's Amendment*.

Chancery Book 7, pp. 367-395   1850   Equity #297
Hezekiah Dotterer, and others vs. Ann Rebecca Barnhart.   Sale of real estate.

John Dotterer (or Dutterow) died 10 April 1850, intestate, leaving widow, Mary Dotterer. Children: Hezekiah Dotterer, of Frederick County; Mary Ann Krise, of Frederick County, wife of Elias Krise; Sophia Ott, of Frederick County, wife of Eli Ott; John W. Dotterer; Joshua Dotterer; Josiah Dotterer; William H. Dotterer; and Elizabeth Barnhart, deceased, wife of William Barnhart, mother of Ann Rebecca Barnhart (of Frederick County). Father was Conrad Dotterer, of Franklin County, PA.
Property formerly situate in Frederick County, now part in Frederick County and part in Carroll County, being parts of *So Far So Good, Lemon's Vineyard, Worth Something, Resurvey on Digg's Lot, Hamilton's Recovery, Six Brothers, Disappointment, Narrow Slipe, Monocacy* and *Settled in Peace.*

Chancery Book 7, pp. 397-439   1851   Equity #329
Benjamin Croft, and wife vs. Benjamin Croft, and others.   Sale of real estate.
John Croft died c. May 1841, intestate, leaving widow, Martha Croft. Children: Benjamin Croft, of OH, husband of Mary Croft (formerly Mary Buckingham); George Croft, husband of Anna Croft (formerly Anna Ruby); John Croft, Jr., deceased, died 1 Jan 1844, husband of Matilda Croft (formerly Matilda Ebaugh and who later became Matilda Algier when she married Nicholas Algier), father of Benjamin Croft and unknown deceased child; Ann Richards, wife of George Richards; Elizabeth Richards, wife of Daniel Richards; and Nancy Croft
Properties formerly situate in Baltimore County, about 26 miles from Baltimore and 4 miles from Hanover Road, near road leading from Brown's Meeting House to Hampstead, one property was a fulling mill, being parts of *Steven's Defense, Hunter's Ridge, Foxes Denn, Wee Bit Enlarged* and *The Trouting Stream.*

Chancery Book 7, pp. 441-461   1851   Equity #341
Samuel Fuss vs. John A. Fuss, Admr., Rebecca Cain, and others.   Sale of real estate to satisfy creditors.
Mary Ann Fuss died June 1851, intestate, an invalid, unmarried and without issue. Brothers and sisters: John Adam Fuss, of Baltimore County; Rebecca Cain, wife of William Cain; Sarah C. Fuss, of Baltimore County; Samuel Fuss, of Baltimore County; Henry D. Fuss, of Baltimore County; and Elizabeth Hays, deceased, wife of Joseph Hays, mother of Daniel F. Hays, Deborah Hays, Joseph T. Hays, and Thomas H. Hays (all of Frederick County).
Property being part of *Terra Rubra.*

Chancery Book 7, pp. 463-508   1845   Equity #175
John Kreglow vs. Barbara Kreglow, and others.   Sale of real estate.
John Kreglow died 29 May 1837, intestate, leaving widow, Barbara Kreglow. Children: John Kreglow; Catherine Marks, of Baltimore City, wife of John Marks; Frederick Kreglow, of IL; George Kreglow, of IN; Lydia Ann Kreglow;

and Anna Elizabeth Fleagle, deceased, died c. 1843, wife of Elijah Fleagle, deceased, mother of Mary Jane Fleagle, of PA, then later Taneytown.
Property formerly situate in Frederick County, being part of *Anxiety Removed.*

Chancery Book 7, pp. 510-529 1852 Equity #348
William Bachman, Guardian to Ezra Jacob Brown vs. Ezra Jacob Brown. Sale of real estate.
Darius Brown died March 1851, intestate, leaving only child, Ezra Jacob Brown.
Property situate in town of Frizzlesburg, being parts of *Molly's Fancy* and *The Resurvey on Share Spring.*

Chancery Book 7, pp. 531-548 1851 Equity #339
Levi Winters vs. Jonathan P. Creager and Elizabeth Creager, his wife. Foreclosure.
Jonathan P. Creager and Elizabeth Creager, his wife.
Property being Lots 66, 67, 68, and 69 of *Winchester's Addition,* and part of *White's Level.*

Chancery Book 8, pp. 1-20 1852 Equity #350
Ezekiel Boring vs. Samuel Wisner, Admr. of John P. Eck, deceased. Sale of real estate to satisfy creditors.
John P. Eck, of Baltimore County, died 15 Oct 1847, intestate, leaving widow, Mary Eck, who became Mary Warner when she remarried and moved to Baltimore City. Children: Barbara Eck, of Baltimore City; Lewis Eck; and William Eck, of Baltimore City.
Property being the southern parts of Lots 8 and 43 in the Town of Manchester.

Chancery Book 8, pp. 21-34 1852 Equity #351
Andrew Powder vs. Elijah Woolery. Foreclosure.
Elijah Woolery and Rachel Woolery, his wife.
Property situate in Woolery (4th) District.

Chancery Book 8, pp. 35-62 1852 Equity #352
Jerome Ebaugh, et als. vs. Rachel Ebaugh, et al. Sale of real estate.
Sabina Ebaugh died 17 Sept 1851, intestate, widow of Conrad Ebaugh, who died 1849. Children: Jerome Ebaugh; Emanuel Ebaugh; Sarah Shipley, wife of Absolom Shipley; Elisabeth Brown, of Baltimore County, wife of Henry Brown; Mary Ausding, of Baltimore County, wife of Ferdinand Ausding; Rachel Ebaugh, of Baltimore City; and Catherine Ebaugh, of Baltimore County.
Sabina's father was Melchour Fowble, late of Baltimore County, farmer, husband of Sabina Fowble. His other children were: Jacob Fowble; Melchor

Fowble; Peter Fowble; Joshua Fowble; Elizabeth Cockey, wife of Joshua F. Cockey; Mary Algier, wife of Henry Algier; Catherine Algire, wife of George Algire; Margaret Benson, wife of Elijah Benson; Susannah Hesson, wife of William Hesson; and John Fowble, father of Richard Fowble, Kenney Fowble, Melchor Fowble, and John Fowble.

Property formerly situate in Baltimore County, being part of *Castle Hannah.*

Chancery Book 8, pp. 64-86   1852   Equity #361

Jacob Buffington, next friend of Caroline O. Maring, and others vs. Caroline O. Maring, and others. Sale of real estate.

David Maring died March 1852, intestate, his wife died few days prior. Children: Caroline Otelia Maring; Ann Eliza Maring; Mary Louisa Maring; Abraham Buffington Maring; Susanna Rebecca Maring; Alice Catherine Maring; and David Albert Maring. The children's uncle was Jacob Buffington.

David Maring was the son of the late John Maring, husband of Catherine Maring. Their other children were: Daniel Maring, husband of Esther Maring; John Maring, husband of Amy Maring; and Anny Maring.

Properties were part of *Resurvey on Owing's Chance, Ohio, Land Stool* and *Addition to Land Stool.*

Chancery Book 8, pp. 88-111   1852   Equity #366

Jacob Mathias as next friend of Eliza Jane McMasters and Rachel Frances McMasters vs. Samuel McMasters, Mary McMasters, his wife, and John Rinehart. Sale of real estate.

Magdalena Rinehart died c. April 1841, testate. Her granddaughter, Mary Sentz intermarried with Samuel McMasters and became known as Mary McMasters, the mother of Eliza Jane McMasters and Rachel Frances McMasters.

Magdalena Rinehart's will mentions her children: George Rinehart, deceased, died 1 May 1845, intestate, father of John Rinehart, Jeremiah Rinehart, Elizabeth Weaver (of Gettysburg PA, wife of Samuel Weaver), Peter S. Rinehart, deceased (died Dec 1847, intestate, husband of Maria Rinehart, father of Sarah A. Rinehart, Rachel A. L. Rinehart, Ann M. M. Rinehart, Elizabeth Rinehart, Susan C. Rinehart, Martha J. Rinehart, and Margaret A. Rinehart; Barbara Lippy, mother of Elizabeth Lippy, Ann Lippy, Joseph Lippy, Magdalena Lippy, William Lippy, and David Lippy; Mary Lippy, deceased, mother of John Lippy, Samuel Lippy, Rebecca Lippy, and Catherine Lippy; Sally Sentz, deceased, died Dec. 1848, widow of Andrew Sentz, mother of Susan Feiser, Isabella Sentz, Sarah Jane Foreman (wife of Absolom Foreman), Catherine Ellen Sentz, and Joshua Sentz; and Elizabeth Everly, wife of David Everly.

Property situate in Town of Manchester.

Chancery Book 8, pp. 113-137 1852 Equity #367
Petition of Joshua Smith as next friend of Hannah E. Frizell, and others. Sale of real estate.
Nimrod Frizell died 13 Dec 1842, testate, leaving widow, Ann Frizell. Children: William Frizell; Ann Eliza Wentz, wife of Valentine Wentz; Ellen Cover, wife of Ephraim Cover; John C. Frizell; Hannah E. Frizell; and Mary Freeze, deceased, wife of Jefferson Freeze, mother of Alfred Freeze, and Mary Ann Freeze (all of OH).
Property being parts of *Molly's Fancy* and *Lookabout.*

Chancery Book 8, pp. 139-162 1852 Equity #373
Mary Roberts, Nancy Wright, Samuel A. Lauver, and others vs. Virginia A. Hergesheimer. Sale of real estate.
Moses Shaw died Feb 1849, testate. Children: Frances Lauver, wife of Samuel A. Lauver; William Shaw; Martha Curry, deceased, mother of Theodore E. Curry, Frances Curry, and Martha Grizelda Curry; Nancy Wright; Mary Roberts; and Ann Thomas, deceased, mother of Martha Griselda Thomas, Frances E. Morrow (wife of John Morrow), Daniel W. Thomas, Virginia A. Hammond (wife of William M. Hammond), Moses S. Thomas, Braxton D. Thomas, Mary Levinia Thomas, and Sarah E. Hergesheimer, deceased (wife of David I. Hergesheimer, mother of Virginia A. Hergesheimer). Also mentions grandson William Martin, parentage not established.
Properties situate in and near Uniontown.

Chancery Book 8, pp. 164-182 1852 Equity #359
Charles Sentz, John Abbott, and others vs. Isabella Sentz, and others. Sale of real estate.
Peter Sentz died May 1852, intestate. Children: Charles Sentz; Margaret Abbott, wife of John Abbott; Mahala Kephart, of Alleghany County, PA, wife of David Kephart; and Asa Sentz, deceased, father of Isabella Sentz, Urias Sentz, and Mahala Sentz.
Property formerly situate in Baltimore County, being part of *Iron Intention.*

Chancery Book 8, pp. 184-212 1852 Equity #374
Elizabeth Legore, and others vs. Joseph E. Hahn, and others. Sale of real estate.
Jacob Legore died c. Dec 1850, testate, leaving widow, Rachel Legore, deceased. Children: Elizabeth Legore; Susannah Hahn, wife of Joseph E. Hahn; John Legore, of Adams County, PA; Ezra Legore; Rebecca Halverstadt, wife of Eli Halverstadt; William H. Legore; Julia Ann Davidson, wife of James Davidson; Ellen Yingling, wife of William H. Yingling; Rachel Legore; Jacob

Legore; Jacob Legore; Jesse H. Legore; and Maria Hawn, deceased, wife of Jesse Hawn, mother of Jesse Hawn.

Jacob's widow, Rachel, was the daughter of John Hull, of Frederick County, who died c. 1832. His other children were: Anna Barbara Keefer, wife of George Keefer; John Hull; Margaret Hesson, wife of Daniel Hesson; Magdalena Hesson, wife of Peter Hesson; Lovis Hesson, wife of Abraham Hesson; Christina Marker, wife of John Marker; Susanna Groff, wife of George Groff; Eleanor Hesson, deceased; and Elizabeth Hesson, wife of Balser Hesson.

Property being parts of *Huckleberry Bottom* and *Durbin's Mistake*.

Chancery Book 8, pp. 213-237   1852   Equity #377
Jacob Storms, and others vs. Catherine Storms, and others.   Sale of real estate.

Henry Storms died 9 Oct 1850, intestate, never married, w/o issue. Brothers and sisters: Jacob Storms, deceased, died Mar 1853, testate, husband of Elizabeth Storms, father of Mary Ann Storms, William Storms, Jacob Storms, Rebecca Williams (wife of John Williams), Elizabeth Aderds (wife of George Aderds), Thomas Storms, Henry Storms, Amon Jesse Storms, Sarah Jane Storms, and Noah Webster Storms; Mary Weakley, wife of William Weakley, mother? of Henry Weakley; Margaret Storms; George W. G. Storms, deceased, died 16 Nov 1851, intestate, husband of Naomi Storms, father of George W. Storms, Jacob L. Storms, William Jesse Storms, Onetta Storms (wife of Jacob J. Storms), Christiana Storms, Sarah Ann Storms (of Baltimore County, wife of William Storms), and Angelina Holly, deceased (died Mar 1849, mother of Ann Onetta Holly and Naomi Mary Holly, [both of Alleghany County, MD]); Catherine Storms; and Christiana Bevard.

Properties being part of *Dean's Comfort, Hickory Ridge* and *James Delight*, one situate on Baltimore-Hanover Turnpike.

Chancery Book 8, pp. 238-257   1851   Equity #336
Absalom Foreman and Sarah Foreman, his wife vs. John Rinehart, Joshua Smith, and Catherine Ellen Sentz.   Partition of real estate.

Magdalena Rinehart died testate. She was the grandmother to Sarah Foreman (wife of Absalom Foreman) and Catherine Ellen Sentz.

Property being parts of *Resurvey on Dairy* and *The Resurvey*.

Chancery Book 8, pp. 258-276   1852   Equity #360
James W. Jordan vs. Mary Jordan, et als.
Sale of real estate to satisfy creditors.

Elias Jordan died 10 April 1852, intestate, leaving widow, Mary Jordan. Children: Mortica W. Jordan; Elias F. Jordan; and Alice A. Jordan.

Property being part of *Deep Valley Resurveyed*.

Chancery Book 8, pp. 277-288 1853 Equity #391
John B. Chenoweth vs. Henry W. Ports. Foreclosure.
Henry W. Ports
Property being part of Lot #9 in division of lands of John Murray, being part of *Transylvania*.

Chancery Book 8, pp. 289-331 1850 Equity #312
Peter Bail and Ludwick Bail vs. Levi Devilbiss, Admr., Peter Nace, and others. Sale of real estate to satisfy creditors.
Lloyd Moals died 1850, intestate, leaving a son, Asbury Moals, as only legal heir. Lloyd also left widow and other children who were all slaves for life, therefore not considered to be legal heirs to his estate.
Property formerly situate in Frederick County, being part of *New Windsor*.

Chancery Book 8, pp. 332-353 1853 Equity #394
Abraham Cassell and Daniel Sullivan vs. Mary M. Sullivan, and others. Sale of real estate to satisfy creditors.
Daniel Sullivan died Feb 1853, testate, leaving widow, Mary M. Sullivan, almost blind, inmate at Alms House, Westminster. Children: Levi Reese Sullivan; and Julia Ann Sullivan, lunatic, inmate at Alms House, Westminster. Brother: William Sullivan.
Property situate about 1 mile from Uniontown.

Chancery Book 8, pp. 354-369 1853 Equity #388
David Crumbacker, and others vs. Jonas Crumbacker, and others. Sale of real estate.
Jacob Crumbacker died c. Sept 1852, intestate, leaving no widow, no children, no lineal descendants. Brothers and sister: John Crumbacker, deceased, father of one unnamed daughter, deceased; Abraham Crumbacker, deceased, father of Ephraim Crumbacker (of Baltimore City), Elizabeth Crouse (wife of James Crouse), and Hannah Englar (widow of Philip Englar); Peter Crumbacker, deceased, father of David Crumbacker, Jesse Crumbacker, Nathan Crumbacker, William Crumbacker, and Elizabeth Crumbacker; Jonas Crumbacker, possibly in VA; and Mary Hammond, deceased, wife of Thomas J. Hammond, mother of Allen C. Hammond, Thomas J. Hammond, George W. Hammond, Caroline A. Hammond, Ann Everly (wife of John L. Everly), Eliza Boyles (wife of James Boyles), Rebecca Kearnes (wife of Henry Kearnes) (all possibly in VA), and Thomsey Bond (of Frederick County, wife of Cornelius Bond).
Property was devised to Jacob by his father, Abraham Crumbacker, farmer, late of Frederick County, who died c. 1795, testate, leaving widow, Elizabeth Crumbacker. Their other children: John Crumbacker; Abraham Crumbacker; Peter Crumbacker; Jonas Crumbacker; and Mary Crumbacker.

Property formerly situate in Frederick County, on north side of Pipe Creek, being part of *Resurvey on The Deeps.*

Chancery Book 8, pp. 370-394   1853   Equity #395
Lydia Borns, and others vs. Edmond Borns, and others.   Sale of real estate and to satisfy creditors.
George Borns died 14 May 1845, intestate, leaving widow, Lydia Borns. Children: Emanuel Borns; George Borns; Sophia Borns, of Baltimore City; Edmond Borns; John Borns, of OH; Simon P. Borns; Amos Borns; Mary A. Borns; Calvin J. Borns; and Charles S. Borns.
George was deeded part of his real property by the following, possibly his brothers and sisters: Jacob Borns, husband of Elizabeth Borns; David Borns, husband of Mary Borns; John Borns, husband of Mary Borns; Daniel Borns; George Nace, husband of Margaret Nace; Abraham Armstrong, husband of Rachel Armstrong; and Margaret Borns.
Properties being parts of *Friendship, The Valley of Jehosephat, Spilters Inclosure, Pleasant Hills* and *Good Luck.*

Chancery Book 8, pp. 395-410   1853   Equity #399
John Ellis and Catherine Ellis, his wife, Mary Stultz, and others vs. Samuel Franklin Stultz, Catherine Stultz, and others.   Sale of real estate.
Sophia Leas died Dec 1851, intestate, leaving husband, Philip Leas, since deceased, and no children. Brothers and sisters: Catherine Ellis, of PA, wife of John Ellis; Mary Stultz; Elizabeth Wilson, wife of William Wilson; Margaret Kemp, wife of Peter Kemp; Hannah Row, wife of Samuel Row; Nicholas Stultz; Ann Dayhoff, deceased, wife of Jacob Dayhoff, mother of Elizabeth Wilson (wife of Thomas Wilson), Polly Dayhoff, Susan Dayhoff, Elias Dayhoff, and Joseph Dayhoff; David Stultz, deceased, father of Mary Ann Stultz, Sophia Otto (wife of Hebert Otto), Eliza Ann Stultz, William Stultz, Samuel Franklin Stultz, Catherine Stultz, and Sarah Jane Stultz; and Sarah Shriner, deceased, wife of John Shriner, mother of Louisa Shriner, William Shriner, James Shriner, Samuel Shriner, and Levi Shriner (all of IL).
Location of property not mentioned.

Chancery Book 8, pp. 412-426   1853   Equity #402
Serepta Shuman, and others vs. Emanuel Shuman, Nathaniel Shuman, and others.   Sale of real estate.
George H. Shuman, son of George Shuman, died 15 Nov 1852, intestate, leaving widow, Serepta Shuman. Children: Mary Cordelia Hoffacker, wife of David Hoffacker; Emanuel Shuman; Nathaniel Shuman; Israel Shuman; and Julia A. Shuman.
Properties being parts of *Grandfather's Gifts* and *Foster's Hunting Ground.*

Chancery Book 8, pp. 427-447   1853   Equity #407
John Roberts and Abraham Appler vs. Ephraim Garner, Savilla Bean, et al. Sale of real estate to satisfy creditors.
Samuel Bean died 15 Jan 1853, intestate, leaving widow, Savilla Bean. Children: Joseph Bean; Ezra Bean; Tabitha Bean; Margaret Bean; and George Bean.
Property situate near Joseph's Eck Mill Race on Big Pipe Creek, being part of *Runneymede Enlarged*.

Chancery Book 8, pp. 448-469   1853   Equity #408
William Roberts and John Roberts vs. Samuel Flegel, John Shoemaker, Americus Shoemaker, and others. Sale of real estate to satisfy creditors.
John Shoemaker died 1852, intestate, leaving widow, Lydia Shoemaker. Children: Magdalena Flegel, wife of Samuel Flegel; John Shoemaker; Caroline Stultz, wife of Henry Stultz; Americus Shoemaker; Henrietta Shoemaker; and Amanda Shoemaker.
Property formerly situate in Frederick County, on public road from Taneytown to David Kephart's Mill, being part of *Resurvey on Brother's Agreement*.

Chancery Book 8, pp. 470-500   1849   Equity #281
Richard W. Condon and William Brandenburg vs. Joshua Barnes, Admr. of Thomas Barnes, and others. Sale of real estate to satisfy creditors.
James H. Barnes died 1849, intestate, never married. Brothers and sisters: Joshua Barnes, of Frederick County, deceased; Thomas Barnes; Ana Leatherwood, wife of Hanson Leatherwood; Eliza Grimes, wife of Joshua Grimes; and Lelitia Elson, of OH, wife of Joseph Elson.
Property formerly situate in Baltimore County, being part of *Batchelor Refuge*.

Chancery Book 8, pp. 501-536   1851   Equity #347
John Rinehart, et als. vs. David Everly, and Elizabeth Everly, his wife, et als. Sale of real estate.
Magdalena Rinehart died April 1841, testate. Children: George Rinehart, deceased, died April 1845, intestate, father of John Rinehart (husband of Margaret Rinehart), Jeremiah Rinehart (husband of Mary Ann Rinehart), Elizabeth Weaver (of Gettysburg PA, wife of Samuel Weaver), and Peter S. Rinehart, deceased (died Dec 1847, husband of Maria Rinehart, father of Sarah A. Rinehart, Rachel A. L. Rinehart, Ann M. M. Rinehart, Elizabeth R. Rinehart, Susan C. Rinehart, Martha J. Rinehart, and Margaret A. Rinehart; Elizabeth Everly, wife of David Everly; Sally Sentz, deceased, died Dec 1848, testate, widow of Andrew Sentz, mother of Susannah Feiser (mother of Sarah Ann Feiser and Susannah Feiser), Mary McMaster, Elizabeth Yiper, Sarah Jane Foreman, Catherine Ellen Sentz, Isabella Sentz and Joshua Sentz; Barbara

Lippy, mother of Elizabeth Ann Lippy, Joseph Lippy, Magdalena Lippy, William Lippy, and David Lippy; and Mary Lippy, deceased, mother of John Lippy, Susan Lippy, Rebecca Lippy, and Catherine Lippy.
Property formerly situate in Frederick County, being parts of *Gotham, Second Addition to Acorn Hill* and *Third Addition to Acorn Hill.*

Chancery Book 8, pp. 537-552   1853   Equity #384
to Chancery Book 9, pp. 1-10
Joshua Murray, et als. vs. Eleanora Murray, et als.   Sale of real estate.
John Murray, of Baltimore County, died c. 1832-33, testate. Children: John Murray, Jr., deceased, died Nov 1835, intestate in Baltimore County, husband of Sarah Murray, who died c. 1846, father of Sarah Chenoweth (wife of John B. Chenoweth), John W. Murray, Kiturah Chenoweth (of IN, wife of William Chenoweth), Elizabeth Fowble (of IN, wife of Andrew Fowble), Joshua S. Murray (of IN), Harriet Garner (of IA, wife of Wesley W. Garner), Isabella J. Hendricks (of MO, wife of Adam Henricks), Eliza Keslinger (of OH, wife of Samuel Keslinger), Susannah Benson (of OH, wife of James Benson), Rebecca Hendricks (of OH, wife of John Hendricks), Deana Aby (of OH, wife of Christian Aby), and Thomas Murray, deceased (d. 15 June 1850, intestate, husband of Catherine Murray, father of Eleanora Murray, John Murray, Charles Murray, Hanson Murray, Whitfield Murray and Columbus Murray; Jabez Murray, deceased, died Aug 1847, intestate, husband of Sarah Murray, father of Joshua Murray, Maria Williams (widow of Amos Williams), Elizabeth Murray, Keziah Barnes (wife of Moses Barnes), and Sarah Shreeve (wife of David Shreeve); William Murray, deceased, died Jan 1849, intestate, father of John P. Murray (of Baltimore City), and Thomas P. Murray, (of IN, father of Ruth Fowble, deceased, died Apr 1847, wife of Richard Fowble, of Baltimore County, mother of Elizabeth Cole [wife of Samuel Cole], Charlotte Fowble [of Baltimore County, wife of Stephen M. Fowble], John T. Fowble [of Baltimore County], and Maria Fowble [of Baltimore County]); Jacob Murray, deceased, died 18 Aug 1852, intestate, never married and w/o issue; Elizabeth Armacost; Rachel Boreing; and Lynda Armacost. Also mentions grandchildren: John Armacost; Elizabeth Boreing; Mary Cox; Keziah Nace; Murray Nace; Emanuel Nace; and Drusill Nace.
Property formerly situate in Baltimore County, on road from Hampstead to Middletown, being part of *Pleasant Meadow Concluded.*

Chancery Book 9, pp. 12-30   1853   Equity #396
Richard Richards vs. Joseph Ebaugh, et als.   Sale of real estate to satisfy creditors.
John Z. Buchen died July 1852, testate, leaving widow, Rachel Buchen. Children: William Buchen; Elizabeth Buchen; George Buchen; David Buchen; and John Buchen.

Property situate in Hampstead District.

Chancery Book 9, pp.32-101   1853   Equity #382
Thomas Jones vs. Joshua Null, and others.   Sale of real estate to satisfy creditors.
Samuel Null, son of Abraham Null (d. c. 1850) and his wife, Catherine Null, died 4 Feb 1853, intestate, leaving widow Susannah Null. Children: Joshua Null; Catherine Hilterbrick, wife of Peter Hilterbrick; George Null; Abraham E. Null; Isaiah Null; Lewis Null, of PA; and Levi Null, deceased, father of Mary C. Null, Jane L. Null, Francis C. Null, and Susannah E. Null (all of PA).
Numerous properties formerly situate in Frederick County, some still in Frederick County, on Monocacy River, near Alloway Creek, being parts of *Addition to Brook's Discovery on the Rich Lands, Frenchman's Purchase, Resurvey on Owing's Chance* and *Galt's Fancy*.

Chancery Book 9, pp. 102-138   1852   Equity #372
Lewis Peters vs. Jacob Peters.   Dissolvement of Partnership
Lewis Peters and his brother, Jacob Peters, co-partners for the purpose of farming, distilling whiskey, merchandizing, etc.
Property situate 4-1/2 miles from Taneytown on Piney Creek, on the east side of road from Taneytown to Littlestown and on road from Maus' Mill to Peter's Tavern, being parts of *Resurvey on Pines* and *Addition to the Pines*.

Chancery Book 9, pp. 140-167   1853   Equity #417
Peter Baile, David Nicodemus, and others vs. Susan Baile, and others.   Sale of real estate.
David Baile, late of Frederick County, died 1833, intestate, leaving widow, Susan Baile. Children: Peter W. Baile; Elizabeth Nicodemus, deceased, wife of David Nicodemus, deceased, mother of Mary Catherine Nicodemus and Eliza Nicodemus; Lydia Roop, of Frederick County, wife of Samuel Roop; and David Baile.
Properties formerly situate in Frederick and Baltimore counties, in Franklin District, on road from Westminster to Old Liberty Road, being parts of *Upper Marlborough, Resurvey on Father's Gift, The Resurvey on Bailes Industry, Brother's Inheritance* and *Fell's Retirement*.

Chancery Book 9, pp. 168-185   1853   Equity #418
Amelia Miller vs. Eliza A. Lockard, and others.   Sale of real estate.
James Lucas, Jr. and wife, Mary Lucas. Children: Amelia Miller, widow of David Miller (died c. 1846-47); and Margaret Lockard, deceased (died c. 1846-47), wife of John Lockard, mother of Eliza Ann Lockard.
Property formerly situate in Baltimore County, being part of *Glendoick*.

Chancery Book 9, pp. 186-219   1853   Equity #409
David W. Nail, and others vs. Daniel L. Shull, and others.   Sale of real estate.
Paul Maurer, of Baltimore County, died 10 April 1853, intestate. Children: Susannah Nail, of Frederick County, wife of David W. Nail; Anna Mary Smelser, wife of David Smelser; Catherine A. Murray, widow of Thomas B. Murray; Sarah Shull, deceased, wife of Daniel C. Shull, mother of Samuel P. Shull, Sarah E. Holmes (wife of William T. Holmes), John H. Shull, Eliza A. Learch (wife of Joseph Learch), Catherine A. Shull, Harriet Porter (wife of George Porter), Kesiah Shull, Amanda Shull, Daniel L. Shull and Mary A. Shull (all of Muskingham County OH); and Elizabeth Drach, deceased, wife of Henry Drach, mother of Daniel L. Drach (of Ashland County OH), Lucretia Snader (wife of Levi W. Snader), Hanson M. Drach, Peter E. Drach, John P. Drach, Winfield S. Drach, Mary L. Drach, and Henry L. Drach.
Properties situate partly in Carroll County and partly in Frederick County, on Sam's Creek, being parts of *Howard's Discovery, Leigh Castle* and *Hills and Valleys.*

Chancery Book 9, pp. 221-263   1850   Equity #313
Anna Maria Lammott, and others vs. Joseph Lammott, and others.
Sale of real estate to satisfy creditors
Jacob Lammott died 4 Oct 1850, testate, leaving widow, Anna Maria Lammott. Children: Jacob Lammott; Catherine Nunemaker, wife of Samuel Nunemaker; Joseph Lammott; Benjamin Lammott; Priscilla Lammott; and Daniel Lammott.
Properties situate c. 2 miles from Manchester on Gunpowder Falls, being parts of *Alltogether too Late, Little Rock, Fox Range, Lammott's Delight, Rome, Lammott's Middle of the World, Plymouth, Stoney Hills, Miner Courses* and *White Oak Bottom.*

Chancery Book 9, pp. 265-276   1854   Equity #426
William Hiteshue vs. Jacob Shockey.   Breach of contract
Jacob Shockey.
Property situate near Washington Road, southeast of Westminster, being part of *Bedford.*

Chancery Book 9, pp. 278-283   1853   Equity #378
Petition of Mary Hall Barnes, Francis Barnes, John Barnes, and others.
Distribute money.
Balinda Barnes, deceased. Children: Mary Hall Barnes; Francis Barnes; Jehu Barnes; George Barnes; and Silas Barnes.
No property mentioned.

Chancery Book 9, pp. 284-306 1854 Equity #425
Samuel Hare and The Bank of Westminster vs. John Jane and Julian Jane, his wife, and others. Sale of real estate to satisfy creditors.
John Hare died Aug 1853, intestate, leaving widow, Catherine Hare. Children: Samuel Hare, of IN; Julian Jane, wife of John Jane; Catherine Hare, of Baltimore County; Sarah Hare; John Hare; George H. Hare; Henry Hare; and Jacob Hare, a lunatic.
Property formerly situate in Baltimore County, being part of *Christopher's Luck*.

Chancery Book 9, pp. 308-320 1854 Equity #430
Isaac Hyde vs. Joshua L. Hyde, Elizabeth A. Hyde and William A. Norris. Sale of real estate to satisfy creditors.
Joshua L. Hyde, who bought land and left area without finishing payments, and his wife, Elizabeth A. Hyde.
Property situate in village of Wakefield.

Chancery Book 9, pp. 322-343 1854 Equity #433
George L. Lippy vs. David Bachman, Admr. of George Gearhart, deceased, and others. Sale of real estate to satisfy creditors.
George Gearhart died 2 Jan 1854, intestate, leaving widow, Lydia Gearhart. Children: Mary J. Gearhart; and Elenora Gearhart.
Property being part of *Cleary's New Holland*.

Chancery Book 9, pp. 344-355 1854 Equity #435
John Lockard vs. Joseph Ritter, et al. To deliver deed.
Joseph Ritter and his wife, Catherine Ritter (she died Nov 1836). Children: John Ritter, of Baltimore County; Martha Ann Brown, of Baltimore City, wife of William H. Brown; and Catherine E. Ritter, of Baltimore City.
Property formerly situate in Baltimore County, being part of *Rochester*.

Chancery Book 9, pp. 356-374 1854 Equity #440
Jesse Sullivan, Margaret E. Sullivan, and others vs. Catharine Sullivan, and others. Sale of real estate.
William Sullivan died Apr 1854, intestate, leaving widow, Catherine Sullivan. Children: Jesse Sullivan; John H. Sullivan; Augustus F. Sullivan; George W. Sullivan; Margaret E. Sullivan; and Mary C. Stoner, wife of George W. Stoner.

Properties formerly situate in Frederick County, 2 miles from Westminster on Littlestown Turnpike, being parts of *Molly's Industry, Bond's Meadow Enlarged* and *Young's Purchase.*

Chancery Book 9, pp. 375-404   1853   Equity #381
Levi Manahan vs. Thomas S. Kelly and Nelly Kelly, his wife, and others. Foreclosure.
William Demmitt, of Frederick County, died Feb or Mar 1837, intestate, leaving Nelly Demmitt, who later married Thomas S. Kelly and became known as Nelly Kelly. Children: Henry Demmitt; and James Demmitt.
Properties formerly situate in Baltimore and Frederick counties, being parts of *The Spike, Hawkins Fancy, Baker's Discovery* and *Evan's Venture.*

Chancery Book 9, pp. 406-421   1854   Equity #444
John Engel, et al. vs. Daniel Engel, et al.   Sale of real estate.
David Engel died 10 Mar 1854, intestate, never married and w/o issue. Brothers and sisters: John Engel, of Frederick County; Abraham Engel, of Frederick County; Hannah Ecker, widow of John Ecker; Mary Widder, of Cumberland County PA, wife of George Widder; Elizabeth Hoffman, of OH, widow of William Hoffman; Susannah Roop, of IA, wife of Joseph Roop; Daniel Engel, husband of Ann Maria Engel; Peter Engel, deceased, father of David Engel, Peter Engel, Lydia Roop (wife of John Roop), Mary Ecker (wife of William Ecker), Susan Cover (wife of Josiah T. Cover), and Hannah Angel (of Philadelphia PA, wife of Adam Angel); and Barbara Deamuth, deceased, mother of David Deamuth.
Property formerly situate in Frederick County, being parts of *Mulberry Bottom, Warfield's Inheritance* and *Leigh Castle.*

Chancery Book 9, pp. 422-456   1854   Equity #439
Joshua Smith vs. Peter Masonheimer.   Sale of real estate.
George Rinehart, of Frederick County, died testate, leaving widow Magdalena Rinehart, who died Apr 1841. Children: George Rinehart, deceased, died Apr 1845, intestate, husband of Rebecca Rinehart, father of John Rinehart (husband of Margaret Rinehart), Jeremiah Rinehart (husband of Mary Rinehart), Peter S. Rinehart (husband of Maria Rinehart), and Elizabeth Weaver (wife of Samuel Weaver); Barbara Lippy, wife of George Lippy (former husband of sister Mary); Mary Lippy, deceased, died May 1816, wife of George Lippy, mother of Rebecca Hesson (wife of Joseph Hesson, of Peter), Catherine Hesson (wife of Isaac Hesson), John Lippy (of IL), and Susannah Porter, deceased (died 1844, wife of John H. Porter, mother of George Porter, Amanda Porter, Maria Porter, Sarah Porter, and Ann Rebecca Porter, all of IL); Elizabeth Everly, wife of David Everly; and Salome Sentz (also known as Sally Sentz), of Baltimore City, widow of Andrew Sentz.

Property formerly situate in Frederick County, being part of *Philipsburgh*.

Chancery Book 9, pp. 457-497   1853   Equity #401
Joseph Arnold, Richard Manning, John Henry Hoppe vs. Caleb Arnold, and others. Sale of real estate and to satisfy creditors.
Joseph Arnold, of Baltimore County, died 1826, testate. Children: Charles Arnold, husband of Margaret Arnold (she died 1845, intestate), father of Caleb Arnold, John Arnold, Henry Arnold, Anthony Arnold, Charles W. Arnold, Joseph Arnold, and Basil Arnold; Eliza Magors; James Arnold; Joseph Arnold; Anthony Arnold; Prudence Arnold; Sarah Arnold; Susannah Arnold; Rachel Fowler; and Mary Lucas, wife of Basil Lucas.
Property formerly situate in Baltimore County, c. 4-1/2 miles from Westminster, being part of *Caledonia*.

Chancery Book 9, pp. 499-516   1854   Equity #441
Francis J. Baumgardner, next friend to Mary L. Baumgardner vs. Mary L. Baumgardner. Sale of real estate.
Helen Baumgardner (formerly Helen Eline) died 11 August 1850, leaving husband Francis J. Baumgardner of MO. Children: Mary L. Baumgardner, of MO; and John F. Baumgardner, deceased, died c. 1851 as infant.
Property situate near Alloway Creek, being part of *Joseph's Chance*.

Chancery Book 9, pp. 517-528   1854   Equity #446
David Best vs. George Schloper and Catherine Schloper, his wife, and others. Sale of real estate.
Jacob Best, of Adams County PA, died Mar 1854. Brothers and sisters: David Best, of Frederick County; John Best, of OH; George Best, of OH; Catherine Schloper, of Frederick County, wife of George Schloper; Elizabeth Bishop, deceased, mother of John Bishop (of CA), Jacob Bishop (of Frederick County), Catherine Hesson (wife of James Hesson), Eve Storb (of Frederick County, wife of John Storb), and Mary Miller (of PA, wife of John Miller); and Rachel Bishop, deceased, mother of Hannah Zimmerman (of Frederick County, wife of George Zimmerman).
Property situate along Baltimore Turnpike, at PA line.

Chancery Book 9, pp. 529-552   1854   Equity #448
to Chancery Book 10, pp. 1-24
Daniel Mitten, and others vs. Rachel Mitten, and others. Sale of real estate.
Miles Mitten died c. Aug 1854, intestate, leaving widow, Rachel Mitten. Children: Daniel Mitten; Noah Mitten; Christena Mitten; Mary Ann Grogg, wife of David Grogg; Catherine Long, wife of William Long; Elmira Mahany, wife of George Mahany; Martha Ann Mitten; Miles A. Brown, wife of Andrew

J. Brown; George A. Mitten; Seranda A. Grumbine, wife of John Grumbine; and Rachel Mitten.
Miles was the son of John Mitten, of Frederick County who died c. 1813, testate, and his wife, Rosina Mitten. Their other children were: William Mitten, father of John Mitten; John Mitten, Jr.; Dulsina Mitten; James Mitten; Thomas Mitten; and Elizabeth Hill, of Orrel, England.
Property formerly situate in Baltimore County, on road from Westminster to Hampstead, being parts of *Rochester, Friendship Completed, Addition to Water Oak Level, Jacob's Lot, Rochester Enlarged* and *Catey's Delight.*

Chancery Book 10, pp. 26-57   1855   Equity #457
Edward F. Spalding, et als. vs. Cecelia M. Spalding. Sale of real estate.
George Spalding died 9 Aug 1854, intestate (will voided), leaving widow, Mary Spalding. Children: Edward F. Spalding; Ann M. Clabaugh, wife of John Clabaugh; Caroline S. Smith, wife of David Smith; Cecelia M. Spalding, deceased, died c. 1856; and Josephine Spalding.
Property being parts of *Goose Quarter* and *Addition to Brook's Discovery on the Rich Lands.*

Chancery Book 10, pp. 58-78   1855   Equity #458
John Marker, Henry Marker, et al. vs. Mary Marker and Elias Marker. Sale of real estate.
David Marker died Jan 1855, intestate, leaving widow, Mary Marker. Children: John Marker, of Frederick County; Henry Marker; Rachel Marker, of Frederick County; Elizabeth Harman, wife of Uriah Harman; Susannah Smelser, wife of William A. Smelser; Catherine Frounfelter, wife of David Frounfelter; and Elias Marker.
Property situate in Wakefield Valley on road from Westminster to New Windsor, being Lot #1 of the division of Eli Haines estate, being parts of *Stevenson's Garden* and *Cornwell.*

Chancery Book 10, pp. 79-89   1855   Equity #463
Ann Regina Warfield, Benjamin Warfield, and others vs. Gustavus Warfield and Elizabeth Warfield. Sale of real estate.
Seth Warfield, of Anne Arundel County, died intestate, leaving widow, Elizabeth Warfield. Children: Ann Regina Warfield; Benjamin Warfield; Eliza Ann Warfield; Lorenzo E. Warfield; Amelia Manalla, wife of Reuben Manalla; Seth H. Warfield; Evan T. Warfield; Caroline Warfield; and Gustavus Warfield.
Property formerly situate in Baltimore County, about 1/4 mile from Woodbine on Baltimore and Ohio Railroad, on Sam's Creek Road, being parts of *Wilkes and Liberty* and *Howard's Resolution.*

Chancery Book 10, pp. 90-114   1855   Equity #462
Henry Wilson, Admr. of Frederick Heiser vs. David B. Earhart, Admr. of George Heiser, et als.   Sale of real estate to satisfy creditors.
George Heiser died 15 July 1838, intestate, leaving widow, Catherine Heiser, w/o issue. He was the son of Frederick Heiser, who died 1 Mar 1846, intestate. Brothers and sisters: David Heiser, husband of Sally Heiser; Jacob Heiser; Susannah Wilson, wife of Henry Wilson; Peter Heiser, of MI, husband of Rebecca Heiser; Catherine Baum, of MI, wife of George Baum; Barbara Mathias, deceased, wife of Henry Mathias, mother of Urias Mathias (of MI, husband of Elizabeth Mathias), Edward Mathias (of OH), Saranda Myers (of OH, wife of Huttle Myers), Susannah Wyans (of OH, wife of James Wyans), Mary Mathias (of OH), Lewis Mathias (husband of Lydia Mathias), and David Weaver (husband of Margaret Weaver); John Heiser, deceased, father of Lewis Heiser (husband of Susannah Heiser), Daniel Heiser (husband of Susan Heiser), Mary Cummings (wife of Henry Cummings), and Catherine Shaffer (somewhere out-of-state, wife of David Shaffer); Daniel Heiser, deceased, father of Sarah Ann Heiser (of PA); and Sarah Foreman, deceased, mother of Henry Foreman (husband of Susannah Foreman).
Property formerly situate in Frederick County, being part of *Gotham*.

Chancery Book 10, pp. 115-157   1855   Equity #465
Lewis Schweigart, et als. vs. Jesse Schweigart, et als.   Sale of real estate.
John Schweigart died 20 Jan 1853, testate, leaving widow, Mary Schweigart. Children: Jesse Schweigart; Cyrus Schweigart; Lewis Schweigart; Anne Frizzel, wife of William Frizzel; Margaret Cassell, wife of Reuben Cassell; Louisa Hiteshue, wife of William Hiteshue; Clementine Schweigart; Sarah Schweigart; Rufus Schweigart, a lunatic; John Schweigart, location unknown; and Mary Cassell, deceased, mother of John Cassell and Elizabeth Cassell.
John was the son of Christian Schweigart who died intestate. John had a deceased sister, Magdalena Kurtz who was the mother of: Israel Kurtz, husband of Maria Kurtz; Lydia Fishburn; Noah Kurtz; Caroline Kurtz; Mary Bixler, wife of Benjamin Bixler; Catherine Myers, wife of John Myers; Jesse Kurtz, of Cumberland County PA; Nancy Bixler, of Franklin County PA, wife of Jacob Bixler; and Sarah Kresler, of Franklin County PA, wife of Frederick Kresler.
Properties formerly situate in Frederick County, on Uniontown Pike about 2-1/2 miles northwest of Westminster and also on Baltimore Pike, being parts of *Resurvey on Good Fellowship, Lamb's Plague, Resurvey on Lookabout* and *Fanny's Meadow*.

Chancery Book 10, pp. 158-177   1855   Equity #470
Abraham Bankert and his wife vs. Mary Herring, et al.   Sale of real estate.
Magadelena Rinehart died. Granddaughters: Susan Bish (formerly Susan Masonheimer), widow of Michael Bish (she remarried and became known as

Susan Bankert, wife of Abraham Bankert), mother of (by first husband) Jacob Bish (of OH), Elizabeth Friermond (of OH, wife of William Friermond), and (by second husband) John Peter Bankert; and Mary Herring (formerly Mary Masonheimer), wife of John Herring, mother of George D. Herring, Angelina A. Herring, Samuel W. Herring, Susannah Herring, William J. Herring, Thomas M. Herring, and Tilghman R. Herring (all of CA).
Property being known as *Stammer's Place.*

Chancery Book 10, pp. 178-197   1853   Equity #411
David Engel, of P. vs. Lydia Gosnell, Admtrx., and others. Sale of real estate to satisfy creditors.
John Gosnell died c. Oct 1851, intestate, leaving widow, Lydia Gosnell. Children: Mary Jane Ensey, wife of Richard L. Ensey; Isabella Gosnell; and Susan Price Gosnell.
Location of property not established.

Chancery Book 10, pp. 198-214   1852   Equity #357
The Commissioners of Primary Schools for Carroll County vs. Calvin Woolery, and others. Sale of real estate to satisfy creditors.
Noah Woolery died 29 April 1852, intestate, leaving widow Sarah Woolery. Children: Calvin Woolery; George Woolery; Mary Jane Woolery; Elizabeth Frances Woolery; Christiana Virginia Woolery; and Martha Ann Woolery. Noah had a brother, Elijah Woolery.
Property being part of *Newfound Bottom Enlarged.*

Chancery Book 10, pp. 215-239   1854   Equity #449
George Mort, next friend of Rebecca Lee Norris, and others vs. Edward Oliver Norris and Sarah Norris, his wife, and Thomas Hook. Sale of real estate.
Edward Oliver Norris and his wife, Sarah Norris. Children: Rebecca Lee Norris; Maria Elizabeth Norris; Martha Emma Norris; and Edward Oliver Norris.
Property situate in Middleburg, being several lots in *Staufer's Addition to Middleburgh.*

Chancery Book 10, pp. 240-256   1855   Equity #480
Josephine E. Warfield, next friend of Mary J. T. Warfield and Ella S. Warfield vs. Mary J. T. Warfield and Ella S. Warfield. Sale of real estate.
Marcellus W. Warfield died June 1855, intestate, leaving widow, Josephine E. Warfield. Children: Mary J. T. Warfield; and Ella S. Warfield.
Property situate in Freedom District, about 1/4 mile from Sykesville.

Chancery Book 10, pp. 257-283 1854 Equity #421
Noah Stocksdale and others vs. Solomon Stocksdale and wife. Sale of real estate.
Elizabeth Lane died testate. Niece and nephew: Nelly Haines, deceased, died 8 Jan 1854, intestate, wife of Edward Haines, w/o issue; and Solomon Stocksdale. Brothers: Noah Stocksdale; John Stocksdale, deceased, father of Emily Billmyer (wife of Daniel Billmyer), Helen Loyd (wife of John L. Loyd), and Edward Stocksdale; and Solomon Stocksdale.
Property situate on Falls, near Finksburg, being part of *Hooker's Meadow Enlarged*.

Chancery Book 10, pp. 285-331 1855 Equity #478
Jonas Ecker and Nathan Hanna vs. Isaac Lambert, et als. Sale of real estate to satisfy creditors.
John Lambert died Mar 1855, intestate, leaving widow, Esther Lambert. Children: Mary Lambert; Rachel S. Drach, wife of Henry Drach; Isaac Lambert; Samuel Lambert; Ellen Lambert; Elizabeth Haines, wife of Reuben Haines; Catherine Fuss, wife of Henry Fuss; Ann Lambert; Jesse Lambert; Jonathan Lambert; and Esther Lambert.
John was the only son of John Lambert who died c. 1838. His sisters were: Elizabeth Lambert; Charlotte Geiger, wife of Peter Geiger; Elinor Metcalf, wife of Joshua Metcalf; and Polly Hide, wife of Isaac Hide.
Property formerly situate in Frederick County, on Little Pipe Creek, about 1-1/2 miles north of New Windsor, being parts of *Resurvey on Black Oak Hill, White Gravel Spring* and *Stevenson's Lot*.

Chancery Book 10, pp. 332-346 1855 Equity #486
J. Henry Hoppe vs. William L. Hoff, Admr. of Nicodemus Sias, and others. Sale of real estate to satisfy creditors.
Nicodemus Sias died 1845, intestate, leaving widow, Ann Sias. Children: Jeremiah Sias; Noah Sias, of IL; Deborah Hoff, wife of William L. Hoff; Sarah Roelky, of Frederick County, wife of William L. Roelky; and Jane Small, of Washington County MD, wife of James Small.
Property situate 5 miles from Westminster on Westminster-Littlestown Pike in town called *Fairview*.

Chancery Book 10, pp. 347-367 1855 Equity #485
James Sykes vs. Samuel Morton, Jr. and William D. Miller. Foreclosure.
Samuel Morton, Jr., and his wife, Kesiah Morton.
Property known as Oakland Factory and farm, situate 1-1/2 miles from Liberty Road, 5 miles from Marriottsville on Baltimore and Ohio Railraod, 2 miles from Westminster Turnpike, formerly in Baltimore County, adjacent to main Falls of Patapsco, being parts of *Bennetts Park, White Oak Bottom* and *Bennetts Chance*.

Chancery Book 10, pp. 368-376 1856 Equity #497
Isaac Rowe vs. Upton F. Wolfe. Foreclosure.
Upton F. Wolfe.
Property situate on road from Union Bridge to Uniontown, being part of *Resurvey on Unity*.

Chancery Book 10, pp. 377-399 1855 Equity #488
John Powder, next friend of Eveline L. Powder, his wife, and others vs. Eveline L. Powder, et als. Sale of real estate.
James M. Gorsuch died 15 July 1852, intestate, leaving widow Mary Gorsuch, who later married John W. Swartzbaugh, Jr., and became known as Mary Swartzbaugh. Children: Eveline L. Powder, wife of John Powder; Henrietta S. Gorsuch; Susanna H. Gorsuch; Ellen M. Gorsuch; James Gorsuch; Sarah A. Gorsuch, of Baltimore County; Henry C. Gorsuch, of Baltimore County; and Thomas F. Gorsuch, of Baltimore County.
James was the son of Joshua Gorsuch (died 1844, of Baltimore County) and his wife Eleanor. Their other children were: Joshua M. Gorsuch; George R. Gorsuch; John L. Gorsuch; William McHenry Gorsuch; Elizabeth Ann Gorsuch; Martha L. Gorsuch; Ellen Maria Gorsuch; and Mary L. Gorsuch. Thomas T. Gorsuch was a cousin of James.
Property situate near Westminster, on Patapsco Falls, being parts of *Rochester, Rochester Resurveyed, Gill's Prospect* and *Bank's Folly*.

Chancery Book 10, pp. 400-414 1847 Equity #212
Henry M. Bennett and Eurith Ann Bennett vs. Mary Ann Bennett, and others. Sale of real estate.
Elisha Bennett was the father of: Jesse Bennett; Wesley Bennett; Charles W. Bennett, father of Mary Ann Bennett, Arabella Bennett, Maria Bennett, Elizabeth Bennett, Charles W. Bennett, Jr., Henry M. Bennett, and Eurith A. Bennett; Perry Bennett; Elizabeth W. Johnson; Sarah Ann Taylor, deceased, mother of Charles Wesley Taylor, and Matilda Taylor; and Mary Ann Bennett, deceased. Elisha had a brother, Benjamin Bennett.
Property situate 1-1/2 miles from Finksburg on Patapsco Falls, on south side of road leading from Ely's Mill to residence of Dr. Elisha Hall.

Chancery Book 10, pp. 415-430 1855 Equity #464
James Owings, and others vs. Andrew Mercer of Richard, Benjamin Warfield and Aletha Warfield, his wife, Ann Regina Warfield, and others. Sale of real estate to satisfy creditors.
Charles W. Warfield died Oct 1854, intestate, leaving widow, Ann Regina Warfield. Children: Charles A. Warfield; Margaretta E. Warfield; Seth N. Warfield; and George E. Warfield.

Property situate near Woodbine, on Sam's Creek Road, on Baltimore and Ohio Railroad, being part of *Wilkes and Liberty*.

Chancery Book 10, pp. 431-444 1856 Equity #508
The Farmers and Mechanics Bank of Carroll County vs. Adam Yingling. Foreclosure.
Adam Yingling and his wife, Margaret Yingling.
Property being parts of *Resurvey on John's Lot* and *Ohio*.

Chancery Book 10, pp. 445-473 1855 Equity #490
George E. Buckingham and Mary Jane Buckingham, his wife, Susan Ann Thomas, et al. vs. George Pickett, et al. Sale of real estate.
Amelia Pickett died Oct 1854, testate, widow of Levin Pickett. Children: Mary Jane Buckingham, wife of George E. Buckingham; Susan Ann Thomas, widow of Henry Thomas, mother of Rachel J. Thomas, and Amelia C. Thomas; Clorida Ripple, wife of Samuel Ripple, mother of Francis M. Ripple, Samuel L. Ripple, Catherine J. Ripple, and Mary Ripple; Charles W. Pickett; Jesse Pickett, deceased, father of George Pickett; and Thomas Pickett, deceased, father of William Henry Pickett, Lucy Ann Pickett, Mary Rosanna Pickett, and James Wesley Pickett (all of Erie County OH).
Properties situate on Woodbine Road, 3/4 mile from Woodbine depot on Baltimore and Ohio Railroad, being parts of *Wilkes and Liberty, Howard's Resolution* and *Minor's Beginning*.

Chancery Book 10, pp. 474-493 1856 Equity #512
Lewis Nicholas and Catherine Nicholas, his wife, et als. vs. David Circle, et als. Sale of real estate.
David Circle died 22 Apr 1854, testate, leaving widow, Lydia Circle. Children: Catherine Nicholas, wife of Lewis Nicholas; William Circle, of OH; David Circle; Lydia A. Circle; Anna Circle; and Lucinda Circle.
Property being part of *Ohio*.

Chancery Book 10, pp. 494-515 1856 Equity #519
Solomon S. Ecker vs. Elizabeth A. Ecker, et als. Sale of real estate.
Samuel Ecker died 31 Aug 1856, intestate, leaving widow Susannah Ecker. Children: Solomon S. Ecker; Elizabeth A. Ecker; Albert Ecker; Ellsworth Ecker; Rachel L. Ecker; Martha E. Ecker; and Samuel Ecker, deceased, died 3 Aug 1857.
Properties in or near New Windsor, known as Lots 9 and 11, and part of 8, being parts of *Five Daughters* and *Stevenson's Garden*.

Chancery Book 10, pp. 516-543 1855 Equity #461
Henry Wilson and wife vs. Jacob Heiser, et als. Sale of real estate and to satisfy creditors.
Frederick Heiser died 1846, intestate, leaving a widow, who died Apr 1854. Children: Susannah Wilson, of MI, wife of Henry Wilson; Peter Heiser, of MI; Catherine Baum, of MI, wife of George Baum; Jacob Heiser; David Heiser; Barbara Mathias, deceased, wife of Henry Mathias, mother of Lewis Mathias, Urias Mathias (of MI), Edward Mathias (of OH), Seranda Myers (of OH, wife of Huttle Myers), Susannah Wyans, (of OH, wife of James Wyans), Mary Mathias, and David Weaver; John Heiser, deceased, father of Lewis Heiser, Daniel Heiser, Mary Comyns (wife of Henry Comyns), and Catherine Shaffer (out of state, wife of David Shaffer); Daniel Heiser, deceased, father of Sarah Ann Heiser (of PA); and Sarah Foreman, deceased, mother of Henry Foreman.
Property formerly situate in Baltimore County, being part of *Gotham*.

Chancery Book 10, pp. 544-566 1854 Equity #420
Peter Senseney, and others vs. Jacob Senseney, and others. Sale of real estate.
Jacob Senseney, Sr., of Frederick County, died 10 Apr 1829, testate, leaving widow, Anna Senseney, who died Jan 1854. Children: Peter Senseney, deceased; Jacob Senseney, out of state, unheard of for 20 years, believed died intestate, husband of Elizabeth Senseney (formerly Elizabeth Crise), father of James Senseney; Elizabeth Christ, wife of Peter Christ; and Catherine Bishop, deceased, wife of Philip Bishop (of PA).
Property formerly situate in Frederick County, being part of *Mountain Prospect*.

Chancery Book 11, pp. 1-26 1856 Equity #506
Christian Long, et als. vs. Julia A. Phillips, et als. Foreclosure.
Uriel Clark Phillips died 17 July 1855, intestate, leaving widow, Julia A. Phillips. Children: Ann M. Phillips; George H. Phillips; Winfield S. Phillips; and William W. Phillips.
Properties situtate on Big Morgan Run, 1-1/2 miles from Moreton's Factory, 2 miles from Beams Mils, being part of *Watson's Trust*.

Chancery Book 11, pp. 28-43 1857 Equity #530
Eliza Krumrine, and others vs. Jacob Krumrine, and others. Sale of real estate.
Henry Krumrine died Mar 1845, intestate, leaving widow, Judith Krumrine. Children: John Krumrine, husband of Eliza Krumrine; William S. Krumrine, deceased, died Dec 1855, intestate, father of Henry Krumrine, and Isaiah Krumrine; Jacob Krumrine; Emanuel Krumrine, deceased, died 15 Sept 1848, intestate, w/o issue; Eliza Krumrine; Anna M. Wentz, wife of Philip Wentz; and Susan M. Shue, of Adams County PA, wife of George Shue.
Property being part of *Ohio*.

Chancery Book 11, pp. 52-72   1857   Equity #533
Daniel Frankforter, et als. vs. Regina Frankforter, et al.   Sale of real estate.
David C. Frankforter died Sept 1852, testate, leaving widow, Anna M. Frankforter. Children: Daniel Frankforter; Conrad Frankforter; Caroline Boring, wife of Jacob W. Boring; Elizabeth Frankforter; Regina Frankforter; and Lavina Frankforter.
Property situate in Manchester, being a tanyard.

Chancery Book 11, pp. 73-82   1857   Equity #547
Margaret Powder, Exrx., and Isaac Powder and John K. Longwell, Exrs. of Andrew Powder, deceased vs. John Powder and wife.   Foreclosure.
John Powder and his wife, Eveline L. Powder.
Location of property not mentioned.

Chancery Book 11, pp. 83-96   1857   Equity #539
Washington Senseney, next friend of Henry Clay Morrison vs. Henry Clay Morrison.   Sale of real estate.
Robert Morrison died 29 Feb 1852, intestate, leaving widow, Louisa G. Morrison, and only child, Henry Clay Morrison.
Property situate in Frederick County, southeast of Emmittsburg, 1 mile from Plank Road, being part of *Jones Fancy*. Probably inherited from John Morrison, who patented property in 1816.

Chancery Book 11, pp. 97-117   1855   Equity #477
The Bank of Westminster, and others vs. Samuel Sanford Payne, and others. Sale of real estate to satisfy creditors.
Elisha D. Payne died c. Dec 1854, intestate, leaving widow, Sarah Payne. Children: Samuel Sanford Payne, of Boston, MA; Ann Elizabeth Payne, of CT; George Washington Payne, of CT; Julia Olivia Payne, of CT; and Fanny Olive Payne.
Property being parts of *Oxmoore, Rochester, Dairy* and *Martin's Mistake*.

Chancery Book 11, pp. 118-146   1857   Equity #542
Levi Caylor, and others vs. Martha Jane Caylor.   Sale of real estate.
Abraham Caylor died 25 May 1857, intestate, leaving widow, Margaret Caylor. Children: Levi Caylor; Amos Caylor; Joel Caylor; Mary Woods, wife of Jesse Woods; Margaret Devilbiss, wife of Frederick A. Devilbiss; Susannah Lindsay, wife of Lewis G. Lindsay; Sarah Morelock, wife of Henry E. Morelock; Elizabeth Lantz, wife of William S. Lantz; and Martha Jane Caylor.
Properties situate 2 miles from Uniontown on road to McKinstry's Mill, being parts of *Margaret's Delight, Pleasant Mountain* and *Myers Good Luck*.

Chancery Book 11, pp. 147-172 1854 Equity #456
James H. Steele, et al. vs. James Becraft, and others. Sale of real estate.
John Becraft (aka John B. Craft), of Baltimore County, died 1828, intestate, leaving widow, Nancy Becraft, who died c. 1831. Children: James Becraft; Peter Becraft, of Baltimore County; Benjamin Becraft, deceased, died 1830, intestate, husband of Louisa Becraft, father of Ann Barnes (wife of George H. Barnes), Cordelia Barnes (wife of William Barnes), and John Becraft (died 1855, w/o issue); Susan Holmes, of OH, wife of Adam Holmes; Elizabeth Jenkins, deceased, died c. 1845, wife of Robert Jenkins (deceased), mother of Nancy Jenkins (of Frederick County), David Jenkins (of Alleghany County MD), John Jenkins (maybe in CA), and Margaret Jenkins (of Washington County MD); Rachel Kelly, deceased, died 1830, wife of John Kelly (deceased), mother of Sarah Duvall (wife of Benjamin Duvall), and David Kelly; and Hester Ann Huff, deceased, died c. 1835, wife of Owen Huff (deceased), mother of Mary A. Huff (died 1850, intestate, w/o issue).
Property formerly situate Baltimore County, in or near Eldersburgh, on new Liberty Road, being parts of *Everet Progress*, *Selmon Purchase* and *Perserverance*.

Chancery Book 11, pp. 174-198 1857 Equity #537
John Waggoner and Elizabeth Waggoner vs. Daniel Benner, Admr. of John Frontfelter, and Sarah Frontfelter. Sale of real estate to satisfy creditors.
John Frontfelter died June 1857, intestate, leaving widow, Rachel Frontfelter. Children: Mary Frontfelter; and Henry Frontfelter.
Property situate on Westminster to Taneytown Turnpike, midway between Westminster and Frizzelsburg, being parts of *Father's Advice*, *Molly's Fancy*, *Addition to Molly's Fancy* and *Resurvey on Lookabout*.

Chancery Book 11, pp. 199-216 1857 Equity #546
John Warner, and others vs. Uriah Warner, et al. Sale of real estate.
Elizabeth Warner died 6 Oct 1857, intestate. Children: Sarah Warner; Lydia Lamberd, wife of John Lamberd; Elizabeth Arther, widow of Joseph Arther; John Warner; David Warner; Jacob Warner; Deborah Warner; George Warner; Emanuel Warner; and William Warner, deceased, intestate, husband of Rebecca Warner, father of Uriah Warner, and Jane Warner.
Property situate on Westminster to Uniontown Road, being part of *Dear Bought*.

Chancery Book 11, pp. 217-230 1858 Equity #557
Benjamin W. Buckingham, Admr. of William Buckingham, deceased vs. Elias Warner and wife. Foreclosure.
Elias Warner and his wife, Mary Warner.

Property being part of *The Ovall*.

Chancery Book 11, pp. 231-243   1858   Equity #571
Samuel A. Lauver vs. John E. Reikel.   Foreclosure.
John Reikel died 7 Nov 1856, intestate, leaving widow, Susannah Reikel, and only child, John E. Reikel.
Property being part of *Bond's Meadow Enlarged*.

Chancery Book 11, pp. 244-263   1856   Equity #495
John Kesselring, and others vs. Samuel Hawk, and others.   Sale of real estate.
George Hawk died 29 Dec 1855, husband of Rebecca Hawk, who died 1834, intestate. Children: Susanna Kesselring, wife of John Kesselring; Mary Keefer, wife of Isaac Keefer; Sophia Heck, wife of Nicholas Heck; Peter Hawk; Samuel Hawk, deceased, died 1841, intestate, husband of Mary Hawk, father of George Peter Hawk (of VA), Mary Jane Hawk, Samuel Hawk, and Daniel Hawk; and Frederick Hawk, deceased, died 1848, intestate, husband of Catherine Hawk, father of Samuel Hawk, and Emanuel Hawk.
Property being part of *Fredericksburg*.

Chancery Book 11, pp. 264-280   1855   Equity #474
Samuel Hesson, and others vs. Samuel Hesson.   Sale of real estate.
Balzer Hesson died 17 May 1855, wife having died prior to husband. Children: Samuel Hesson, husband of Rachel Hesson; Jacob Hesson; Catherine Blankert, wife of Joseph Blankert; Rachel Hesson; Elizabeth Frier, of Adams County PA, wife of Philip Frier; and William Hesson.
Property formerly situate in Frederick County, in Myers District, about 2 miles from Maus's Mill, being parts of *Carroll's Range* and *Unity*.

Chancery Book 11, pp. 280-312   1853   Equity #412
Cornelia R. Delaplane and E. A. Clabaugh vs. Michael Mackley, and others. Sale of real estate to satisfy creditors.
Michael Mackley and his wife, Bridget Mackley. Children: Jacob Mackley; Margaret Otto, wife of George Otto; John Mackley; David Mackley; Emanuel Mackley; William H. Harrison Mackley; James Mackley; and Samuel F. Mackley.
Property situate near Middleburg, being Lot 5 of *Stuffer's Addition to Middleburg*.

Chancery Book 11, pp. 313-340   1855   Equity #468
Zadock M. Waters vs. Virginia Waters and Ann Eliza Waters.   Sale of real estate.

Thomas Hood, of Howard District of Anne Arundel County MD. Children: John Hood; Henry Hood; and Elizabeth Waters, deceased, died c. 1852, wife of Zadok Waters, mother of Virginia Waters, and Eliza Ann Waters.
Property situate in Howard County and Carroll County (in part formerly Baltimore County) at Hood's Mill, being parts of *Buck Forest, Concord* and *Hoods Fine Soil Forest.*

Chancery Book 11, pp. 341-352   1857   Equity #532
Robert J. Jemison, Trustee vs. Benjamin Jemison. Sale of real estate to satisfy creditors.
Robert Jemison, of Frederick County, died testate (will written 1815). He devised land to son Benjamin Jemison, who was declared a lunatic. Robert J.Jemison was appointed trustee.
Property being parts of *Watson's Delight* and *Second Addition to Brooks Discovery on the Rich Lands.*

Chancery Book 11, pp. 353-366   1858   Equity #573
Jonas Grace, and others vs. Emily Jane Sellman. Sale of real estate
Michael Grace died 9 Aug 1858, intestate. Children: Jonas Grace; Catherine Newcomer, wife of Henry Newcomer; and Catherine Sellman, deceased, wife of Henry Sellman, mother of Emily Jane Sellman, Caroline Louise Sellman, and Mary Catherine Sellman.
Property situate near Taneytown, about 3/4 miles from town on Uniontown Road, being part of *Lind's Bottom.*

Chancery Book 11, pp. 368-376   1858   Equity #589
John P. Kaufman, & others vs. Abraham Haines, and others. Sale of real estate.
George Kaufman died 1821, intestate, leaving widow, Margaret Kaufman, deceased. Children: John P. Kaufman; Caroline Haines, wife of George Washington Haines; Margaret Campbell, of OH, wife of Edward Campbell; Mary Ann Kaufman, of OH; Sophia Haines, wife of Abraham Haines; and Salomi Baker, wife of Meshak Baker. Widow, Margaret, also had a daughter, Susannah Lescaleet.
Property formerly situate in Frederick County, being part of *Resurvey on Mount Pleasant.*

Chancery Book 11, pp. 377-392   1855   Equity #475
Ann Rebecca Barnhart vs. Lemuel H. Dotterer, and others. Sale of real estate to satisfy creditors.
John W. Dotterer died Apr 1855 intestate, leaving widow, Juliann Dotterer. Children: Lemuel H. Dotterer; Mary J. Dotterer; and Emma C. Dotterer.
Property situate on Pipe Creek, being part of *So Far so Good.*

Chancery Book 11, pp. 393-408 1856 Equity #510
Joseph A. Eck vs. Samuel T. Eck, and others. Sale of real estate to satisfy creditors.
Joseph Eck died 15 Jan 1856, leaving widow, Barbary Eck. Children: Henry T. Eck; Mary Ann Kuhns, of Adams Co PA, wife of Paul Kuhns; Helen M. Weaver, wife of Louis H. P. Weaver; Joseph A. Eck; Samuel T. Eck; Willilam J. Eck; Ann Rebecca Eck; and Harriet E. Eck.
Property formerly situate in Frederick County, being a grist mill, being part of *Ross's Range*.

Chancery Book 11, pp. 409-438 1858 Equity #572
William G. Bausemer and Daniel Byers, Exrs., and Ellen Byers vs. William G. Byers,␣et al. Sale of real estate.
John A. Byers died c. April 1842, intestate, leaving widow, Ellen Byers, who died 3 Nov 1857, testate. Children: William G. Byers, of parts unknown; Susannah Byers; Daniel Byers; Elizabeth Bausemer, wife of William G. Bausemer; and John Franklin Byers.
Property formerly situate in Frederick County, on the Westminster to Littlestown Turnpike, being parts of *Brown's Vexation, Ben's Fancy, Clover Valley, Rattlesnake Denn, Cool Spring, Stevenson's Conclusion* and *Second Amendment*.

Chancery Book 11, pp. 439-454 1858 Equity #556
John Hess, Jr., vs. Jonathan Plaine. Foreclosure.
Jonathan Plaine.
Property being parts of *Dunblane, Arnold's Desire* and *Arnold's Desire Resurvey*.

Chancery Book 11, pp. 453-467 1858 Equity #558
George W. Gilliss, et als. vs. Elijah Gilliss, et als. Sale of real estate.
Alexander Gilliss died Oct 1854 intestate, leaving widow, Elizabeth Gilliss. Children: George W. Gilliss; Cecelia Jenkins, wife of Rezin T. Jenkins; Thomas H. Gilliss; Rebecca E. Gilliss; Rachel R. Gartrell, wife of Edward Gartrell; Elijah Gilliss; Gassaway Gilliss; and Francis Gilliss.
Property formerly situtate in Baltimore County, being parts of *Bachelors Refuge* and *Lapland*.

Chancery Book 11, pp. 468-482 1859 Equity #599
James Hood, et als. vs. Basil Runkels, et als. Foreclosure.
Jacob Mentzer died Mar 1858, intestate, leaving widow, Rachel Mentzer. Children: Catharine Runkles, wife of Basil Runkles; Mary E. Runkles, wife of Basil Runkles; Samuel Mentzer; John Mentzer; Thomas Mentzer; Francis Mentzer; William Mentzer; and Lewis Mentzer.
Property being parts of *Limestone Ridge, Good Will* and *Favor and Ease*.

Chancery Book 11, pp. 483-505 1856 Equity #504
Eliza Krumrine vs. Henry Krumrine, and others. Sale of real estate to satisfy creditors.
William S. Krumrine, of Hy, died Dec 1855, intestate, leaving widow, Elizabeth Krumrine. Children: Henry Krumrine; and Isaiah Krumrine.
Property being part of *Ohio*.

Chancery Book 11, pp. 506-515 1857 Equity #525
John McKinney, and others vs. James A. Dayhoff, and others. Sale of real estate.
Philip Hines died 1838, intestate. Children: Mary Hines; Ann McKinney, wife of John McKinney; Elizabeth Shriner, deceased, died c. 1851, intestate, wife of Christian Shriner, mother of Philip Shriner (of Frederick County), Mary Shriner, Hannah Shriner, Catherine Little (wife of Henry Little), and Ann Arnold (wife of Joseph Arnold); and Hannah Dayhoff, deceased, died c. 1856, intestate, wife of Elias Dayhoff, mother of James A. Dayhoff, Josiah Dayhoff, John T. Dayhoff, Margaret A. Dayhoff, and William H. Dayhoff.
Property situate in Middleburg, being part of *Stoffer's Additon to Middleburg*.

Chancery Book 11, pp. 516-527 1858 Equity #590
Nicholas D. Norris, Exr. of Nicholas Dorsey, deceased vs. Reuben Benson and wife. Foreclosure.
Reuben Benson and his wife, Margaret Benson.
Location of property unknown.

Chancery Book 11, pp. 528-545 1858 Equity #580
Petition of Joseph Evans. Sale of real estate.
John Evans died May 1841, testate, leaving a widow, who died 13 Sept 1858. Children: Joseph Evans, of Leavenworth, Kansas Territory; Lewis Evans; Levi Evans; Susannah Evans; Catherine Woolery, wife of Nimrod Woolery; William Evans; and Elizabeth Taylor, wife of Samuel Taylor.
Property formerly situate in Baltimore County, on road from Charity Meeting House to Brown's Meeting House, being part of *Stain's Neglect*.

Chancery Book 12, pp. 1-14 1860 Equity #641
William Myers, et als. vs. Frederick H. Myers. Sale of real estate.
David Myers died 23 May 1859, leaving widow, Elizabeth Myers. Children: William Myers; John Myers; Catherine Feeser, wife of George W. Feeser; and Frederick H. Myers.
Property formerly situate in Frederick County, being part of *Ohio*.

Chancery Book 12, pp. 15-30 1858 Equity #560
Elizabeth Ulrich, the mother and natural guardian of David Ulrich vs. David Ulrich, and others. Sale of real estate and to satisfy creditors.
Samuel Ulrich died c. Mar 1858, intestate, leaving widow, Elizabeth Ulrich, and only child, David Ulrich.
Property situate on Patapsco Falls.

Chancery Book 12, pp. 31-48 1858 Equity #582
Henry Bixler and Joseph Wimer vs. Lydia Bixler, et als. Sale of real estate.
George Bixler died c. Sept 1854, testate, leaving widow, Lydia Bixler. Children: Jacob Bixler; Henry Bixler; Jesse Bixler; George Bixler; Eliza Shaffer, widow of Samuel Shaffer, deceased (died 1 Aug 1857); Ann Greenholtz, wife of James W. Greenholtz; Mary Bixler; and Ellen Bixler.
Property situate near Manchester, being part of *Iron Intention*.

Chancery Book 12, pp. 49-67 1859 Equity #612
John McKellip, William A. McKellip, and others vs. Anna McKellip, and others. Sale of real estate.
James McKellip died May 1859, intestate. Children: John McKellip; William A. McKellip; James H. McKellip; Mary Elizabeth McKellip; Anna McKellip; Joseph A. McKellip; and Maggie C. McKellip.
Properties near Taneytown, being parts of *Addition to Brook's Discovery on the Rich Lands*, *New York* and *Heads Good Luck*.

Chancery Book 12, pp. 68-83 1859 Equity #610
Cornelius Wilson, and others vs. Robert W. Wilson, and others. Sale of real estate.
John Wilson died 1849, intestate, leaving widow, Penelope Wilson.
Children: Cornelius Wilson; Nathan Wilson; Robert W. Wilson; Mary Ellen Wilson; Joseph Wilson; Joshua Wilson; Nicholas Wilson; Levi L. Wilson; and Susan Ann Brashears, of Kansas Territory, wife of John Brashears.
Property being parts of *Windsor Forest* and *Colross*.

Chancery Book 12, pp. 84-102 1857 Equity #545
John Rinehart, Exr. of Joseph Baust vs. Elizabeth Baust. Sale of real estate and to satisfy creditors.
Sidney Baust, of Frederick County, died c. 1856, widow of Valentine Baust. Children: Upton Currans, eldest son, whereabouts unknown; and Joseph Baust, deceased, died May 1857, testate, leaving widow, Elizabeth Baust (formerly Elizabeth Garner), father (with former wife) of John Baust, William Baust,

Samuel Baust, Sarah Baust, Sidney Byers (wife of David Byers), Mary Jane Baust, and Isabelle Baust.
Property being parts of *Error's Corrected* and *Molly's Fancy*.

Chancery Book 12, pp. 102-137   1862   Equity #708
George Jacobs vs. Thomas S. Jacobs. Partition of land.
John Jacobs, of Baltimore County, died 1818, intestate. Children: George Jacobs; and Richard Jacobs, deceased, died June 1861, testate.
Numerous properties formerly situate in Baltimore County, on Deer Park, Nicodemus, and Washington Roads, being parts of Indian Town, Harryforde, *Buckingham's Good Will, Stevenson's Manor, Stevenson's Manor Corrected, Jacob's Venture, Barnes Level Resurveyed, Campbell's Search, Wilmots Manor Resurveyed* and *Additon to School Lot*.

Chancery Book 12, pp. 138-161   1858   Equity #569
Eliza Steffey, mother and next friend to Cecelia Steffy vs. Cecelia Steffey, and others.   Sale of real estate.
John Steffey died Oct 1846, intestate, leaving widow, Eve Steffey, who died intestate several days later. Children: Michael Steffey, deceased, died 1 Oct 1857, intestate, husband of Eliza Steffey and father to Cecelia Steffey (both of Lancaster County PA); and Mary Crumrine, wife of William Crumrine.
Property formerly situate in Baltimore County, near Hanover to Reisterstown Turnpike, being parts of *Matter's Choice* and *Troy*. Being Lots 2 and 9 of the division of Eve Steffey's father's estate.

Chancery Book 12, pp. 162-177   1860   Equity #631
Robert Wilson and George Wilson vs. Jacob Koontz, and others.
Sale of real estate to satisfy creditors.
David Hape died 2 Nov 1859, intestate, leaving widow, Louisa Hape, and only child, James Madison Hape, of PA.
Property situate in Middleburg, being part of *Dry Lodging*.

Chancery Book 12, pp. 177-188   1860   Equity #651
Upton Koons, and others vs. Eliza Koons, and others.   Sale of real estate.
Henry Koons died Jan 1854, intestate, leaving widow, Eliza Koons. Children: Upton Koons; Catherine A. Koons; Ann R. Stuller, wife of John Stuller; Jacob H. Koons; James H. Koons, of Franklin County PA; Emily I. Koons, of Franklin County PA; and Susan W. Haugh, wife of John Haugh.
Property situate on road from Robert's Mill to Taneytown, being part of *Resurvey on Brother's Agreement*.

Chancery Book 12, pp. 188-199 1861 Equity #696
John F. Buffington vs. Edwin A. Arter, Admrs. of Francis Smith, deceased, Lucinda Smith, and others. Sale of real estate to satisfy creditors.
Francis Smith died Apr 1861, leaving widow, Lucinda Smith. Children: Emma I. Smith; and Martha Elizabeth Smith.
Property being Lot 11 in New Windsor, being part of *Five Daughters*.

Chancery Book 12, pp. 200-208 1861 Equity #668
Porcius Gilliss vs. Susan A. Thomas. Foreclosure.
Henry Thomas died 1853, intestate, leaving widow, Susan A. Thomas.
Property being part of *Washington*.

Chancery Book 12, pp. 208-221 1861 Equity #694
Frederick Mering vs. William M. Mering, and others. Sale of real estate.
George Mering, of Frederick County, died Sept 1860, intestate. Children: Frederick Mering; William Marshall Mering; Joanna Mering; Luther Mering; and Margaret Mering.
Properties situate in Frederick County and in Bruceville, being part of *Good Intent, Fuss Purchase* and *Gist's Forrest*.

Chancery Book 12, pp. 222-229 1861 Equity #672
Harry B. Shroeder vs. Mary Newman (late Gugel), Admr. of Henry Gugel, deceased, and others. Sale of real estate to satisfy creditors.
Henry Gugel, formerly of Baltimore County, died 7 Jan 1860, intestate, leaving widow, Mary Gugel, who later married William Newman and became known as Mary Newman, and only child, Wilhemina Gugel (all of Baltimore County).
Property situate in Finksburg.

Chancery Book 12, pp. 230-237 1862 Equity #722
Jesse Hann, and others vs. David Wantz and Rachel Wantz, his wife. Sale of real estate.
Abraham Hann died 5 Oct 1862, intestate. Children: Jesse Hann; Elizabeth Miller, wife of Lewis Miller; Daniel Hann, of KS; Eva Stonesifer, of York County PA, wife of Levi Stonesifer; Anna Mary Rudolph, of York County PA, wife of Daniel Rudolph; Samuel Hann; and Rachel Wantz, wife of David Wantz.
Properties formerly situate in Frederick County, being part of *Durbin's Mistake*.

Chancery Book 12, pp. 238-246 1860 Equity #655
Henry B. Strevig, and others vs. Lydia Strevig, et al. Sale of real estate.
John Strevig, Jr., died 7 Aug 1860, intestate. Children: Henry B. Strevig, husband of Mary A. Strevig; Ephraim Strevig; Elizabeth Bucher, wife of Adam Bucher;

Ann Peterman, wife of Benjamin Peterman; Sarah Stonesifer, wife of Joshua Stonesifer; Polly Lammott, wife of John H. Lammott; William Strevig, of York County PA, husband of Sophia Strevig; John Strevig, of York County PA, husband of Maria Strevig; Lydia Strevig; and Edward Strevig.
Properties formerly situate in Baltimore County, being parts of *Stump's Lot, Smiths Field* and *Coutz Lot.*

Chancery Book 12, pp. 247-269 1861 Equity #684
Elizabeth Henry, and others vs. Sarah A. Henry, and others. Sale of real estate and to satisfy creditors.
Jacob Henry died 22 May 1861, intestate, leaving widow Catherine Henry. Children: Elizabeth Crowl, wife of John Crowl; Lavina Crowl, wife of George Crowl; Rebecca Keefer, wife of William Keefer; David Henry, husband of Catherine M. Henry; Leah Crowl, wife of Elias Crowl; Daniel Henry, of Montgomery County OH, husband of Louisa Henry; Nicholas Henry, of Montgomery County OH, husband of Matilda Henry; Jacob Henry, of Montgomery County OH; Catherine Petre, of Preble County OH, wife of Michael F. Petre; and Michael Henry, deceased, died Feb 1860, father of Sarah A. Henry, William D. Henry, Mary C. Henry, Lydia A. R. Henry, Catherine E. Henry, Nicholas I. Henry, Samuel I. Henry, and Michael M. Henry.
Property situate near Westminster, being part of *William's Luck.*

Chancery Book 12, pp. 269-283 1861 Equity #688
John Adam Fuss vs. Isaac C. Baile, Admr. of Thomas Townsend, deceased, and others. Sale of real estate to satisfy creditors.
Thomas Townsend died Apr 1861, leaving widow, Mary Townsend. Children: Charles B. Townsend; Isaac W. Townsend; John R. Townsend; Lydia E. Townsend; Joseph C. Townsend; William F. Townsend; Evan T. Townsend; and Jesse O. Townsend.
Property being parts of *Resurvey on Good Will, Bethel* and *Recovery Unexpected.*

Chancery Book 12, pp. 284-288 1861 Equity #665
Petition of Levi T. Bennett. Sale of real estate.
Eli Bennett died Mar 1840, testate, leaving widow, Rachel Bennett, who died c. Feb 1861. Brothers and sister of Eli were: Elisha Bennett; Benjamin Bennett, deceased; Thomas Bennett; Samuel Bennett, deceased; and Margaret Brown. Nephews and nieces: Levi T. Bennett; Rebecca M. Zepp; Ruth E. Crawford; Honor Prugh; Nimrod Shreeve; Benjamin Bennett; Mary Murray; Juliet Thomas; Jesse L. Bennett; Joshua Bennett; Samuel M. Bennett; Eli R. Bennett; Rebecca Moss; Catherine Bennett; Harriet Bennett; Matilda Finch; Lloyd Brown; Jesse Brown; Rezin Brown; George Brown; and Honor Brown.
Property being part of *Batchelor's Refuge.*

Chancery Book 12, pp. 289-296   1861   Equity #671
Peter Engel vs. Elizabeth Kenell and Nathan Kenell.   Sale of real estate to satisfy creditors.
Andrew Kenell died 1860, intestate, leaving widow, Elizabeth Kenell, and only child, Nathan Kenell.
Property being part of *Resurvey on Mount Pleasant*.

Chancery Book 12, pp. 296-306   1861   Equity #683
John S. Crawford vs. Margaret Dods.   Sale of real estate.
Margaret Dods, a lunatic, died June 1862, testate. Brother and sisters: George Dods, deceased, father of two sons (all of Scotland); Ann Crawford, deceased, testate, mother of John S. Crawford (father of Ann Crawford and Sarah Crawford); and ____ Landers, deceased, mother of William Landers, Robert Landers, James Landers, Harriet Morrison, and Margaret Groff.
Properties situate in Baltimore City on Paca and Saratoga Streets, in Uniontown, and in New Windsor.

Chancery Book 12, pp. 307-318   1862   Equity #711
Washington Irons vs. Samuel Nichols and wife, et als.   Sale of real estate.
Isaac Irons died 29 Aug 1861, intestate. Children: Rachel Nichols, wife of Samuel Nichols; Catherine Randall, wife of Vachel Randall; Ann Gist, wife of John Gist; Washington Irons; Clara Uhler, wife of William Uhler; Mary Upperco, deceased, mother of Eleanor Green (of Baltimore County, wife of John Green), John Thomas Upperco (of Baltimore County) and Isaac Upperco, deceased (father of George Upperco and John Upperco, both of Baltimore County); Sarah Nace, deceased, mother of Sarah I. Patterson (of OH, wife of Joseph J. Patterson); Joshua Irons, deceased, father of John Irons (of MS); Isaac Irons, Jr., deceased, father of James Irons, Andrew Irons, and Emma Merrick (wife of Joseph Merrick), all of PA; and John B. Irons, deceased, father of Edward D. Irons (out-of-state).
Property formerly situate in Baltimore County, being part of *Speculation*.

Chancery Book 12, pp. 319-325   1858   Equity #586
Lemuel W. Gosnell, and others vs. Robert J. Jemison.   Partition of real estate.
Robert J. Jemison
Property in Taneytown District on Piney Creek, being parts of *Watson's Delight* and *Second Addition to Brook's Discovery on the Rich Lands*.

Chancery Book 12, pp. 325-332   1861   Equity #691
James Bankert vs. Henry Bankert, and others.   Sale of real estate to satisfy creditors.

Christina Bankert died 4 Feb 1849, widow of John Bankert, of Jacob. Children: James Bankert, husband of Sarah Bankert; and Henry Bankert.
Property formerly situtate in Frederick County, being part of *Cool Spring*.

Chancery Book 12, pp. 332-342   1859   Equity #609
Jacob Young vs. Julian Smith and Michael Morelock, Admrs. of Joel Smith, deceased, and others. Sale of real estate to satisfy creditors.
Joel Smith died 7 Apr 1859, intestate, leaving widow, Juliann Smith. Children: Missouri Smith; Martha Smith; Mary Smith; Ezra Smith; William Smith; and Augustus Smith.
Properties being parts of *Brown's Plague Resurvey*, *York Company Defense* and *Resurvey on Lookabout*.

Chancery Book 12, pp. 343-354   1858   Equity #570
Jacob H. Christ vs. Sarah E. Parrish, Admx. of Richard Parrish, and others. Sale of real estate to satisfy creditors.
Richard Parrish died Nov 1857, leaving widow Sarah E. Parrish. Children: Mary Virginia Parrish; Charles Albert Parrish; and a girl born c. 1858.
Property was some of the lots purchased from Equity #420 (Chancery Book 10, pp. 544).

Chancery Book 12, pp. 355-368   1851   Equity #343
John Powell, et als. vs. Jacob H. Powell. Sale of real estate.
Moses Powell went to parts unknown in 1805, reported to have died in KY c.1841, leaving widow, Esther Powell, who died c. June 1851, testate. Children: John Powell, deceased, died c. 1858, of Adams County PA; and Jacob Powell, deceased, died 1858, father of Julia Ann Kaufman (wife of John P. Kaufman), Elizabeth Waggoner (wife of William Waggoner), Savilla Riggler (of Preble County OH, wife of George Riggler), Matilda Powell, Caroline B. Powell (of Preble County OH), and Jacob H. Powell (of Frederick County).
Esther Powell must have been previously married for in her will she also mentions sons: John Byers; and Peter Byers. Her grandchildren: John Byers; Mary Byers; Elizabeth Byers; Susan Byers; and Henry Byers.
Property formerly situate in Frederick County, being parts of *Foglesong's Hott* and *Stevenson's Conclusion*.

Chancery Book 12, pp 368-381   1858   Equity #553
Mathias Mann vs. William H. Warner, Admr. of Richard P. Buckingham, and others. Sale of real estate to satisfy creditors.
Richard P. Buckingham, of Frederick County, died Jan 1857, intestate, leaving no widow or lineal descendants. Brother and sisters: Mary E. Warner, wife of

William H. Warner; Cordelia Shipley, wife of Thomas Shipley; Minerva A. Skidmore, wife of James Skidmore; and Thomas B. Buckingham.
Property being parts of *Last Resurvey on Sheridan's Range* and *Eppington Forest.*

Chancery Book 12, pp. 381-396   1858   Equity #584
The Manchester Savings Institute vs. Peter Hax, Admr. of George Adam Hersh, deceased, and others. Sale of real estate to satisfy creditors.
George Adam Hersh died 6 Oct 1858, intestate, leaving widow, Elizabeth Hersh. Children: Caroline Hax, of York County PA, wife of Peter Hax; Catherine Myers, of Baltimore City, wife of Charles Myers; Christiana Kake, of Baltimore City, wife of Philip Kake; Polly Stoffle, wife of Sebastian Stoffle; Rebecca Shultz, of Baltimore City, wife of John Shultz; Elizabeth Hersh, of Baltimore City; and Sophia Hersh.
Property being parts of *Little Britton Enlarged, Everything Needful Corrected* and *Three Brothers.*

Chancery Book 12, pp. 397-414   1853   Equity #400
Joseph Baugher, Jeremiah Fisher and Alexius Baugher vs. John George Mihm and Ezekiel Boring   Foreclosure.
John George Mihm, of Baltimore City, and Ezekiel Boring, of Manchester. Ezekiel Boring died c. 1861, testate, leaving children: Jacob W. Boring; Catherine Ringer; and possibly Margaret Sentz.
Property situate in Manchester, being parts of Lots 4 and 42.

Chancery Book 12, pp. 415-426   1857   Equity #531
John Myers, Samuel Myers, Jacob Myers, et al. vs. Joel Myers, et al.   Sale of real estate.
Jacob Myers died Mar 1857, intestate. Children: John Myers; Samuel Myers; Jacob Myers; Henry Myers; Emanuel Myers; Noah Myers; Rebecca Bankert, wife of Abraham Bankert; Catherine Haifley, wife of David Haifley; Mary Wentz, wife of John Wentz; Rachel Wentz, wife of Emanuel Wentz; and Elizabeth Myers, deceased, wife of David Myers, mother of Joel Myers, Alford Myers, Ann Louisa Myers, and Julia Ann Herring (an illegitimate daughter before marriage).
Property formerly situate in Frederick County, in Myers District, being parts of *The Resurvey on Patience Care* and *Ohio.*

Chancery Book 12, pp. 426-436   1860   Equity #632
The Bank of Westminster vs. Benjamin W. Buckingham, et als.   Sale of real estate to satisfy creditors.
William Buckingham died Sept 1857, intestate, leaving widow, Nancy M. Buckingham. Children: Caroline E. Buckingham; and Mary Buckingham.

Property being part of *Resolution*.

Chancery Book 12, pp. 436-447 1859 Equity #624
Ephraim Warehime, et ux., and et al. vs. Nelson Warehime and Sevilla Starner. Sale of real estate.
Conrad Warehime died c. Feb 1858, intestate, leaving widow, Catherine Warehime. Children: Ephraim Warehime, husband of Susannah Warehime; Manassa Warehime; Henry Warehime, husband of Susannah Warehime; John S. Warehime (or Thomas Warehime), husband of Seranda Warehime; Noah Warehime; Mary A. Bixler, wife of Elias Bixler; Sarah Lippy, wife of Jacob Lippy; Sevilla Starner, wife of John Starner; and Nelson Warehime.
Property being parts of *North Canton, Well's Care Enlarged, Ormley, Iron Intention, Partnership, Good Luck, Sapling Ground* and *Gist's Ambition*.

Chancery Book 12, pp. 448-468 1858 Equity #567
David Orendorff and wife, and others vs. Susan Reese, and others. Sale of real estate.
John Reese died 11 Mar 1858, intestate, leaving widow, Susan Reese. Children: Jacob G. Reese; Rebecca Orendorff, wife of David Orendorff; Ann Marie Reese; Simon Jonas Reese; Doratha Dixon, of Frederick County, wife of Haines Dixon; Elizabeth Danner, of Frederick County, wife of David W. Danner; Ellen Barnes, of Frederick County, wife of Washington Barnes; Sarah Miller, of Frederick County, wife of David E. Miller; Catharine Byers, of St. Joseph, MO, wife of Noah Byers; Sophia Reese; John Reese; Absalom Reese; Noah Reese; and Washington Reese.
One of the properties was conveyed to John Reese by the heirs of Henry Grammer, deceased, by his widow, Rebecca Grammer and their children: Ann Mary Leister, wife of Henry Leister; Rachel Lantz, wife of George Lantz; Andrew Grammer, husband of Dorothy Grammer; Simon J. Grammer, husband of Rebecca Grammer; and Henry B. Grammer.
Properties formerly situate in Baltimore County, some in Cranberry Valley which is about 3 miles from Westminster on the road to Manchester, and others on the road from Westminster to Hampstead, being parts of *New Farm, Time Enough Yet, Reece's Industry Resurveyed, Newport, Iron Intention, Little Profit, Molly's Delight, Zebulon's Fancy* and *Hickory Ridge Resurveyed*.

Chancery Book 12, pp. 469-489 1858 Equity #566
Lydia Crawmer, et als. vs. Lucinda Crawmer, et als. Sale of real estate.
Henry Crawmer, late of York County PA, died August 1857, intestate, leaving widow, Lydia Crawmer. Children: Lewis W. Crawmer, of Pickaway County OH; Harriett Garnett, wife of Henry Garnett; Catherine Garnett, wife of William Garnett; Rebecca Crawmer, of York County PA; Henry W. Crawmer, of York

County PA; John W. Crawmer, of York County PA; Jacob W. Crawmer, of York County PA; and Lucinda Crawmer, of York County PA.
Property formerly situate in Frederick County, on the Maryland-Pennsylvania line, being part of *Old Germany*.

Chancery Book 12, pp. 490-516   1857   Equity #527
Catherine Bennett vs. Amanda Mercer, Admrx. and Hanson T. Bartholow, Admr. of Gustavus Mercer, deceased, and others. Sale of real estate.
Gustavus Mercer died June 1856, intestate, leaving widow, Amanda Mercer. Children: Thomas B. Mercer; Mary C. Mercer; Littlewood S. Mercer; Emily R. Mercer; Amanda E. Mercer; Isabella A. Mercer; Virginia B. Mercer; and Serena H. Mercer.
Property was previously devised by Andrew Mercer, of Anne Arundel County MD, c. 1825, to his son, Richard Mercer. Andrew's will also mentions his widow, Ruth Mercer, and their other children: John Mercer; Joshua Mercer; and Andrew Mercer; and also grand-daughter, Ruth Mercer. When Richard died in 1855, intestate, the property was inherited by his three children, Andrew Mercer, William Mercer, and Gustavus Mercer. One of the sons, William Mercer died Nov 1856, intestate, leaving widow, Lydia Mercer and children: Joseph F. Mercer; Susan M. Mercer; Richard Mercer; William H. Mercer; Elizabeth M. Mercer; and Salome A. Mercer, all of Clark County IL.
Property situate formerly in Baltimore County, part being in Howard County, which was once a part of Anne Arundel County, being parts of *Henry's Mills* and *Pleasant Springs*.

Chancery Book 12, pp. 517-536   1857   Equity #543
George W. Lamott vs. George W. Gorsuch, Admr. of William Griffie, and others. Sale of real estate to satisfy creditors.
William Griffie died Sept 1856, testate, leaving widow, Louisa Griffie. Children: Mary Elizabeth Griffie; and Thomas Vinton Haines, a stepson.
Property was conveyed to him by his father, William Griffie, Sr., situate on Deer Park Road, being parts of *Stevenson's Deer Park and Trouting Stream* and *Wilmott's Meadows*.

Chancery Book 12, pp. 537-550   1860   Equity #635
Joshua T. Cockey vs. Rufus J. Winterode and Mary Ann Winterode. Foreclosure.
Rufufs J. Winterode and his wife, Mary Ann Winterode, of York County PA.
Property situate in the Hampstead District, being parts of *Penelope and Thomas Cockey's Deysburg*, *Addition to Penelope and Thomas Cockey's Deysburg* and *Singery's Chance Resurvey*.

Chancery Book 13, pp. 1-15   1863   Equity #745
Petition of Rachel Wentz, and others.   Sale of real estate.
Valentine Wentz, aka John Valentine Wentz, died Feb 1843, testate, leaving widow, Rachel Wentz. Children: David Wentz; John Wentz; Valentine Wentz, deceased, died Feb 1860, intestate, husband of Ann E. Wentz, father of Charles V. Wentz and Eliza J. Wentz; Elizabeth Myers, widow of Samuel Myers; Jacob Wentz; Samuel Wentz; Eve Humbert, wife of William Humbert; Nancy Crowl, wife of Henry Crowl; Rachel Koontz, wife of Jacob Koontz; and Susanna Bonsack, of Montgomery County IN, wife of Daniel Bonsack.
Properties formerly situate in Frederick County, being parts of *Clear Meadow, The Crooked Rounds* and *The Resurvey on Locust Neck.*

Chancery Book 13, pp. 16-31   1863   Equity #738
John Wilson vs. John W. Crabbs, and others.   Sale of real estate to satisfy creditors.
Frederick Crabbs died Oct 1861, intestate, leaving widow, Matilda Crabbs. Children: John W. Crabbs; Elizabeth Buffington, wife of William A. Buffington; William J. Crabbs; Andrew J. Crabbs; George W. Crabbs; Charles E. Crabbs; and Rachel Crabbs.
Property situate on Big Pipe Creek, between Taneytown and Union Bridge.

Chancery Book 13, pp. 32-51   1863   Equity #743
Albert Koons vs. Charles Franklin Reck, and others.   Sale of real estate.
John Koons died 20 Sept 1862, intestate, leaving widow, Margaret Koons. Children: Albert Koons; Eleanore Reck, deceased, died Aug 1862, intestate, wife of Henry Reck, mother of Charles Franklin Reck, and James Calvin Reck; and Lucretia Reck, deceased, died Sept 1852, intestate, wife of Charles Reck, mother of Margaret Lucretia Reck.
Property situate in Middleburg District, being part of *Bedford.*

Chancery Book 13, pp. 52-60   1863   Equity #739
Uriah J. Morelock vs. Jesse T. Myers, his wife, and John H. Diffenbaugh. Foreclosure.
Jesse T. Myers and his wife, Susan Catherine Myers.
Property situate in Frizzleburg, being part of *Molly's Fancy.*

Chancery Book 13, pp. 61-78   1863   Equity #733
Walter C. Roberts vs. Francis N. Roberts, and others.   Sale of real estate.
Henry H. Roberts died Feb 1853, testate, leaving widow, Catherine Ann Roberts, who later married John H. Uhler and became known as Catherine Ann Uhler. She died Nov 1861. Children: Walter C. Roberts; Francis N. Roberts;

Mary Elizabeth Roberts; Virginia S. Roberts; Henry S. Roberts; San Salvador Roberts; and Kate A. Roberts.
Property situate on Baltimore-Reisterstown Turnpike, being parts of *Barbadoes* and *James' Purchase*.

Chancery Book 13, pp. 79-92   1863   Equity #729
Petition of Elizabeth Storm. Sale of real estate.
Christoper Storm, of Frederick County, died 1812, testate, leaving widow, Mary Ann Storm, who died 3 Jan 1860. Children: Elizabeth Storm; Ann M. Classon, wife of John Classon; Margaret Wivel, wife of Anthony Wivel; Anthony Storm, deceased; Mary A. Storm, deceased, died 1816, intestate; Catherine Burke, deceased, died 1821, intestate, wife of John Burke, deceased (died 1839).
Property formerly situate in Frederick County, being part of *Troublesome Job*.

Chancery Book 13, pp. 93-104   1859   Equity #628
James W. Jordan vs. James W. Jordan, Admr. of Samuel Blizzard, deceased, and others. Foreclosure.
Samuel Blizzard died Oct 1859, intestate. Children: Ann Rebecca Blizzard; Catherine Ellen Blizzard; John Lewis Blizzard; and Belinda Virginia Blizzard.
Property being part of *Cumberland*.

Chancery Book 13, pp. 105-119   1863   Equity #728
Isaac Dern and Sarah Hann, Exrs. vs. Lucinda Mackley, and others.
Completion of sale.
Mathias Hann died 1860, testate. Hann bought land from Equity #525 (Chancery Book 11/506), but never received deed to property. He agreed to sell property to Jacob S. Mackley who never completed payments before he died in 1862, in Frederick County, intestate. Jacob left widow, Lucinda Mackley and children: Milton O. Mackley, of Adams County, PA; Mary C. Mackley; and Samuel D. Mackley.
Property situate in Middleburg, known as *Hine's Lot*.

Chancery Book 13, pp. 120-141   1859   Equity #596
Thomas Gorsuch, et als. vs. Mary Gorsuch. Sale of real estate.
Benjamin Gorsuch died 13 Sept 1858, intestate, leaving widow, Sarah Gorsuch. Children: Thomas Gorsuch; Dennis H. Gorsuch; Robert D. Gorsuch; Jane Gorsuch; Ellen Goodwin, wife of Thomas Goodwin; and Mary Gorsuch, an idiot.
Properties being parts of *Lawrence's Disappointment, Lawrence's Industry, The Resurvey on Father's Gift, Hawk's Fancy, Dorsey's Mill Frogg, Upper Marlborough* and *Tevis's Adventure*.

Chancery Book 13, pp. 142-157 1859 Equity #626
John H. Conaway, et al. vs. William P. Conaway. Sale of real estate.
Reuben Conaway died 7 Dec 1858, intestate. Children: John H. Conaway; Cordelia Cristwell, wife of James V. Cristwell; Susannah Picket, wife of Wesley Picket; William P. Conaway; Lucinda Conaway; Louisa G. Conaway; Charles V. Conaway; Reuben N. Conaway; and Mary J. Conaway.
Reuben was the son of John Conaway, of Baltimore County, who died c. 1837, testate, leaving widow, Amelia Conaway. Their other children were: Louisa Shipley, wife of Grove Shipley, Jr.; Cornelius H. Conaway; John C. Conaway; Cordelia Shipley, wife of John Shipley; Columbus H. Conaway; Lloyd N. Conaway; and Charles W. Conaway.
Property devised by father, formerly situate in Baltimore County, on New Liberty Road, being parts of *Monzie* and *Dorsey's Industry*.

Chancery Book 13, pp. 158-169 1859 Equity #616
George W. Storms, et al. vs. Josephine Storms, et al. Sale of real estate.
Christiana Storms died 3 Feb 1859, intestate, leaving no lineal descendants. Brothers and sisters: George W. Storms; Jacob D. Storms; William J. Storms; Sarah Ann Storms, of Baltimore City; Aretta Storms, deceased, mother of Josephine Storms, James F. Storms, and William P. Storms; and Angelina Holby, mother of Anaretta Holby, and Naomi Mary Holby.
Properties obtained from Equity #376 (Chancery Book 14, pp. 152&c., George Storms real estate), being parts of *Hickory Ridge Resurveyed* and *Dean's Comfort*.

Chancery Book 13, pp. 170-187 1860 Equity #640
David Roop and John Roop, Jr., Exrs. of John Roop, Sr., et al. vs. David Reese, Admr. of John Byers, Elizabeth Byers, et al. Sale of real estate to satisfy creditors.
John Byers died c. May 1860, intestate, leaving widow, Elizabeth Byers. Children: Andrew Jackson Byers; Frederick Washington Byers; Mary Ann Rebecca Snider, wife of Michael Snider; Elizabeth Jane Byers; Ezra David Byers; Ellen R. Byers; Rachel Ann Byers; and John Henry Byers.
Property being part of *Lookabout*.

Chancery Book 13, pp. 188-211 1862 Equity #704
Hanson T. Webb and John Myers, of Joseph, vs. Jacob Babylon and James N. Kelley. Sale of real estate to satisfy creditors.
Jacob Babylon, formerly of Union Township, Adams County PA.
Property being parts of *Molly's Fancy* and *High Spring*.

Chancery Book 13, pp. 212-234 1861 Equity #695
Michael Murphy vs. Jeremiah Tomey, Exr. of Daniel Tomey, deceased, and others. Sale of real estate to satisfy creditors.
Daniel Tomey died Feb 1861, testate, leaving widow, Mary Tomey. Children: Catherine Tomey; Jeremiah Tomey; and Daniel Tomey, who was born after death of father. Nephews (sons of sister): John Sullivan; and Jeremiah Sullivan. Brother: Jeremiah Tomey.
Property being parts of *Mount Pleasant Enlarged.*

Chancery Book 13, pp. 235-248 1863 Equity #751
Levi Valentine, et al. vs. Rebecca Valentine, et al. Sale of real estate.
Jacob Valentine died Aug 1863, intestate, leaving widow, Rebecca Valentine. Children: Levi Valentine; William Valentine; Ann Rebecca Baker, wife of Levi Baker; Mary Ellen Shriner, wife of Isaac Shriner; Josiah Valentine, of Frederick County; Ezra Valentine, of Baltimore City; Milton Valentine, of PA; and Lydia Levinia Bowers, deceased, wife of Joel Bowers, mother of William Ellsworth Bowers.
Property being part of *New London.*

Chancery Book 13, pp. 249-265 1860 Equity #648
Elizabeth Storms, Jacob Storms, et als. vs. Noah Webster Storms. Sale of real estate.
Jacob Storms died 18 Mar 1853, testate, leaving widow, Elizabeth Storms. Children: Mary Ann Storms; William W. Storms, of Baltimore City, husband of Sarah Storms; Jacob Storms; Rebecca Williams, of Baltimore City, widow of John Williams; Elizabeth Adrian, of Baltimore City, wife of George Adrian; Thomas Storms, husband of Margaret Storms; Henry Storms, wife of Mary Storms; Amon Jesse Storms; Sarah Jane Storms; and Noah Webster Storms.
Jacob was the son of Jacob Storms and his brothers and sisters were: George Storms, husband of Naomi Storms; Mary Weakly, wife of William Weakly; Christian Beverde; Margaret Storms; and Catherine Storms.
Properties being parts of *White's Level* or *Friendship Completed, Frogg's Forest, Jacob's Beginning, Hale's Venture Resurveyed* and *Petersburgh Resurveyed.*

Chancery Book 13, pp. 266-279 1858 Equity #568
Elias Crawmer vs. Henry W. Steffy, Andrew Yeagle, et al. Sale of real estate to satisfy creditors.
George Yeagle died 25 Feb 1858, intestate, leaving widow, Anna Yeagle, who died Mar 1858. Children: Andrew Yeagle; Mary Yeagle; Anna E. Yeagle; John Yeagle; Nicholas Yeagle; Caroline Yeagle; and George Yeagle.
Property situate 8 miles northeast of Manchester on road from Stick's Store to Shaeffer's Mill, being parts of *Venus's Harbor* and *Dehoof's Pleasure.*

Chancery Book 13, pp. 280-294 1859 Equity #613
Lewis Green vs. John Davidson, Admr. of Benjamin Taylor, et al. Sale of real estate to satisfy creditors.
Benjamin Taylor died 3 Sept 1858, intestate, leaving widow, Mary A. Taylor. Children: Francis A. Taylor; Noah W. Taylor; and Deborah Taylor.
Properties being parts of *German Town, McQueen's Choice, Foxes Forest* and *Rockey Point.*

Chancery Book 13, pp. 295-311 1862 Equity #724
Joseph Wilson, and others vs. William Wilson, and others. Sale of real estate.
William Wilson, Sr., died Nov 1849, intestate, leaving widow, Elizabeth Wilson. Children: Joseph Wilson; Jacob Wilson; George Wilson; Elizabeth Shew, wife of Henry Shew; Nancy Row, wife of Isaac Row; Mary Ann Durbin, wife of John Durbin; William Wilson; Catherine Edwards, of Knox County OH, widow of Moses Edwards; Susannah Shuey, deceased, wife of John Shuey, mother of Mary J. Hilbetts, Elizabeth Shuey, Debora Shuey, Nancy Shuey, Susannah Shuey, Sarah Shuey, Monro Shuey, and Lucinda C. Shuey (all out of state).
Properties formerly situate in Frederick County, on Little Pipe Creek, being parts of *Wilson's Inheritance* and *Resurvey on Susan's Fancy.*

Chancery Book 13, pp. 312-334 1864 Equity #782
Daniel Richards, et als. vs. Catherine Richards, et als. Sale of real estate.
George Richards, Sr., died 16 July 1863, intestate, leaving widow, Ann Richards. Children: Daniel Richards; Jacob Richards; Elizabeth Miller, wife of Jacob Miller; Nancy Shaffer, wife of Henry A. Shaffer; Bethsheba Brown, wife of N. A. Brown; Belinda Houck, wife of George Houck; Sarah Lynch, wife of George Lynch; Catherine Fowble, wife of William Fowble; Harriet Shaffer, wife of Adam Shaffer; and George Richards, deceased, father of Richard R. Richards, Catherine Richards, Lucretia Richards, William Richards, Alice Richards, Laura Richards, James Richards, and Samuel Richards.
Properties being parts of *Trouting Streams Corrected, Brown's First Attempt, Hale's Venture Resurveyed, Jacob's Beginning* and *Blenheim.*

Chancery Book 13, pp. 335-348 1864 Equity #758
Chancery Book 14, pp. 458-460
David Engel vs. Benjamin W. Bennett, Admr. of Benjamin Bennett, et al. Sale of real estate to satisfy creditors.
Benjamin Bennett died 15 Dec 1862, intestate, leaving widow, Elmira DeMerville Bennett. Children: John W. Bennett; Mary A. Bennett; Asberry F. Bennett; and Edward L. Bennett.
Property being parts of *Resurvey on Hard Bargain, The Addition* and *Dorsey's Mill Frogg.*

Chancery Book 13, pp. 349-355   1864   Equity #790
Petition of Henry Shule, et al.   Sale of real estate.
Henry Keefer, of Frederick County, died 7 Mar 1829, testate, leaving widow, Sarah Keefer, deceased. Children: Jacob Keefer, deceased; Thomas Keefer, deceased; Catherine Otto, deceased; and Susanna Hann, deceased. Susanna's sole heirs were Henry Shule; Catharine Clinging; Mary A. Miller; Sarah Hahn; Isaiah Hahn; and Elizabeth Hahn.
Property formerly situate in Frederick County.

Chancery Book 13, pp. 356-377   1863   Equity #756
Chancery Book 14, pp. 221-223
John H. Conaway, et al. vs. Amelia Conaway, William P. Conaway, et al.   Sale of real estate.
Reuben Conaway died 1858. Children: John H. Conaway; Susan E. Picket, wife of Wesley Picket; Cornelia Creswell, wife of James V. Creswell; William P. Conaway; Levina McQuay, wife of David N. McQuay; Louisa G. Conaway; Charles Conaway, deceased, intestate, unmarried, w/o issue; Reuben N. Conaway; and Mary Jane Conaway.
Property formerly situate in Baltimore County, commonly known as *The Home Farm*, on Liberty Road, being parts of *Monzie* and *Dorsey's Industry*.

Chancery Book 13, pp. 378-399   1864   Equity #772
Susan Price and Ruth Price vs. Joshua Bosley, et al.   Sale of real estate.
John Price, of Baltimore County, died c. June 1825, testate, leaving widow, Catharine Price, who died 25 Feb 1864. Children: Susan Price; Ruth Price; Mary Ann Bosley, deceased, died 14 Apr 1849, wife of Joshua Bosley, mother of Catherine Bixler (wife of Jesse Bixler), Joshua W. Bosley, John W. Bosley, David Bosley, Mary J. Bosley, Edward W. Bosley, Ruth A. Bosley, and Sarah Shaffer, deceased (died 10 Feb 1859, wife of Henry Shaffer, mother of Mary A. E. Shaffer); Violet Frank, wife of John Frank; Samuel Price, husband of Catherine Price; Keziah Price, deceased, died c. 1826, as infant, w/o issue; John Coltrider Price, husband of Leah Price; Amon Price, husband of Elizabeth Price; and Jeremiah Price, deceased, died c. 1826, as infant, w/o issue.
Properties formerly situate in Baltimore County, one in Hampstead, other being parts of *Richard's Hunting Ground* and *Thornback's Addition*.

Chancery Book 13, pp. 400-422   1864   Equity #793
Ezekiah D. Bowersox, and others vs. Jeremiah Bowersox, and others.   Sale of real estate.
Daniel Bowersox died Dec 1863, intestate, leaving widow, Mary Bowersox, who died June 1864. Children: Ezekiah D. Bowersox, husband of Mary Bowersox; Absalom Bowersox, husband of Susan Bowersox; Mandilla Beightel, wife of

Henry Beightel; Julian Snyder, of Adams County PA, wife of Solomon Snyder; George A. W. Bowersox, of Adams County PA, husband of Mary Bowersox; Jeremiah R. Bowersox, deceased, died 15 July 1864, testate, husband of Catherine Bowersox (who died 13 Aug 1864), father of Elizabeth Bowersox, Jeremiah Bowersox, Isabella Bowersox (died 17 Sept 1864, as infant, w/o issue), Absalom Bowersox, and John T. Bowersox (died 22 July 1864, intestate, w/o lineal descendants).
Property being parts of *John's Delight, Addition to John's Delight, John's Lott* and *Resurvey on High Germany*.

Chancery Book 13, pp. 423-436   1865   Equity #813
Wesley Bloom, et al. vs. Mary Bloom.   Sale of real estate.
Jacob Bloom died c. 1862, intestate, leaving widow, Mary Bloom. Children: Margaret Babylon, wife of Jeremiah Babylon; Mary C. Bloom; Martha Jane Bloom; Anna E. Wilson, deceased, died c. 1864, wife of John W. Wilson, mother of George Wilson and Franklin H. Wilson; Wesley Bloom; Josiah Bloom; George W. Bloom; Isaac Bloom; David Bloom; William H. Bloom; Philip H. Bloom; and Ann S. Eyler, wife of Samuel Eyler.
Properties situate in District 1, being part of *Resurvey on Brothers Agreement*.

Chancery Book 13, pp. 439-478   1858   Equity #583
Christian Long, et al. vs. Ludwick Long.   Sale of real estate.
Henry Long died 1854, intestate, w/o issue, a lunatic. Brothers and sisters: Christian Long; Jacob Long, of VA; Peter Long, of OH; George Long, of OH; Margaret Arbaugh; Catherine Bish, of PA, wife of Jacob Bish; Conrad Long, deceased, father of Jacob Long, Jr., Catherine Long, Margaret Long, and Lucy Long (all of OH); and Ludwick Long.
Properties situate on Patapsco Falls, being parts of *Loveall's Prospect, Addition to Loveall's Prospect, John's Desire, Oxmoore, Wilmott's Purchase, Little Chance, Aspen Hill, Snake Denn, Hale's Venture Resurvey* and *Vine Yard*.

Chancery Book 13, pp. 479-488   1865   Equity #830
Nathan Crumbacker and Elizabeth Crumbacker vs. David Crumbacker, et al.   Partition of real estate.
Ann Crumbacker died 1856, intestate. Children: Nathan Crumbacker; Elizabeth Crumbacker; William Crumbacker, husband of Lydia Crumbacker; and David Crumbacker, husband of Elizabeth Crumbacker.
Properties formerly situate in Frederick County, being parts of *Something, Log Cabin* and *Carmack's Chance*.

Chancery Book 13, pp. 488-500 1864 Equity #780
Jesse Schweigart, et al. vs. Elizabeth Cassell, et al. Sale of real estate.
Mary Schweigart died 28 Apr 1863, intestate. Children: Jesse Schweigart; Lewis Schweigart; John Schweigart, out of state; Sarah Schweigart; Ann Frizzell, wife of William Frizzell; Margaret Cassell, wife of Reuben Cassell; Louisa Hiteshue, wife of William Hiteshue; Clementine Mering, wife of George T. Mering; Cyrus Schweigart, husband of Sevilla Schweigart; Rufus Schweigart, lunatic; and Mary Cassell, deceased, mother of John T. Cassell, and Elizabeth Cassell.
Property situate near Westminster, being part of *Fanny's Meadow.*

Chancery Book 13, pp. 501-514 1864 Equity #776
Jesse E. Stem, et als. vs. Deborah J. Stem, et als. Sale of real estate.
Jacob Stem died 1855, testate, leaving widow, Mary Ann Stem, who died Feb 1864. Children: Jesse E. Stem, of Frederick County; Julia Ann Ingells, wife of Hanson T. Ingells; David E. Stem; John Henry Stem; Joseph T. Stem; Deborah J. Stem, of Baltimore City; William L. Stem; Charles Wesley Stem; Leanna V. Stem; and Lucinda Stem.
Property formerly situate in Frederick County, 3 miles from New Windsor.

Chancery Book 13, pp. 515-529 1864 Equity #775
Elisha J. Cook vs. Sarah A. Lambert and Uriah P. Lambert, Extrs, et al. Sale of real estate to satisfy creditors.
Abraham Lambert died Sept 1862, testate, leaving widow, Sarah Lambert. Children: George W. Lambert; Elizabeth Ann Otto, wife of Evan Otto; Uriah P. Lambert; Mary Jane Clingal, wife of William Clingal (who went to parts unknown); Sarah Ellen Lambert; and Abraham Augustus Lambert.
Location of property not established.

Chancery Book 13, pp. 530-541 1864 Equity #788
David E. Morelock vs. Christian Yingling and wife. Foreclosure.
Christian Yingling and his wife, Mary Yingling.
Property situate on 1/2 mile from Stone Road on the road to Grove's Mill, being part of *Resurvey on Weaver's Lot.*

Chancery Book 13, pp. 543-554 1863 Equity #740
James Bosley vs. Levi S. Winterode. Sale of real estate to satisfy creditors.
Levi S. Winterode.
Property situate on Reisterstown-Hanover Turnpike, being part of *Nace's Tavern.*

Chancery Book 14, pp. 1-10 1864 Equity #757
Andrew Smeach vs. William Minter. Sale of real estate to satisfy creditors.
William Minter.
Property situate on Westminster-Manchester Road, being part of *Iron Intention*.

Chancery Book 14, pp. 11-26 1861 Equity #682
Samuel Shunk, et al. vs. Elizabeth Shunk, et als. Sale of real estate.
Daniel Shunk died Mar 1860, intestate, leaving widow, Elizabeth Shunk, of Frederick County. Children: Samuel Shunk; George Shunk; John Shunk; Benjamin Shunk; Priscilla Stoner, deceased, died 25 Mar 1864, of Frederick County, wife of William Stoner; Mary Angel, of Frederick County, wife of David Angel. Properties formerly situate in Frederick County, about 1 mile from Union Bridge, being parts of *Bedford* and *Resurvey on Unity*.

Chancery Book 14, pp. 27-39 1860 Insolvent Docket #1 p.115
Petition of Noah Plowman, Insolvent.   Sale of real estate to satisfy creditors.
Noah Plowman.
Property situate in Myers District.

Chancery Book 14, pp. 40-53 1864 Equity #796
David Palmer, next friend to Israel Ann Grove vs. Israel Ann Grove and Julian Grove. Sale of real estate to satisfy creditors.
Israel Grove died 18 Aug 1864, intestate, leaving widow, Juliann Grove, and only child, Israel Ann Grove, who was born 19 Aug 1864.
Juliann was the daughter of John Weaver. His eldest daughter was Mary Palmer, wife of David Palmer.
Property being parts of *Lammott's Middle of the World, Alltogether Too Late, White Oak Bottom* and *Curpoy*.

Chancery Book 14, pp.54-66 1864 Equity #783
Solomon S. Ecker, et al. vs. Upton S. Poole. Sale of real estate.
Esther Poole died Apr 1864. Children: Hettie A. Ecker, wife of Solomon Ecker; Margaret E. Poole; Sarah C. Gaither, of Frederick County, wife of George Gaither; Matilda Poole, of Frederick County; Jesse H. Poole, of Baltimore City; Joseph I. Poole, of PA; Lucretia Giles, of MN, wife of Aquilla Giles; and Upton S. Poole.
Property situate in New Windsor, being part of *Hibbard's Addition*.

Chancery Book 14, pp. 67-89 1864 Equity #767
William G. Bansemer and his wife vs. Susan Bansemer, Amanda Byers, et al. Sale of real estate.
John A. Byers died 1842, intestate, leaving widow, Helena Byers, who died 1857, testate. Children: William G. Byers; Susan Bansemer, deceased, died c. 1861, wife of Augustus Bansemer, mother of Susan Bansemer (of Baltimore City); Elizabeth Bansemer, of Baltimore City, wife of William G. Bansemer; Daniel Byers, deceased, died c. 1861, husband of Amanda Byers, father of Ellen C. Byers, and George S. Byers; and John Franklin Byers, of IN.
Helena Byers, in her will, mentions her following slaves: Jane Ann Gibson; David Sikins; Samuel Gibson; Richard David Robbison; Samuel Owings Gibson; Charles Allen Gibson; and Lindy Hunt.
Property being part of *Resurvey on Lookabout.*

Chancery Book 14, pp.90-107 1864 Equity #781
Jacob Powel, et al. vs. John Powel. Sale of real estate.
Jacob Powel, Sr., of William, died 21 Apr 1855, testate, leaving widow, Elizabeth Powel, who died 1 May 1864. Children: Jacob Powel, husband of Hannah Powel; Ephraim Powel, husband of Nancy Powel; David Powel, husband of Eliza Powel; Rachel Kump, of Adams County PA, wife of Peter Kump; Elizabeth Moore, of Fulton County IL, wife of David Moore; and John Powel, migrated to OH, not heard from for c. 30 years.
Property being parts of *Ohio* and *Keefer's Range.*

Chancery Book 14, pp. 108-119 1864 Equity #771
Francis H. Orendorf vs. Emanuel Trine. Foreclosure.
Emanuel Trine.
Property situate on Westminster-Manchester Road, being part of *Loveall's Enlargement.*

Chancery Book 14, pp. 120-142 1864 Equity #806
David W. Harner, next friend to Charles Harner, and in his own right, and others vs. Charles Harner, and others. Sale of real estate.
Michael Harner died 1854, intestate, leaving widow, Elizabeth Harner. Children: David W. Harner; Eliza Zentz, wife of David Zentz; Lydia Staley, wife of Alfred Staley; Sarah Lynn, of Adams County PA, wife of David Lynn; Eli Harner, of Adams County PA; Mary Messinger, wife of Ephraim Messinger; Rebecca Jones, insane, wife of Ephraim Jones; Noah Harner, deceased, died July 1863, intestate, husband of Joanna Harner, father of Charles Harner (all of Adams County PA).
Properties formerly situate Frederick County, being part of *Ohio.*

Chancery Book 14, pp. 143-151 1865 Equity #824
Esther Williams, and others vs. Adam Danner and wife. Sale of real estate.
James McIlhenny died Sept 1862, testate. He devised land to sister, Jane Maria McIlhenny, who died 3 Apr 1865, intestate, w/o lineal descendants. Brothers and sisters: Esther Williams, of Cumberland County PA, widow of Abraham Williams; John McIlhenny, deceased, father of Mary Plank (wife of Peter Plank), and Elizabeth McIlhenny, (all of Cumberland County PA); Samuel McIlhenny, deceased, father of Henrietta Johnson (wife of David Johnson), Eliza M. McIlhenny, Elmira McIlhenny, Mary McIlhenny, and James McIlhenny (all of Cumberland County PA); Nancy King, deceased, mother of William King (of Dauphin County PA); Margaret Reid, deceased, mother of John Reid, Alexander H. Reid, and Hugh F. Reid (all of OH); Sarah Cassatt, deceased, mother of David Cassatt (of Adams County PA); and Alexander McIlhenny, father of Elizabeth R. Danner (wife of Adam Danner).
Property being parts of *Addition to Brook's Discovery on The Rich Land* and *Rich Land.*

Chancery Book 14, pp. 152-171 1852 Equity #376
George Washington Gilmore Storms, et als. vs. William Jesse Storms, et als. Sale of real estate.
George Storms died 16 Nov 1851, intestate, leaving widow, Naomi Storms. Children: George Washington Gilmore Storms, of PA; William Jesse Storms; Jacob L. Storms; Aritta Storms; Sarah Ann Storms, of Baltimore, wife of William Storms; Angelina Holly, deceased, wife of Albert Holly, mother of Ann Aretta Holly, and Naomi Mary Holly (all of Alleghany County MD); and Christiana Storms.
Properties situate about 3 miles east of Westminster, near branch of Patapsco Falls, being parts of *Dean's Comfort, Hickory Ridge Resurveyed* and *Lane's Delight.* Another situate in Westminster, on Washington Road, being part of *White's Level* or *Friendship Completed.*

Chancery Book 14, pp. 172-184 1864 Equity #786
James Shorb, and others vs. Abraham Shorb and William Thomas Shorb. Sale of real estate.
Conrad Shorb died Oct 1863, intestate, leaving widow, Catherine Shorb. Children: John Shorb; James Shorb; Samuel Shorb; Ann Ohler, of Frederick County, wife of John Thomas Ohler; Washington Shorb; Edward Shorb; Abraham Shorb; and William Thomas Shorb.
Properties formerly situate in Frederick County, being parts of *New London, Third Additon to New London* and *Terra Rubra.*

Chancery Book 14, pp. 185-200 1864 Equity #769
Joseph Bromwell vs. Levi S. Winterode and Maria Winterode, his wife. Foreclosure.
Levi S. Winterode, and his wife, Maria Winterode. They moved to Baltimore County in the spring of 1864.
Property being part of *Gittinger's Glade* and *Nace's Tavern*.

Chancery Book 14, pp. 201-211 1863 Equity #744
Jacob Sellers, et als. vs. Belinda Ann Sellers and Amanda E. Sellers. Sale of real estate.
Peter Sellers died c. May 1863, intestate, leaving no lineal descendants. Brothers and sisters: Jacob Sellers, husband of Ruth Sellers; Mary Brown, wife of Jacob Brown; Catherine Wagoner, widow of Philip Wagoner; Samuel Sellers; George Sellers, deceased, father of Serepta Sellers, Rachel Sellers, Belinda Ann Sellers, Anna M. Caltrider (wife of Jacob Caltrider), and Amanda E. Sellers; John Sellers, deceased, husband of Sallie Sellers, father of Mary Sellers; and Elizabeth Hann, mother of Sabrina L Hann.
Peter was the son of George Sellers, Sr., who died c. 1859, testate, and his wife, Ann Mary Sellers, deceased. George's will also mentions their other children: John Sellers; George Sellers; Jacob Sellers; Samuel Sellers; Catherine Wagner, wife of Philip Wagner; and Magdalena Brown, wife of Jacob Brown: and a granddaughter, Philipinia Louisa Hahn.
Location of property not established.

Chancery Book 14, pp. 213-220 1864 Equity #795
Petiton of Moses Shaw, Trustee of Fanny Dorsey. Foreclosure.
Fanny Dorsey d. 17 May 1865, intestate.
Property situate on road leading from New Windsor to McKinstry's Mill, being part of *The Agreement*.

Chancery Book 14, pp. 224-240 1865 Equity #819
Peter B. Smith vs. Jeremiah H. Smith, Adm. of Joel Kerchner, deceased, Elizabeth A. Kerchner, et als. Sale of real estate to satisfy creditors.
Joel Kerchner died 19 Nov 1864, leaving widow, Elizabeth A. Kerchner. Children: George W. Kerchner; and Peter Kerschner.
Joel purchased land from Margaret Ellen Woodrow, who died Mar 1864, intestate, before she gave him a deed to property. She was the widow of Granville Woodrow and mother of George W. Woodrow (of Fulton County IL), John D. Woodrow (of Fulton County IL), Mary E. Woodrow, and Benjamin F. Woodrow.
Property was situate in Hampstead District.

Chancery Book 14, pp. 241-260   1864   Equity #798
Mary Alice Fogle, and others vs. Michael Fogle, and others. Sale of real estate and to satisfy creditors.
David Fogle died Aug 1864, intestate, leaving widow, Mary Alice Fogle, w/o original descendants. Brothers and sisters: John Fogle; Joseph Fogle; Nancy Newcomer, wife of Isaac Newcomer; and Michael Fogle.
Properties situate near Taneytown, being part of *Resurvey on Brother's Agreement*.

Chancery Book 14, pp. 261-287   1862   Equity #717
William N. Burgoon, et als. vs. David N. Burgoon, et als. Sale of real estate.
William Burgoon died 21 Apr 1862, testate, leaving widow, Sarah Burgoon. Children: William N. Burgoon; Aaron Burgoon; Mary Slyder, of Frederick County, wife of Peter Slyder; David N. Burgoon, of IL; Francis N. Burgoon; Susannah Burgoon; Edith Burgoon; John Burgoon; and Rachel Miller, deceased, wife of John Miller, mother of Rachel Miller.
Properties formerly situate in Frederick County, on road from Union Mills to Hanover, being parts of *Hill Spring, Jacob's Lot, Bankert's Amendment* and *Ohio*.

Chancery Book 14, pp. 288-308   1864   Equity #800
Ezekiah D. Bowersox, next friend to Elizabeth Bowersox, and others vs. Elizabeth Bowersox, and others. Sale of real estate.
Jeremiah R. Bowersox died 15 July 1864, leaving widow, Catherine Bowersox, who died 13 Aug 1864, intestate. Children: Elizabeth Bowersox; Jeremiah Bowersox; Isabella Bowersox, deceased, died 17 Sept 1864, w/o issue; and Absalom Bowersox.
Catherine was the daughter of Adam Humbert, who died 20 May 1854, and his wife, Elizabeth Humbert, who died 1 Nov 1863.
Property being part of *Leonard's Lott* and *Ohio*.

Chancery Book 14, pp. 309-328   1865   Equity #849
Uriah B. Mikesell, Adm. of William B. Mikesell, deceased, vs. Anna M. Mikesell and Elizabeth Mikesell. Sale of real estate and to satisfy creditors.
William B. Mikesell died 14 Apr 1863, intestate, leaving widow, Elizabeth Mikesell. Children: Uriah B. Mikesell; Anna M. Mikesell; and Elizabeth Mikesell, deceased, died 12 Jul 1865, intestate, w/o issue.
Properties formerly situate in Frederick County, being parts of *New Germany, Chestnut Ridge, The Resurvey on Halfer Stadt* and *Phillipsburgh*.

Chancery Book 14, pp. 329-355 1865 Equity #858
Henry H. Gore and wife, Elias Stocksdale, guardian and next friend to Rebecca Jane Stocksdale and Susanna Stocksdale vs. Rebecca Jane Stocksdale and Susanna Stocksdale. Sale of real estate.
William Whalen, of Baltimore County, died 16 Oct 1864, intestate, leaving widow, Susan Whalen. Children: Ann Rebecca Gore, of Baltimore County, wife of Henry H. Gore; and Martha Stocksdale, deceased, wife of Elias C. Stocksdale, mother of Rebecca Jane Stocksdale, and Susanna Stocksdale.
Properties situate in Carroll, Baltimore and Frederick counties. The Carroll County property situate on Morgan Run, south of Nicodemus Road, being parts of *Wilmot's Wilderness*, *William's Defense*, *Adam's Garden*, *Beasman's Discovery Corrected*, *Conaway's Venture Improved*, *Conaway's Improvement*, *Bower's Chance*.

Chancery Book 14, pp. 356-372 1865 Equity #832
Frederick Fowble and Anna Fowble vs. Daniel Null, Caroline Null and Mary A. Null. Foreclosure.
Absalom Null died 1862, testate, leaving widow, Caroline Null, of Baltimore City, and only child, Mary Agnes Null. His brother was Daniel Null.
Property being part of *The Addition to Landaff*.

Chancery Book 14, pp. 373-387 1865 Equity #828
Peter Greenwood vs. George Hoffman and Henry Hoffman.
Partition of real estate.
Philip Greenwood died 1849, intestate, leaving widow, Mary Greenwood. Children: Peter Greenwood; John Greenwood, of Frederick County, husband of Ann Maria Greenwood; Abraham Greenwood, husband of Caroline V. Greenwood; William Greenwood, husband of Minerva A. Greenwood; Ann Maria Devilbiss, wife of Adam A. Devilbiss; Sophia Snader, wife of David W. Snader; and Mary C. Hoffman, deceased, died 1864, intestate, wife of Henry Hoffman, mother of George Hoffman (of Frederick County).
Property being parts of *Resurvey on the Deeps*, *Poplar Spring*, *Resurvey on Walnut Bottom*, *Hull's Neglect* and *Mount Pleasant*.

Chancery Book 14, pp. 388-404 1865 Equity #838
John Myers, of Jacob, Admr. of Samuel Myers, deceased, vs. Elizabeth Myers, widow of Samuel Myers, deceased, and others. Sale of real estate to satisfy creditors.
Samuel Myers, of Jacob, died 1861, intestate, leaving widow, Elizabeth Myers. Children: Josephus Myers; Reuben Myers; Ann E. Myers; and Susan Alice Myers.
Properties being parts of *Erb's Pleasure* and *Dyer's Mill Forest*.

Chancery Book 14, pp. 405-421 1864 Equity #801
Absalom H. Bowersox, prochim ami of Elizabeth Bowersox, Jeremiah Bowersox and Absalom Bowersox vs. Elizabeth Bowersox, Jeremiah Bowersox, Absalom Bowersox and J. William Earhart, surv. Exr. of Jeremiah R. Bowersox. Sale of real estate.
Jeremiah R. Bowersox died 15 July 1864, testate, leaving widow, Catherine Bowersox, who died 13 Aug 1864. Children: Elizabeth Bowersox; Jeremiah Bowersox; Absalom Bowersox; Isabella Bowersox, deceased, died 17 Sept 1864, intestate; and John Thomas Bowersox, deceased, died 22 July 1864, intestate. Jeremiah's brother was Ezekiah D. Bowersox.
Property being part of *Ohio*.

Chancery Book 14, pp. 422-444 1865 Equity #850
Josiah E. Mehring and wife, Edward Spangler and wife, and others vs. Harriet Mehring, and others. Sale of real estate.
John Mehring, of John, died June 1865, in Germany Township, Adams County PA, intestate, leaving widow, Harriet Mehring, of Adams County PA. Children: (with first wife, Amy Mehring, who died Mar 1852) Isaiah E. Mehring, of Adams County PA, husband of Sarah J. Mehring; Mary C. Spangler, of Adams County PA, wife of Edward Spangler; Jonathan F. Mehring, of Adams County PA; Margaret E. Hilterbrick, wife of George Hilterbrick; Ellen C. Crownover, wife of Samuel Crownover; John O. Mehring, of Adams County PA; Emma M. Mehring, of Adams County PA; and Lydia A. Mehring, of Adams County PA; (with second wife and widow, Harriet Mehring) Solomon D. Mehring, of Adams County PA; Alverta M. Mehring, of Adams County PA; and Harriet R. Mehring, of Adams County PA.
Properties being parts of *Ohio*, *Resurvey on Owings Chance* and *The Exchange*.

Chancery Book 14, pp. 445-457 1866 Equity #869
Frederick Taney, et als. vs. Charles Calvin Taney, et als. Sale of real estate.
Elmira Taney died Oct 1861, intestate, leaving husband, Frederick Taney. Children: (with former husband, Abraham Sherfy) Christopher Columbus Sherfy, of Otoe County, Territory of Nebraska; John Thomas Sherfy, of Parke County, IN; (with present husband, Frederick Taney) Charles Calvin Taney; Elmira Alice Taney; Ann Missouri Taney; and Solomon Frederick Taney.
Property situate in Frizzleburg, being part of *Molly's Fancy*.

Chancery Book 14, pp. 461-473 1865 Equity #837
John S. Stansbury vs. Susan E. Kalkman, Frederick W. Kalkman, and others. Foreclosure.
Alexander E. Kalkman died 29 Oct 1863, intestate, leaving widow, Susan E. Kalkman. Children: Frederick W. Kalkman; Alexander E. Kalkman; and Maria L. Kalkman.

Property situate on Baltimore and Ohio Railroad, being part of *Mount Pleasant Enlarged.*

Chancery Book 14, pp. 474-504   1865   Equity #863
Chancery Book 17, pp. 292-297
John Paul Murray, and others vs. Whitfield Murray and William Columbus Murray. Sale of real estate.
Thomas B. Murray, son of John Murray, died May 1850, tesate, leaving widow, Catherine Ann Murray, who died July 1864, intestate. Children: John Paul Murray; Charles Milton Murray; Elenora Murray; Whitfield Murray; and William Columbus Murray.
Properties situate in Carroll, Baltimore and Frederick counties, some on or near Reisterstown-Hanover Turnpike, being parts of *Merryman's Meadows, Sportsman's Hall, Landaff, Howard's Discovery* and *Leigh Castle.*

Chancery Book 14, pp. 505-522   1864   Equity #807
William W. Smelser, et als. vs. Mary Smelser, widow of David Smelser, deceased, et al. Sale of real estate.
David Smelser died 10 Feb 1864, testate, leaving widow, Mary Smelser. Children: William W. Smelser; Mary E. Frownfelter, wife of John Frownfelter; David P. Smelser; Virginia C. Smelser; and John P. Smelser.
David was the son of Michael Smeltzer (who died c. 1831, testate) and his wife, Mary Smeltzer, of Frederick County. Their other children were: George Smeltzer; Mary Morris; Catherine Winrode; and Sallly Lantz.
Properties being parts of *The Resurvey on Good Will, Bethel* and *Recovery Unexpected.*

Chancery Book 14, pp. 523-536   1865   Equity #867
Lydia Hoffacker, next friend, and others vs. Henry Jacob Hoffacker. Sale of real estate.
Jeremiah H. Hoffacker died Sept 1865, leaving widow, Lydia Hoffacker, and only child, Henry Jacob Hoffacker. Lydia was the daughter of Henry H. Miller.
Property formerly situate in Baltimore County, being in the Hampstead District about 1/2 mile east of Turnpike, and about 1-1/2 miles from Hampstead, being parts of *Penelope and Thomas Cockey's Deysburgh, Addition to Penelope and Thomas Cockey's Deysburgh, Singery Chance Resurveyed* and *Foster's Hunting Ground.*

Chancery Book 14, pp. 537-550   1866   Equity #874
William Fuss, and others vs. Samuel Angel, and others. Sale of real estate.
Lavinia Fuss, daughter of Elizabeth Shaner, wife of William Fuss (who plans to move his family West). Children: John Henry Fuss; and William Edward Fuss.

Property situate near road from Taneytown to Double Pipe Creek, being part of *Resurvey on Terra Rubra*.

Chancery Book 15, pp. 1-11   1865   Equity #821
Lydia Koutz, mother and next friend to John Koutz and Henry Koutz vs. John Koutz and Henry Koutz. Sale of real estate.
Nathan Koutz died 13 Mar 1865, intestate, leaving widow, Lydia Koutz. Children: John Koutz; and Henry Koutz.
Property being parts of *Sugar Valley* and *Beaver Trap*.

Chancery Book 15, pp. 12-27   1865   Equity #842
Eli Fuhrman, and others vs. Amelia Fuhrman. Sale of real estate.
Henry Fuhrman, formerly of York County PA, died 10 Jan 1858, testate, leaving widow, Elizabeth Fuhrman, who died 13 July 1865. Children: John Fuhrman, deceased, died July 1863, intestate, husband of Rachel Fuhrman, father of George Fuhrman, Urias Fuhrman, and Amelia Furhman (of York County PA); Eli Fuhrman, husband of Rebecca Fuhrman; Conrad Fuhrman, husband of Polly Fuhrman; Catherine Fuhrman; Julia Ann Mencha, of York County PA, wife of Martin Mencha; and Lewis Fuhrman, deceased, father of Salonous Fuhrman, and Malinda Fuhrman (both of York County PA).
Property formerly situate in Baltimore County, being part of *Caltrider's Lot*.

Chancery Book 15, pp. 28-44   1865   Equity #836
Jeremiah Malehorn & wife vs. Susannah Malehorn, & others. Sale of real estate.
Elizabeth Malehorn died Dec 1863, testate, w/o issue. Brothers and sister: Catherine Malehorn, deceased, died 1863, intestate, unmarried and w/o issue; John Malehorn, deceased, died 1865, husband of Susannah Malehorn, father of Jeremiah Malehorn (husband of Catherine Malehorn), Ann Worley (wife of William Worley), Andrew J. Malehorn (husband of Ella B. Malehorn), Martha A. Worley (wife of Jacob Worley), Catherine Malehorn, Lucinda Malehorn, Oliver P. Malehorn (of PA, husband of Mary Malehorn), Samuel Malehorn (of IL, husband of Sarah Malehorn), Franklin P. Malehorn (husband of Amanda C. Malehorn), and Mary J. Malehorn; and Jacob Malehorn, father of Mary Holmes (of Harford County MD, wife of William Holmes), Jane Laff (of Harford County MD, wife of Elias F. Laff), Adeline Moss (of St. Mary's County MD, wife of James Moss), and George W. Malehorn (of parts unknown).
Property being part of *Rochester*.

Chancery Book 15, pp. 45-58   1864   Equity #804
Samuel Crooks, et als. vs. Caroline Crooks, et als. Sale of real estate.
Henry Crooks died 5 Mar 1861, intestate, leaving widow, who died 1 May 1863. Children: Samuel W. Crooks; Susannah Crooks; Sarah Crooks; Rachel M.

Crooks; Richard S. T. Crooks; Nelson M. Crooks; John Crooks, deceased, died 1847, father of Susannah Owings (wife of George W. Owings), Elizabeth A. Taylor (wife of William H. Taylor), Mary E. Crooks, and John H. Crooks; and Alexander W. Crooks, deceased, died 1852, father of Sarah E. Crooks, Caroline Crooks, Florida Crooks, and Samuel A. Crooks (all of Washington D.C.).
Property formerly situate in Baltimore County, being part of *Kin Fauns*.

Chancery Book 15, pp. 59-73   1865   Equity #839
William H. Irving, husband and next friend of Mary E. Irving vs. Emeline Harris, and others. Sale of real estate.
William Haines died Mar 1855, intestate, leaving widow, Emaline Haines. Children: Mary E. Irving, wife of William H. Irving (he was later in Baltimore City Jail); Eurith E. Haines; Martha N. Haines; Levi U. Haines; and Tabitha Haines.
Property situate in the 4th District, on Nicodemus Road, being part of *Morgan's Tent*.

Chancery Book 15, pp. 75-96   1858   Equity #561
Jacob Reese vs. Caroline R. Raymond, Admtx. of James Raymond, deceased, and others. Sale of real estate to satisfy creditors.
James Raymond died Jan 1858, intestate, leaving widow, Caroline R. Raymond. Children: Ann E. Raymond; and Calvin C. Raymond.
Property situate in Westminster, being part of *Addition to Water Oak Level*.

Chancery Book 15, pp. 97-110   1865   Equity #855
Jesse Philips, and others vs. Asbury Philips, and others. Sale of real estate.
Alexander Philips died intestate, leaving widow Milkey Philips, who died intestate. Children: Jesse Philips; Asbury Philips; Edwin J. Philips; Thomas Philips; George W. Philips; Emily Jane Wilson, wife of Levi L. Wilson; Catherine Brown, wife of Elias Brown; Alexander Philips; Elias Philips; and Lewis H. Philips.
Property being part of *Caledonia* or *Edinburgh*.

Chancery Book 15, pp. 111-129   1865   Equity #831
John L. Hoover, and others vs. Catherine Hoover, and others. Sale of real estate.
Daniel Hoover died 16 Aug 1864, testate, leaving widow, Catherine Hoover. Children: John L. Hoover, husband of Mary Ann Hoover; Harriet A. Worthington, wife of Benjamin Worthington; Daniel L. Hoover, deceased, father of James B. Hoover, Robert H. Hoover, and David B. Hoover; and Adam L. Hoover, deceased, father of Daniel Hoover; Conrad Hoover; Thomas W. Hoover; Edward R. Hoover; Francis Hoover; and Eugene B. Hoover.

Property situate on road from Hampstead to Gross's Mill, being parts of *Fowble's Barren Hills* and *Newfoundland.*

Chancery Book 15, pp. 130-148   1860   Equity #657
William A. Albaugh vs. William Wilson, Admr. of Rezin Stevens, deceased, and others. Sale of real estate to satisfy creditors.
Rezin Stevens died Apr 1860, testate, leaving widow, Mary Stevens. Children: Clemson Stevens, of St. Louis MO; Rezin Stevens, of Dayton OH; William Stevens, of Dayton OH; Samuel Stevens, of Dayton OH; Charity Gasshide, of Baltimore County (or Howard County), wife of James Gasshide; Mary Batson, wife of George Batson; and John Stevens, deceased, died c. 1858, father of Henry Stevens, deceased (died Dec 1860, as infant), George Stevens, David Stevens, and Mary Stevens.
Property situate in Warfieldsburgh, being part of *Rich Meadow.*

Chancery Book 15, pp. 149-164   1864   Equity #809
Eliza H. Hoover, and others vs. Joseph Shaeffer, and others. Sale of real estate to satisfy creditors.
Daniel L. Hoover died 13 Apr 1864, intestate, leaving widow, Eliza H. Hoover. Children: James B. Hoover; Robert H. Hoover; and David B. Hoover.
Daniel L. Hoover's brother, Adam L. Hoover, died 15 July 1864, testate, leaving widow, Polly Hoover. Children: Daniel Hoover; Conrad Hoover; Thomas W. Hoover; Edward R. Hoover; Francis Hoover; and Eugene B. Hoover.
Daniel and his brother, Adam, were engaged in merchandising, prior to 1860, as partners in store in Finksburg, then partnership was dissolved.
Property situate near Hampstead, being parts of *Transylvania Resurveyed* and *Little Addition.*

Chancery Book 15, pp. 165-193   1865   Equity #822
Chancery Book 17, pp. 364-365
John Nusbaum, and others, Admrs. of John Babylon, deceased vs. Samuel Babylon, and others. Foreclosure.
John Babylon died Mar 1862, intestate, leaving widow, Catherine Babylon. Children: Andrew Babylon, of Dark County OH, husband of Sarah Babylon; Susan Morelock, wife of Samuel Morelock; Elizabeth Morelock, of Dark County OH, wife of Daniel Morelock; Mary C. Hively, wife of Jacob Hively; Emanuel Babylon, out-of-state, husband of Caroline Babylon (of Carroll County); Sarah L. Babylon; Uriah J. Babylon; Rachel A. Babylon; and (by former wife, Rachel Babylon, deceased) Amanda Lindley, deceased, died 10 Dec 1867, intestate, wife of Jared L. Lindley, mother of Abra Lindley, Mary E. Lindley, Barbara E. Baker (wife of Samuel Baker), Susan E. Lindley, James Franklin

Lindley, Hannah Jane Lindley, John Lindley, and Stephen Douglas Lindley (all of Wood County OH).
Property situate on Taneytown Road, being parts of *Molly's Fancy* and *Resurvey on Lookabout.*

Chancery Book 15, pp. 194-202   1865   Equity #852
Moses Shaw, Admr. of Jeremiah Key, deceased, vs. Stephen Key.
Sale of real estate to satisfy creditors.
Jeremiah Key died Sept 1864, leaving son and only heir, Stephen A. Keys.
Property being part of *Shepherd's Retirement.*

Chancery Book 15, pp. 204-228   1865   Equity #818
William H. Blizzard, and others vs. Elias Nelson Blizzard, and others.
Sale of real estate and to satisfy creditors.
Elias Blizzard died c. 1850, intestate, leaving a widow, Hyanthe Blizzard, who died 1864, intestate. Children: illiam H. Blizzard; Samuel H. Blizzard; Rachel R. Wagner, deceased, died Dec 1865, intestate, wife of Henry Wagner, mother of Hiram C. Blizzard (born before marriage), Rachel R. Wagner, Sarah L. Wagner, William H. Wagner, and Charles Wagner; Ruth E. Blizzard; George Blizzard; Elias Nelson Blizzard; John Blizzard; and Martha E. Blizzard.
Property being parts of *Glendoick* and *William's Delight.*

Chancery Book 15, pp. 229-239   1866   Equity #871
Joshua Smith, Trustee vs. Nathaniel Shipley and wife.   Sale of real estate.
Philip Nicodemus died 1855, testate. Children: Abraham Nicodemus, deceased, father of four children; Valentine Nicodemus, deceased, died June 1863; Mary Brown; Elizabeth Nicodemus; Isaac Nicodemus; Abigail Cassell; Deborah Pearre; Susanna Baile; Jacob Nicodemus; and Washington Nicodemus. Philip had sisters: Mary Nicodemus, deceased, died 1865 and Sophia Nicodemus, deceased, died 1865.
Property being parts of *York Company Defense* and *Resurvey on Father's Gift.*

Chancery Book 15, pp. 240-254   1866   Equity #887
Emanuel Koontz, & others vs. Margaret A. Koontz, & others. Sale of real estate.
Jacob Mehring, died Feb 1865, testate, leaving wife, Mary. In his will, he mentions - brothers and sisters: Catherine Mehring; Elizabeth Mehring; Susan Mehring; Lydia Mehring; George Mehring, deceased; John Mehring, deceased; and Mary Mehring, deceased; brothers-in law and sisters-in-law: Catherine Wampler; Christian Royer; Jesse Royer; Jehu Royer; Anna Weybright, deceased; Louisa Englar; and William Koontz; and nephew - Amos Merhring Royer. Others mentioned, but relationship not determined: Emanuel Koontz, husband of Louisa C. Koontz; Rebecca Weybright, wife of Samuel Weybright; Lydia Morrison, wife of Samuel Morrison; and Elias Koontz,

husband of Sarah A. Koontz, father of Margaret A. Koontz, Mary E. Koontz, Jacob M. Koontz, and Elias G. Koontz.
Property situate in Westminster, on Taneytown Road, being part of *Fanny's Meadow*.

Chancery Book 15, pp. 255-267 1866 Equity #789
Thomas Parker Scott, Exr. vs. John J. Baublitz.
Sale of real estate to satisfy creditors.
Susan G. Cockey, later known as Susan G. Ritner, deceased, of Baltimore City, died c. 1857, testate. Heirs: Rachel R. Cockey, sister; Thomas Cockey, brother, father of Thomas Cockey, Ann Cockey, and Sally Cockey; Mary Bussey, niece; Dr. J. F. C. Cockey, nephew; and Emma Duvall, niece.
Property situate part in Carroll County and part in Baltimore County.

Chancery Book 15, pp. 268-289 1866 Equity #873
Charles H. Fogg and Susan L. Fogg, his wife, in her right and as next friend, and others vs. Stephen Smith, and others.   Sale of real estate.
Philip Smith died 4 Dec 1860, intestate, leaving widow, Rebecca Smith, who died 14 Dec 1865, intestate. Children: Ann Rebecca Smith; Samuel H. Smith; Henry T. Smith; William J. Smith; Francis M. Smith; Mary Henrietta Smith, deceased, died 17 Nov 1864, unmarried, w/o issue; Louisa Adeliza Smith, deceased, died 30 Jan 1866, unmarried, w/o issue; and Susan L. Fogg, wife of Charles H. Fogg.
Christian Miller was the grandmother of Philip and his brother, Stephen. In her will (c.1861), she mentions other grandchildren: Absalom Smith; William Smith; Mary E. Smith; and Amanda Smith.
Properties being parts of *Addition to Brook's Discovery on the Rich Lands* and *Second Addition to Brook's Discovery on the Rich Lands*.

Chancery Book 15, pp. 290-303 1865 Equity #865
William Derr, and others vs. Mary Derr, and others.
Sale of real estate to satisfy creditors.
George W. Derr died 30 Apr 1860, intestate, leaving widow, Mary Derr. Children: John Derr; Samuel Derr; Harriett Sprinkle, wife of Henry Sprinkle; William Derr; George W. Derr; Mary Hesson, wife of Abraham Hesson; Jacob F. Derr; Noah Derr; Amanda J. Derr; Martha E. Rumby, wife of Thomas Benton Rumby; and Sarah Sprinkle, deceased, died intestate, wife of Henry Sprinkle, mother of Ida Mary Sprinkle, Simon Peter Sprinkle, and Theodore Sprinkle.
Property situate in Hampstead District, on old Hampstead-Westminster Road, about 3 miles from Westminster, being part of *The Trouting Streams Corrected*.

Chancery Book 15, pp. 304-328 1865 Equity #840
James W. Jordan vs. Rebecca Smith, Admtx. of Washington Smith, deceased, Richard Smith, and others. Sale of real estate to satisfy creditors.
Washington Smith died c. Jan 1864, intestate, leaving widow, Rebecca Smith. Children: Julia A. Smith; and Daniel W. Smith.
Properties formerly situate in Baltimore County, being parts of *Peach Brandy Forest, Point Esprite* and *Rochester.*

Chancery Book 15, pp. 329-344 1865 Equity #861
Chancery Book 17, pp. 360-363
Lucy Houck, et als. vs. Joseph Armacost, et als. Sale of real estate.
William Houck died 4 Mar 1854, testate, leaving widow, Lucy Houck. Children: Jacob Houck; George Houck; Elias Houck; Elizabeth Ebaugh, widow of John Ebaugh, deceased (she later remarried and became known as Elizabeth Koons); Catharine Armacost, deceased, died 5 Feb 1863, intestate, wife of Joseph Armacost, mother of Elizabeth Hoffman (of Baltimore County, wife of William D. Hoffman), Lucinda Abbott (wife of John Abbott), Ellen Armacost (of Baltimore County, wife of Christopher Armacost), Rebecca Cullison (of Baltimore County, wife of Wesley Cullison), Melchor Armacost (of Baltimore City), William Armacost, George Armacost, Julia A. Armacost, and Mary E. Armacost; Julian Allgire, wife of Melchor Allgire; William Houck, father of Julian Fowble (wife of Francis Fowble); and Lucy Houck, deceased, died 23 May 1867, unmarried, and w/o issue.
Property formerly situate in Baltimore County, being part of *Landaff.*

Chancery Book 15, pp. 345-355 1866 Equity #914
Eliza H. Hoover, et als. vs. Polly Hoover, et als. Sale of real estate.
Daniel L. Hoover died 1864, intestate, leaving widow, Eliza Hoover. Children: James B. Hoover; Robert H. Hoover; and David B. Hoover.
Daniel held property jointly with brother, Adam L. Hoover, who died in 1864, testate, leaving widow, Polly Hoover. Children: Daniel Hoover; Conrad Hoover; Thomas W. Hoover; Edward Hoover; Francis Hoover; and Benton Hoover.
Properties situate in IA and IL.

Chancery Book 15, pp. 356-381 1865 Equity #812
The Farmers Mechanics Bank of Carroll County vs. Elias Myerly, Admr. of Frederick Ritter, deceased, and others. Sale of real estate to satisfy creditors.
Frederick Ritter died 9 Feb 1864, intestate. Children: Margaret Myerly, wife of Elias Myerly; Anna M. Stein, widow of George Stein; John (aka Jacob) Ritter, of Lancaster County PA, father of Lavinia Krantz, wife of Edward T. Krantz, and Amanda Kopp, wife of J. Alfred Kopp.

Frederick Ritter was the son of John Ritter, whose other children were: Michael Ritter, husband of Polly Ritter; Lewis Ritter, of Cumberland County PA, wife of Ann Ritter; Jacob Ritter, husband of Magdalena Ritter; Mary Crumrine, wife of Daniel Crumrine; Catherine Humburg, wife of George Humburg; and Barbara Hinkle, wife of George Hinkle.

Properties formerly situate in Baltimore County, being parts of *Iron Intention* and *Landaw*.

Chancery Book 15, pp. 382-404   1865   Equity #810
Eliza H. Hoover, next friend of James B. Hoover, and others vs. James B. Hoover, and others. Sale of real estate.

Daniel L. Hoover died 13 April 1864, intestate, leaving widow, Eliza H. Hoover. Children: James B. Hoover; Robert Hoover; and David B. Hoover.

Daniel was the son of Daniel Hoover, who died Aug 1864, and his wife, Catherine Hoover.

Properties situate near Hampstead, being parts of *Transylvania Resurveyed, Murray's Ridge, Transylvania, Petersburg, Stricker* and *Little Addition*.

Chancery Book 15, pp. 405-414   1865   Equity #829
Petition of John H. Lammotte, next friend of Andrew L. Bowser. Sale of real estate to satisfy creditors.

Andrew L. Bowser, a lunatic, needed to be sent to Mount Hope Hospital, near Baltimore City. He was the son of Barbara Shirick, deceased, and brother to Charlotte Bowser, Solomon Bowser, and Joseph Bowser. John H. Lammotte was his cousin.

Property location not determined, but was devised to him and his sister by his mother.

Chancery Book 15, pp. 415-429   1866   Equity #868
Levi Beecher and Elias Beecher vs. Noah Beecher, and others. Sale of real estate.

Eve Beecher died 14 Nov 1865, intestate, wife of Levi Beecher. Children: Elias Beecher, of York County PA; Noah Beecher; Anna Mary Elizabeth Beecher; and William Henry Beecher.

Properties situate in and near Manchester, being Lots 31 and 67, and part of *Dey's Adventure*.

Chancery Book 15, pp. 430-444   1865   Equity #853
Henry E. Masonheimer, and others vs. Andrew Brison and wife, and others. Sale of real estate.

Magdalena Rinehart died testate. Her grandson, Frederick Masonheimer was the father of: Henry E. Masonheimer; Elizabeth Parker, of Alleghany County

PA, wife of James E. Parker; Julia A. Fletcher, of Alleghany County PA, wife of James Fletcher; Sarah Hersperger, of Alleghany County PA, widow of James Hersperger; Catherine Masonheimer, of Alleghancy County PA; Jacob Masonheimer, of Laurence County PA; Nathaniel Masonheimer, of KY; Mary Brison, out of state (whereabouts unknown), wife of Andrew Brison; Alfred Masonheimer; Frederick Masonheimer; William Masonheimer, deceased, died 13 Oct 1839; Abagail Masonheimer, deceased, died 22 Dec 1856; and Jane Masonheimer, deceased, died 29 Aug 1855.

Property being parts of *Ohio* and *Bankert's Amendment.*

Chancery Book 15, pp. 445-464 1866 Equity #911
Thomas Rudisel, and others vs. Mary E. Rudisel, and Tobias Rudisel, Jr. Sale of real estate.
Ludwick Rudisel died, leaving widow, Nancy Rudisel, who died 9 Sep 1861, intestate. Children: William Rudisel, died 16 Oct 1866, intestate, unmarried, w/o issue; Tobias Rudisel, deceased, died Dec 1863, leaving widow, Mary Jane Rudisel, father of Mary E. Rudisel, and Tobias Rudisel, Jr.; Thomas Rudisel; Alice Motter, of Frederick County, wife of Lewis Motter; Sarah Grabill, of Frederick County, wife of Peter Grabill; Ann Rudisel; and Margaret Rinedollar, wife of William Rinedollar.
Properties situate in and near Taneytown.

Chancery Book 15, pp. 465-478 1866 Equity #906
Rachel Nace, mother and next friend to Jane Nace and Charles L. Nace vs. Jane Nace and Charles L. Nace. Sale of real estate.
Peter Nace died Jan 1866, intestate, leaving widow, Rachel Nace. Children: Jane Nace, and Charles L. Nace.
Properties being part of *New Windsor.*

Chancery Book 15, pp. 479-519 1866 Equity #890
Henry L. Fringer vs. Martha A. Stocksdale, and others. Foreclosure.
Noah B. Stocksdale died Dec 1865, intestate, leaving widow, Martha A. Stocksdale. Children: William Nelson Stocksdale; Keziah Van Julia Stocksdale; and Mary Jane Stocksdale (all of Baltimore County).
Property situate part in Carroll County and part in Baltimore County, 2 miles from Hampstead on Hampstead-Reisterstown Turnpike, being parts of *Hooker's Meadow Resurveyed, Point Patience, Paris* and *Well's Inheritance.*

Chancery Book 15, pp. 520-532 1866 Equity #882
Jacob Albaugh, and others vs. Dianna Tipton, Thomas Tipton, and others. Sale of real estate.

William Albaugh died Dec 1865, intestate, leaving widow, Elizabeth Albaugh, who died Mar 1866. Children: Jacob Albaugh; Edmond Albaugh; Abraham Albaugh; Margaret Sharer, wife of Jacob Sharer; Elizabeth Albaugh; Dallas Albaugh; Dianna Tipton, wife of Thomas Tipton; Emily Jane Albaugh; and Catherine Krantz, deceased, died Oct 1865, wife of Willilam Krantz, mother of Edward H. Krantz.
Property formerly situate in Baltimore County, being part of *Everything Needful Corrected.*

Chancery Book 15, pp. 533-546 1866 Equity #912
Anthony J. Jackson, grandfather and next friend to Samuel J. Toop, and others vs. Samuel J. Toop, and others. Sale of real estate to satisfy creditors.
Ann Elizabeth Bruce, daughter of Anthony J. Jackson, died Oct 1866, intestate, widow of Isaac Bruce. Children: (by deceased former husband) Samuel J. Toop; Mary E. Toop; Amanda Toop; (by deceased husband, Isaac Bruce) Susan L. Bruce; and Isaac E. M. Bruce.
Property situate on road from Westminster to Manchester.

Chancery Book 16, pp. 1-14 1866 Equity #880
Sophia Rhodes vs. Eveline Woolery and Azariah Oursler, Admrxs. of Elijah Woolery, deceased. Sale of real estate to satisfy creditors.
Elijah Woolery died April 1865, intestate, leaving widow, Eveline E. Woolery, and only child, Ellsworth Woolery.
Property situate near road from Sandymount Meeting House to Brown's Meeting House, being part of *Stain's Neglect.*

Chancery Book 16, pp. 16-28 1860 Insolvent Docket #1, p. 124
Edwin Shipley vs. George W. Lammott. Insolvency.
Edwin Shipley.
Property being part of *Buck's Forest.*

Chancery Book 16, pp. 29-43 1865 Equity #846
Francis T. Birely, and others vs. Mary Catharine Bireley, and others. Sale of real estate.
William Birely died Feb 1852, intestate, leaving widow, Elizabeth Birely, of Frederick County. Children: Francis Thomas Birley; Maggie Ann Cash, wife of Lewis Cash; Jacob Birely; Mary Catherine Birely, of Frederick County; and Sarah Ellen Birely, of Frederick County.
William was the son of Jacob Birely, of Frederick County, who died c. 1847, testate. William's brothers and sisters were: David Birely; Lewis Birely; Mary Ecker, wife of David Ecker; and Elizabeth Norris, wife of Nimrod Norris.

Property situate on Little Pipe Creek, with a small part in Frederick County, being parts of *Resurvey on Clark's Discovery, Black Flint* and *Friendship.*

Chancery Book 16, pp. 44-56 1865 Equity #851
Elizabeth Loveall, next friend of Margaret Loveall vs. Margaret Loveall. Sale of real estate.
John Loveall died c. Nov 1862, testate, leaving widow, Elizabeth Loveall. Children: John Thomas Loveall; and Margaret Ann Loveall.
His mother was Lucinda Loveall, and he had a sister, Lydia Cullison.
Property formerly situate in Baltimore County, being parts of *John's Lot Enlarged, Brown's Lot, Brown's Contrivance* and *Stansbury's Grove.*

Chancery Book 16, pp. 57-68 1866 Equity #898
Frances Cookson, mother and next friend of Joseph Cookson, and others vs. Joseph Cookson, and others. Sale of real estate.
Levi Cookson died July 1866, intestate, leaving widow, Frances Cookson. Children: Joseph Cookson; Robert L. Cookson; and Mary E. Cookson.
Property being parts of *Myer's Resurvey* and *Resurvey on Black Oak Hill.*

Chancery Book 16, pp. 69-80 1866 Equity #904
Hester A. Wolf, widow, et als. vs. Hollis A. Wolf. Sale of real estate.
William Wolf died testate, leaving widow, Hester A. Wolf, of Baltimore City. Children: Laura Wolf; Hollis Wolf; and Josephine C. Ray, wife of Benjamin Ray (all of Baltimore City).
Property situate on Main Street in Westminster, being part of *Timber Ridge Resurveyed.*

Chancery Book 16, pp. 81-90 1865 Equity #834
Elizabeth Snader, and others vs. Martha C. Snader, and others. Sale of real estate.
Philip Snader died Feb 1864, intestate, leaving widow, Elizabeth Snader. Children: Mary C. Wolf, wife of Samuel Wolf; Eliza J. Shriner, wife of Ezra Shriner; Evan T. Snader; Jesse W. Snader; William H. H. Snader; Jacob W. Snader; Martha C. Snader; and Ezra L. Snader.
Property situate on Church Street in New Windsor, being Lot 9, being part of *Five Daughters.*

Chancery Book 16, pp. 91-102 1860 Equity #656
Henry A. Sellman vs. John Wagoner, Admr. of John K. Dell, and others. Sale of real estate to satisfy creditors.

John K. Dell died c. Oct 1859, intestate, leaving widow, Harriet Dell. Children: Mary E. Wagoner, wife of John Wagoner; Cecelia Ingleman, wife of Palmer Ingleman; Martha Dell, deceased, died Dec 1863, intestate, and w/o issue; John Dell; Jerome Dell; and Mathilda Dell.
Property situate on Deer Park Road, being part of *Kin Faunes*.

Chancery Book 16, pp. 103-113   1867   Equity #949
Margaret M. E. Lowe, et als. vs. Jesse M. Lowe, Trustee.
Sale of land held in trust.
Jesse M. Lowe, husband of Margaret M. E. Lowe, father of Clarence Willie Lowe, Silas Conn Lowe, and Jesse Marion Lowe (wife and children of Baltimore City).
Property being parts of *Progress, Additional Progress* and *Dorsey's Delama*.

Chancery Book 16, pp. 114-141   1864   Equity #791
Elizabeth Barnes, and others vs. Solomon Barnes, and others.   Sale of real estate.
Joshua Barnes died 1853, testate, leaving widow, Elizabeth Barnes, deceased. Children: Joshua Tevis Barnes; Solomon Barnes; Mary Williams, wife of Benjamin Williams; Elizabeth Shipley, deceased, widow of Frederick Shipley; Naomi Upperco, deceased, wife of Benjamin Upperco, of Baltimore County; Eurith Demoss, deceased, wife of Thomas Demoss, mother of Mary Warner (wife of Elias Warner), Nimrod Demoss, Laura Hooker (widow of James Hooker), Lewis D. Demoss, Jehu Demoss, John Demoss, and Jane Demoss; and William Barnes (left state 15 years ago and never heard from).
Location of properties not established.

Chancery Book 16, pp. 142-168   1866   Equity #876
James A. Albaugh and Milton W. Warfield vs. William A. Webb, Admr. of Presley Zepp, deceased, and others.   Sale of real estate to satisfy creditors.
Presley Zepp died c. Sept 1864, intestate. Children: Artimus R. Zepp; William Presley Zepp; John J. Zepp; Margaret E. V. Zepp; Laura F. Zepp; and Anna Lee Zepp.
Property situate partly in Howard County, being parts of *Larkin the Second* and *The Blooming Plains Resurveyed*.

Chancery Book 16, pp. 170-195   1851   Equity #346
Mordecai Gist vs. States L. Gist.   Sale of real estate to satisfy creditors.
States L. Gist, lunatic. Children: Mary Gist; Joseph Mordecai Gist; Independence Gist; Branford Porcher Gist; Elizabeth Sarah Gist; and Richard Joshua Gist. Brother: Mordecai Gist.
Location of properties not established.

Chancery Book 16, pp. 196-202 1867 Equity #954
William Crichton vs. The Maryland Copper Company of Carroll and Baltimore Counties. Foreclosure.
The Maryland Copper Company of Carroll and Baltimore Counties.
Location of properties not established.

Chancery Book 16, pp. 203-232 1863 Equity #726
The School Commissioners of Carroll County vs. Samuel G. Harden, Admr. of William H. Harden, deceased, and others. Sale of real estate to satisfy creditors.
Willilam H. Harden died Sept 1862, intestate, leaving widow, Amanda C. Harden. Children: Joseph W. Harden; Nicholas Harden; & Louisa R. Harden.
Properties being parts of *Stepney Causeway* and *Buck's Park*.

Chancery Book 16, pp. 233-241 1866 Equity #905
George Crabbs and others vs. Elias G. Reed, and others. Sale of real estate.
George Crabbs died 1859, testate, leaving widow, Mary Crabbs. Children: John Crabbs, deceased; George Crabbs, husband of Susan Crabbs; William Crabbs, husband of Ann Crabbs; Frederick Crabbs; Catherine Snider, wife of Levi Snider; Eliza Reed, wife of Elias G. Reed; and Mary Shoemaker, wife of Americus Shoemaker.
Properties situate on Big Pipe Creek, commonly known as the *Home* or *Mill Property*, and *Shoemaker Farm*.

Chancery Book 16, pp. 242-260 1865 Equity #811
Horatio N. Gambrill vs. Andrew G. Ege. Release of mortgage.
Andrew Ege, now out of state, mortgagee, and James Piper, deceased, mortgagor.
Property situate in Taneytown, known as *Antrim*.

Chancery Book 16, pp. 261-282 1867 Equity #926
Louisa R. Horn and Philip C. Horn vs. Mary Horn, Admrx. of John S. Horn, deceased, and others. Sale of real estate to satisfy creditors.
John S. Horn died Nov 1866, intestate, leaving widow, Mary Horn, and no lineal descendants. Brothers and sisters: Philip C. Horn; George M. Horn, of Baltimore City; Mary L. Cunningham, wife of William A. Cunningham; Laura C. Reese, of Baltimore City, wife of Andrew Reese; and Lovinia C. Harvey, deceased, wife of John E. Harvey, mother of Jacob A. Harvey, and Charles W. Harvey (both of Baltimore City).
Property situate in Wakefield Valley, on Western Maryland Railroad Line, being parts of *Stevenson's Garden*, *Stansbury Plains* and *Strawberry Mead*.

Chancery Book 16, pp. 283-302 1866 Equity #893
J. Henry Hoppe vs. Hanson G. Clemson, and others. Foreclosure.
Thomas C. Nelson died 31 May 1866, intestate, leaving widow, Mary E. Nelson. Children: Hamilton Nelson; and Thomas Nelson.
Property being parts of *Thomas's Resurvey on the Deeps, The Resurvey on Walnut Bottom, Hills and Valleys* and *The Agreement.*

Chancery Book 16, pp. 303-316 1866 Equity #913
Henry Germand vs. Nicholas Leipolt Foreclosure.
Nicholas Leipolt.
Property being parts of *Eight Sisters* and *Addition to Curpoy.*

Chancery Book 16, pp. 317-335 1865 Equity #823
Jacob Bowers vs. Michael Stier, and others. Sale of real estate to satisfy creditors.
John Stier died 20 Nov 1864, leaving widow, Barbara Stier, and no lineal descendants. Brothers and sisters: Michael Stier, of Adams County PA, husband of Lydia Stier; Jacob Stier, deceased, died c. 1834, father of Elias Stier (husband of Caroline Stier), Jacob Stier (husband of Anna Stier), and Jonas Stier (of Adams County PA, husband of Rebecca Stier); Molly Bushman, deceased, wife of Henry Bushman, deceased, mother of Eli Bushman, and Louisa Leopard (of Cumberland County PA, wife of Jacob Leopard; Susannah Yeagerline, deceased, wife of John Yeagerline, deceased, mother of Louisa Zentz (wife of Daniel Zentz), and Mary Shilt (wife of Samuel Shilt); Mary Stonebreaker, deceased, wife of Henry Stonebreaker, deceased, mother of Joseph Stonebreaker (husband of Lydia Stonebreaker), Ann Valentine (widow of Thomas Valentine), Mary A. Hahn (wife of Benjamin Hahn), John Stonebreaker (of Harford County MD), and Eliza Moser (of Frederick County, wife of Daniel Moser, out of state); and Catherine Feeser, out of state in parts unknown, wife of Jacob Feeser, mother of George Bushman, of Carlisle PA.
Property formerly situate in Frederick County, being parts of *Owings Second Chance* and *The Resurvey on Hibernia.*

Chancery Book 16, pp. 336-374 1864 Equity #797
Theodore Carpenter, next friend to Solomon Carpenter, and others vs. Solomon Carpenter, and others. Sale of real estate.
Henry Shuler died 20 Nov 1863, in Baltimore City, testate. His cousin was Theodore Carpenter, father of Solomon Carpenter, William H. Carpenter, Hoesa Carpenter, and Jane E. Carpenter (all of Randolph County IN. Also mentioned in his will, but relationships undetermined were: Juliann Beecher, of Miami County IN, wife of William Beecher, mother of Mary A. Hatterman (wife of Isaac Hatterman), Henry Beecher, William Beecher, Elmira Abler

(wife of William D. Abler), Matilda Beecher, Juliann Beecher (wife of William V. Beecher), all of Miami County IN, and Harriet Dague (of Franklin County OH, wife of George Dague); Susan Shunk, of York County PA, wife of Michael Shunk, mother of a son and a daughter (married to Levi Eckert), both of York County PA; Samuel Messinger, deceased, father of Mary A. Flickinger (of Adams County PA, wife of Thomas Flickinger), Sarah Shuler (of York County PA, wife of John Shuler), Samuel Messinger, Anna Harner (wife of James Harner), Ephraim Messinger, Susanna Messinger, Martin Messinger, and John Messinger; David Myers, deceased, father of William Myers, John Myers, Catherine Feeser (wife of George W. Feeser), and Frederick H. Myers; Anna May Werner, wife of Thomas Werner; Maria Flickinger, wife of William Flickinger; Mary Lowe, of York County PA, wife of Andrew Lowe; Jessiah Sheeler, husband of Lucinda Sheeler; Peter Robenstien, father of Eli M. Robenstien, George Robenstien, and Amelia Robenstien (all of York County PA); and John Robenstien, father of Elias Robenstien, Eliza Baumgartner (wife of Samuel Baumgartner), Sarah Houck (wife of Jacob H. Houck), Amanda Nace (wife of Eli Nace), and Amelia Stegner (wife of Ephraim Stegner), all of York County PA.

Properties being parts of *Lewis Luck, Shoemaker's Lot, Dyer's Mill Forest* and *Resurvey on Dyer's Mill Forest.*

Chancery Book 16, pp. 375-389   1865   Equity #848
Joseph E. Hahn, and others vs. John Study, and others.   Sale of real estate.
Peter Erb, of Frederick County, died c. Jan 1836, testate, leaving widow, Elizabeth Erb. Children: John Erb; and Margaret Hahn, deceased, died 9 July 1865, wife of Jacob Hahn, Jr., mother of Joseph E. Hahn, Rebecca Hahn, Eliza Study (wife of John Study), Sarah Hull (wife of Isaac Hull), Jacob Erb, deceased, died c. Aug 1840, intestate, (husband of Mary Erb, who later married William Tagg, and became known as Mary Tagg, father of Jesse Hahn, who died 15 Aug 1840, intestate and w/o issue), and Abraham E. Erb (husband of Mary G. Erb).

Property formerly situate in Frederick County, being parts of *Patience Care, Ohio, Locust Neck* and *Laurel Bank.*

Chancery Book 16, pp. 390-413   1867   Equity #960
George Gummel, et als. vs. Jacob Gummel, et als.   Sale of real estate.
Jacob Gummel died 3 Oct 1866, intestate, husband of Elizabeth Gummel, deceased. Children: George Gummel; Sarah Snyder, wife of David A. Snyder; Lydia Ann Bummond, wife of Elisha Bummond; Elizabeth Shaeffer, wife of Lewis Shaeffer; Clara Yingling, wife of Jacob Yingling; Jacob Gummel; and Amanda E. Gummel.

Properties formerly situate in Baltimore County, being parts of *Stansbury's Prospect, Bachelor's Prospect, John's Beginning* and *Iron Intention.*

Chancery Book 16, pp. 414-428 1867 Equity #940
Daniel Engel and Theresa Ann Engel, his wife, and Daniel Engel, next friend to Charles F. Zile vs. Lewis C. Zile and Charles F. Zile. Sale of real estate.
Abraham Zile died 1855, intestate, leaving widow, Theresa Ann Zile, who later married Daniel Engel and became known as Theresa Ann Engel. Children: Lewis C. Zile; William Henry Zile; John T. Zile; Martha Hull, wife of Eli Hull; Penelope Zile; Mary A. H. Zile; and Charles F. Zile.
Property formerly situate in Baltimore County, being part of *Shadrack's Last Shift Resurveyed*.

Chancery Book 16, pp. 429-454 1866 Equity #908
Chancery Book 18, pp. 30-34
Margaret Ann Bowersox, et als. vs. Mary A. Ecker, Admrx. of William Ecker, deceased, et als. Sale of real estate to satisfy creditors.
William Ecker died Nov 1865, intestate, leaving widow, Mary A. Ecker. Children: Susanna Englar, wife of Uriah Engler; James M. Ecker; Eliza J. E. Barnes, of Frederick County, wife of John T. Barnes; and Eugene Ecker.
Properties formerly situate in Frederick County, being parts of *Timber Hills, Resurvey on Woman's Content* and *Resurvey on Timber Hills*.

Chancery Book 16, pp. 455-477 1866 Equity #892
Chancery Book 32, pp. 219-230
Michael Ott vs. Isabella C. Reaver. Sale of real estate and to satisfy creditors.
Ulrich Reaver died in 1860's, intestate, leaving widow, Isabella C. Reaver, a lunatic, who was the daughter of Michael Ott. Children: George Reaver; Mary Reaver; Sarah Reaver; Samuel Reaver; and Hamilton Reaver.
Property situate on road from Taneytown to Gettysburg, being part of *Addition to Brook's Discovery on the Rich Lands*.

Chancery Book 16, pp. 478-499 1866 Equity #888
John Lammott vs. Joseph Bowser. Sale of real estate.
Joseph Bowser, a lunatic.
Property being part of *Complication Corrected*.

Chancery Book 16, pp. 500-515 1867 Equity #928
George Becker, and others vs. John Becker. Sale of real estate.
Michael Becker, formerly of Baltimore County, died 6 Sept 1866, intestate, leaving widow, Elizabeth Becker. Children: George Becker, of Percy County PA; John Becker, of KY; Ephraim Becker; Catherine Brilhart, wife of Isaac Brilhart; Abdol Becker; Jeremiah Becker; Emeline Kneller, wife of David Kneller; and Edmond Becker.

Properties formerly situate in Baltimore County, near Hanover-Reisterstown Road, being part of *Nace's Tavern*.

Chancery Book 16, pp. 516-536 1867 Equity #933
Mary Rinehart, and others vs. Susanna Rinehart, and others. Sale of real estate.
Joseph Rinehart died 4 Oct 1866, intestate, by accident in Hanover PA, leaving widow, Catherine Rinehart. Children: Mary Rinehart; Elizabeth Buck, of York County PA, wife of Solomon Buck; William Henry Rinehart; Louisa Housefel, wife of Andrew Housefel; George Rinehart; Catherine Miller, wife of George Miller; Susannah Rinehart; Eli Rinehart; Amelia Rinehart; and Mary Ruoff, deceased, died 1865, wife of Jacob Ruoff, mother of George Ruoff, and Jacob Ruoff (both of Philadelphia PA).
Properties being parts of *Long Hill, Troy* and *Everybody's Land*.

Chancery Book 16, pp. 537-546 1865 Equity #866
Daniel Plaine vs. Samuel Plaine. Foreclosure.
Samuel Plaine.
Property being part of *Resurvey on the Deeps*.

Chancery Book 17, pp. 1-24 1867 Equity #948
George Dern, and others vs. Jane Dern, and others. Sale of real estate.
Frederick Dern died 10 May 1867, testate; his wife, Elizabeth Dern, having died c. 1861. Children: George Dern; Sophia Dern; Eliza Dern; Catherine R. Wilhide; Washington Dern, of OH; and Frederick Dern, deceased, died Nov 1863, intestate, father of Jane Dern, Ann E. Dern, and Elizabeth Dern.
Frederick was the son of Sophia Dern, of Frederick County, who died 1830, testate, who was also mother to: William Dern; and Isaac Dern, deceased.
Properties being parts of *Terra Rubra* and *Resurvey on Terra Rubra*.

Chancery Book 17, pp. 26-48 1868 Equity #995
Daniel S. Herring, Committee, Joshua W. Herring, Sarah Fringer and George Fringer, Exrs of Jacob Fringer, deceased vs. Catherine Fetterling, Lunatic. Sale of real estate to satisfy creditors.
Catherine Fetterling, a lunatic, was the aunt of Sarah Fringer, of Baltimore City, widow of Jacob Fringer, who died Aug 1861. Their children were: Caroline V. Fringer; George N. Fringer; Emily J. C. Fringer; Winfield K. Fringer; and Margaret Ann Forester, wife of John Forester.
Property situate on Main Street in Westminster, being Lot 30, being part of *The Resurvey on Timber Ridge*.

Chancery Book 17, pp. 49-75 1867 Equity #975
Joseph Wolfe, Trustee vs. Sarah Wolfe, and others. Sale of real estate.

Abraham Wolfe died c. Nov 1863, testate, leaving widow, Sarah Wolfe. Children: John Martin Wolfe; Daniel Wolfe; Mary Wright, wife of Isaac Wright; Susan Repp, of Johnson County MO, wife of Ephraim R. Repp; Margaret Wolfe; Charles Wolfe, of Monroe County OH; Rebecca Shunk, of Monroe County OH, widow of John Shunk; Elizabeth Switzer, of Johnson County IA, widow of John Switzer; Joseph Wolfe; and maybe Samuel Wolfe.
Property situate on Sam's Creek, partly in Frederick County.

Chancery Book 17, pp. 76-91   1865   Equity #859
Catherine E. Shoemaker, et al vs. Henry A. Shoemaker, et al. Sale of real estate.
John Shoemaker, son of Abraham Shoemaker (who died c. 1854) died 10 July 1864, intestate, leaving widow, Catherine E. Shoemaker. Children: Alice J. Shoemaker; Henry A. Shoemaker; David M. Shoemaker; Emma C. Shoemaker; and Clara E. Shoemaker.
Property formerly situate in Frederick County, being part of *Eping Forest.*

Chancery Book 17, pp. 92-111   1867   Equity #959
Thomas Coltrider vs. Keziah Coltrider, and others.
Dispute.
Joshua Coltrider died c. Mar 1863, testate, leaving widow, Keziah Coltrider. Children: James Coltrider; Susan Armacost, wife of Melchor Armacost; Thomas Coltrider; Elizabeth Ann Coltrider; and Margaret J. Clark, of Baltimore County, wife of Francis Clark.
Property situate in Hampstead District on the Middletown Road, about 2-1/2 miles northeast of Hampstead, being parts of *Green Veisenburg, Murray's Ridge* and *Foster's Pleasant Meadows.*

Chancery Book 17, pp. 112-124   1867   Equity #953
William Bevard vs. Margaret Storms. Sale of real estate to satisfy creditors.
Margaret Storms, lunatic, had sisters: Catherine Storms; and Christiana Bevard.
Property being part of *Hale's Venture Resurveyed.*

Chancery Book 17, pp. 125-140   1867   Equity #962
William M. Englar, and others vs. Sarah V. Baile and Charles E. Cassell. Sale of real estate.
Isaac Haines died July 1851, intestate, leaving widow, Mary Haines, who died Sept 1863. Children: Eliza Baile, deceased, died Nov 1850, wife of Isaac C. Baile, mother of Mary J. Englar (wife of William M. Englar), Nathan K. Baile, and Sarah V. Baile; and Mary J. Cassell, deceased, died Aug 1850, wife of Abraham Cassell, deceased, who died 1862, mother of Charles E. Cassell.
Property formerly situate in Frederick County, being parts of *Stevenson Garden* and *Cornwell.*

Chancery Book 17, pp. 141-152 1868 Equity #994
In the Matter of Sale under Mortgage made by William W. Stamp to Isaac W. Jewett. Foreclosure.
William H. Stamp and his wife, Clarinda J. Stamp, of Baltimore City.
Property being parts of *Buck Bottom, Lime Stone Ridge* and *The Valley of Strife.*

Chancery Book 17, pp. 153-171 1867 Equity #970
Samuel Fieser, and others vs. Paul Reinecker, and others. Sale of real estate.
Jacob Fieser, son of Adam Fieser, died 21 May 1838, leaving widow, Rebecca Fieser, who later married Simon Leppo (who died 1850) and became known as Rebecca Leppo. Children: Samuel Fieser, husband of Margaret Fieser; John Jacob Fieser, husband of Elizabeth Fieser; David Fieser, husband of Sevilla Fieser; John Fieser, husband of Eliza Fieser; and Anna Maria Reinecker, deceased, died 3 Mar 1860, intestate, wife of Paul Reinecker, mother of Anna Reinecker, deceased (died 6 Apr 1862, intestate, unmarried and w/o issue), Mary E. Kump (wife of Josiah Kump), David H. Fieser, Mandella Fieser, and Ellen J. Fieser.
Jacob Fieser had brothers: Adam Fieser and David Fieser.
Property formerly situate in Frederick County, being parts of *Bankert's Amendment, Resurvey on John's Lot* and *Ohio.*

Chancery Book 17, pp. 172-205 1866 Equity #907
John Cover of T. vs. William H. Hook and wife. Foreclosure.
William H. Hook and his wife, Mary T. Hook.
Property situate in Franklin District, about 5 miles from Westminster, 3/4 mile from Washington Road, being part of *Hopewell.*

Chancery Book 17, pp. 206-219 1868 Equity #999
Wesley Carson vs. Elizabeth Carson, et als. Sale of real estate.
George Carson died Nov 1865, intestate, leaving widow Elizabeth Carson, who was the sister of George K. Frank and Jacob K. Frank.
Children: Wesley Carson; Elias Carson; Mary E. Carson; Caroline Carson; George Carson; Abarilla Carson; and Sarah A. Carson, all of Baltimore County.
Property being part of *Grandfather's Gift.*

Chancery Book 17, pp. 220-237 1867 Equity #963
David W. Trine, and others vs. Richard Manning, and others. Sale of real estate.
Mary Dorothy Trine died 1861, intestate, wife of Samuel Trine.
Children: David W. Trine, husband of Martha Trine; Rachel Ebaugh, wife of Jesse Ebaugh; Emanuel Trine, husband of Susannah Trine; Lydia Lightner, of

Eaton County MI, wife of Jacob Lightner; Rebecca Heiser, of Eaton County MI, wife of Peter Heiser; and Mary Everly, deceased, died 1853, wife of Joseph Everly, mother of Levi D. Everly, and Alice A. Everly, all of Fulton County IL.
Property being part of *Loveall's Enlargement.*

Chancery Book 17, pp. 238-257   1868   Equity #992
John E. Gaither, and others vs. Elvira Gaither, and others.   Sale of real estate.
Warner Gaither died 1857, intestate, leaving widow, Elvira Gaither. Children: John E. Gaither; Susan Thompson, of Howard County MD, wife of Charles R. Thompson; Rachel P. Hewitt, wife of Septemius Hewitt; and James W. Gaither.
Property being parts of *Mount Pleasant Enlarged* and *Concord.*

Chancery Book 17, pp. 258-275   1868   Equity #989
William Henry Rinehart vs. Catherine Rinehart, and others.
Completion of sale.
Joseph Rinehart died 4 Oct 1866, leaving widow, Catherine Rinehart. Children: William Henry Rinehart; Mary Rinehart; Elizabeth Buck, wife of Solomon Buck; Louisa Housefel, wife of Andrew Housefel; George Rinehart; Catherine Miller, wife of George Miller; Susannah Rinehart; Elias Rinehart; Amelia Rinehart; Mary Ruoff, deceased, mother of George Ruoff and Jacob Ruoff, both of Philadelphia PA.
Properties formerly situate in Baltimore County, being parts of *Heidelburg, Nottenstot, Three Brothers, Neighbor* and *Stoney Hills.*

Chancery Book 17, pp. 276-291   1867   Equity #939
William R. Curry vs. George W. Pilson. Sale of real estate to satisfy creditors.
George W. Pilson, of Baltimore County.
Property being parts of Resurvey on the Deeps, Resurvey on *Walnut Bottom* and *Mount Prospect.*

Chancery Book 17, pp. 298-327   1866   Equity #896
William Sharretts, next friend of Clara Ellen Harner and Augustus Jacob Harner vs. Clara Ellen Harner and Augustus Jacob Harner. Sale of real estate.
Augustus Harner died Dec 1863, leaving widow Ann Maria Harner. Children: Clara Ellen Harner; and Augustus Jacob Harner, all of Adams County PA.
Augustus was the son of Michael Harner, Jr., deceased, of Germany Township, Adams County PA, and Elizabeth Harner, and the grandson of Michael Harner, Sr. and his wife, Suzen Harner. Brothers and sisters of Augustus: Jacob Harner; Levi Harner; Sylvester Harner; Lydia Harner; Elizabeth Harner; Catherine Harner; and Ellen Harner.
Property partly in Adams County PA.

Chancery Book 17, pp. 328-347   1867   Equity #923
James Murray and wife vs. Joseph D. Barnes and James Penn.
Partition of real estate.
Thomas Barnes died Feb 1860, intestate, leaving widow, Miranda Barnes. Children: (by first wife, Elizabeth Dorsey Barnes, deceased, died Feb 1854, intestate) Sarah Murray, wife of James Murray; Lucy A. Penn, deceased, died Mar 1862, wife of James Penn, mother of Elizabeth Penn, deceased (died 1862); and Joseph D. Barnes.
Property situate on east side of Washington Road, being parts of *Dorsey's Thicket Resurvey, Long Trusted Resurveyed* and *John's Chance.*

Chancery Book 17, pp. 348-359   1867   Equity #947
Sarah Weekly, next friend and mother of Emily J. Weekly and William Michael Weekly vs. Emily J. Weekly and William Michael Weekly.
Sale of real estate.
William Weekly, Sr., and wife, Mary Weekly, conveyed land to Sarah Weekly, for life. Children of Sarah: Emily J. Weekly; and William Michael Weekly.
Property being Lot 6 in the division of real estate of Jacob Storms.

Chancery Book 17, pp. 366-382   1868   Equity #1001
John T. Ways vs. Caroline Buckingham, and others.
Sale of real estate to satisfy creditors.
Ephraim Buckingham died 15 Apr 1868, intestate, leaving widow, Caroline Buckingham. Children: George E. Buckingham; Elizabeth Buckingham; Harriet Ways, wife of John T. Ways; Margaret McCleary, wife of John McCleary; John Buckingham; Mary Buckingham; and Teresa Pickett, deceased, intestate, wife of Jesse Pickett, mother of George Pickett, of Howard County MD.
Property being part of Washington.

Chancery Book 17, pp. 383-401   1868   Equity #1007
Samuel Fitze, and others vs. Elizabeth Fitze, and others.   Sale of real estate.
George Fitze died 2 July 1868, intestate, leaving widow, Elizabeth Fitze. Children: Samuel Fitze, husband of Mary Ann Fitze; Matilda Coltrider, wife of Daniel Coltrider; Catherine Beggs, wife of Richard Beggs; Mary Ann Brown, wife of Peter Brown; and Joseph Fitze, deceased, intestate, father of Jacob Fitze, Amos Fitze, Elizabeth C. Fitze, Susannah R. Fitze, Mary J. Fitze, and Ellen M. Fitze.
Property formerly situate in Frederick County, being parts of *The Will Restored* and *Resurvey on Lookabout.*

Chancery Book 17, pp. 402-441   1868   Equity #997
Daniel Long, and others vs. Lenah Long, and others.   Sale of real estate.
Christian Long died Feb 1861, testate, leaving widow, Lenah Long.

Children: Daniel Long; Lydia A. Long; Elizabeth Long; Sarah A. Long, of Howard County MD; William L. Long, of Howard County MD; Emeline C. Long, of Howard County MD; Lucinda A. Evans, wife of Kinzy Evans; Eliza C. Lockard, wife of William H. Lockard; and Angeline V. Long.

Property formerly situate in Baltimore County, on the Patapsco, on Western Maryland Railroad Line, being parts of *Zachariah's Conclusion, John's Desire, Oxmoore, Loveall's Prospect, Aspen Hill* and *Wilmot's Purchase.*

Chancery Book 17, pp. 442-450 1868 Equity #1004
Petition of Jacob H. Houck. Sale of real estate.

Jacob Houck, of Baltimore County, died testate, leaving widow, Elizabeth Houck, who died Apr 1868. Children: David Houck, deceased, died c. 1855, intestate, father of Ellen Lower (wife of Levi Lower), Eli Houck, Henry Houck, Catharine Shue (wife of Jeremiah Shue), Margaret Hoffacker (wife of Jeremiah Hoffacker), and Amelia Houck; Elizabeth Kreidler, deceased, died 1837, intestate, wife of Peter Kreidler, mother of Edward Kreidler; Susannah Masemore, deceased, died 1851, intestate, wife of John Masemore, mother of Jacob Masemore; John Houck; Jacob Houck; Polly Styner, wife of Peter Styner; Catherine Bachman, wife of David Bachman; and Rebecca Houck.

Property formerly situate in Baltimore County, on Manchester-Hanover Turnpike, being part of *Coltrider's Lot.*

Chancery Book 17, pp. 451-470 1867 Equity #973
James H. Steele, next friend to John William Steele, and others vs. John William Steele, and others. Sale of real estate.

John T. Steele died c. Aug 1863, testate, leaving widow, Ann A. Steele. Children: Joseph Henry Steele; James E. Steele, deceased, died 25 Dec 1866, unmarried and w/o issue; John William Steele; Emma Kate Steele; and Charlotte A. Steele. John had brothers: James H. Steele, of Frederick County; and Dr. J. W. Steele.

Property situate on Gillis Falls, being parts of *Eppington Forest* and *Red Oak Ridge.*

Chancery Book 17, pp. 471-485 1867 Equity #920
Josiah J. Cover vs. Sarah A. Barnes, Exr. of Nathaniel Barnes, and others. Sale of real estate to satisfy creditors.

Nathaniel Barnes was in Army and was killed at Lafayette GA on 12 Oct 1864, intestate, leaving widow, Sarah A. Barnes. Children: Wesley F. Barnes; Ira Nathaniel Barnes; and Robert E. Barnes.

Property being part of *Eppington Forest.*

Chancery Book 17, pp. 486-507 1867 Equity #965
Edwin J. Crumrine, and others vs. Lydia Crumrine, and others.
Sale of real estate.
William J. Crumrine died Sept 1867, leaving widow, Lydia Crumrine. Children: Edwin J. Crumrine; Ellen V. Wheeler, wife of William B. Wheeler; Mary F. Crumrine; and Laura K. Crumrine.
Properties being parts of *German Church, Everything Needful Corrected* and *Dey's Adventure*.

Chancery Book 17, pp. 508-527 1867 Equity #961
Chancery Book 18, pp. 4-9
Chancery Book 23, pp.267-273
John Ezra Shoemaker, and others vs. Araminta M. Shoemaker, and others.
Sale of real estate.
William Shoemaker died Dec 1863, leaving widow, Maria R. Shoemaker. Children: Araminta M. Helterbrick, wife of Henry Helterbrick; Samuel C. Shoemaker; Soloman S. Shoemaker; Anna F. Shoemaker; Edward E. Shoemaker; Oliver B. Shoemaker; Jacob L. Shoemaker, deceased; John Ezra Shoemaker; George A. Shoemaker; and William Albert Shoemaker.
Properties situate near Taneytown, one on Gettysburg Road about 8 miles from Taneytown, one on Monocacy River and the Bullfrog Road about 4 miles from Taneytown, and one in Frederick County, being parts of *Addition to Brook's Discovery on the Rich Lands, Frenchman's Purchase* and *Good Luck*.

Chancery Book 17, pp. 528-541 1869 Equity #1039
David Cassell, Guardian vs. Charles E. Cassell. Sale of real estate.
Abraham Cassell died Apr 1862, intestate, wife having died c. 1850, leaving only son and heir, Charles Ellsworth Cassell.
Property situate in Wakefield, being parts of *Stevenson's Garden* and *Cornwell*.

Chancery Book 17, pp. 542-552 1865 Equity #847 to Book 18, pp. 1-3
John J. Baumgartner, and others vs. Mary L. Baumgartner, and others.
Sale of real estate.
John Baumgartner died 16 Jan 1853, intestate, husband of Margaret Baumgartner, deceased. Children: William H. Baumgartner, deceased, of St. Louis MO, died 19 Sept 1853, intestate, husband of Catherine Baumgartner, of St. Louis MO (who later remarried and became known as Catherine Lee), father of Olivia Woodruff (of St. Louis MO, wife of Hamilton W. Woodruff), John J. Baumgartner (of St. Louis MO), Francis A. Baumgartner, and Margaret H. Baumgartner; Francis J. Baumgartner, deceased, of St. Louis MO, died 5 Jan 1861, intestate, husband of Caroline Baumgartner, of St. Louis MO (who later remarried and became known as Caroline Gresfeld), father of Mary L. Baum-

gartner, and John J. Baumgartner; Mary L. Kerr, widow of Francis J. Kerr; John J. Baumgartner, husband of Margaret Baumgartner; Elizabeth Baumgartner; Magdalena Gilbert, of Baltimore City, wife of Lewis Gilbert; Harriet A. Baumgartner; and Margaret O. Baumgartner, of Baltimore City.
Property formerly situate in Frederick County, being parts of *Troublesome Job* and *Owings Second Chance.*

Chancery Book 18, pp. 10-29   1865   Equity #827
Ephraim Cover, and others vs. Henry Cover, and others.   Sale of real estate.
Tobias Cover died Apr 1865, intestate, at Uniontown, leaving widow, Elizabeth Cover. Children: Ephraim Cover, of Frederick County; John Cover; Samuel Cover; Mary Jane Davis, wife of John W. Davis; Margaret Ann Jordan, wife of John W. Jordan; Frances E. Cookson, widow of Levi Cookson; James B. Cover; Thomas B. Cover, of Baltimore County; Henry Cover; and Charles Cover, deceased, died 1860, intestate, father of Columbus Cover, and Mary C. Cover.
Property situate in Uniontown District, near Uniontown, being parts of *Retirement Corrected* and *Resurvey on Stephen's Purchase.*

Chancery Book 18, pp. 35-51   1868   Equity #1011
John Bentz, et als. vs. Martin Seif, et als.   Sale of real estate to satisfy creditors.
Frederick Frankforter died, leaving widow, Louisa Frankforter, who later married Martin Seif in June 1866 and became known as Louisa Seif. She died 13 Apr 1868, intestate, and w/o issue.
Property being parts of *Rinehart's Folly Resurveyed* and *Good Luck.*

Chancery Book 18, pp. 52-66   1869   Equity #1036
Michael Scanborn vs. Emma R. Ripples, and others.   Foreclosure.
Francis M. Ripples died Feb 1867, intestate, leaving widow, Emma R. Ripples. Children: S. Marian Ripples; Cobb Ripples; and Mary C. Ripples (all live in Baltimore City).
Property partly situate in Howard County, being parts of *Bunker Hill Fortified, Stophels Meadow, Bachelor's Refuge* and *Larkin the Second.*

Chancery Book 18, pp. 67-83   1868   Equity #1025
Thomas Rudisel vs. Mary A. Naill, and others.   Foreclosure.
William Naill died Aug 1868, intestate, leaving widow, Mary A. Naill. Children: Henry C. Naill; David W. Naill; and Sophia A. Naill.
Property being part of *Resurvey on Brothers Agreement.*

Chancery Book 18, pp. 84-111   1868   Equity #1006
Mary S. Grove by her next friend, Jacob Grove vs. George W. Lamott, Admr., and others.   Sale of real estate to satisfy creditors.
George Trumbo died 17 July 1868, intestate, in Westminster, no widow, w/o issue. Sisters: Mary C. Lamott, widow of Abraham Lamott; and Hannah Grove, deceased, died 1838, wife of Jacob Grove, mother of Augustus G. Grove (of AL), Lewis J. Grove (of Baltimore City) and Hannah Winebrenner (of Adams County PA, wife of John Winebrenner).
Property situate near and in City of Westminster, some on Washington Road, being parts of *Peach Brandy Forest*, *Caledonia*, and Lot 7 of *Friendship Completed*.

Chancery Book 18, pp. 112-130   1869   Equity #1044
William Ebaugh vs. John N. Johnson.   Foreclosure.
John N. Johnson and his wife, Mary N. Johnson, of 32 Harford Avenue, Baltimore City.
Property being part of *Frankfort* or *Stansbury Grove*.

Chancery Book 18, pp. 131-148   1869   Equity #1068
Peter Bixler, and others vs. Mary Koontz, and others.   Sale of real estate.
Barbara Bixler died c. Apr 1869, intestate. Children: Peter Bixler, husband of Priscilla Bixler; Daniel Bixler; Elizabeth Mikesell, widow of William B. Mikesell; Rebecca Mikesell, wife of Peter B. Mikesell; Susanna Schaeffer, wife of David Schaeffer; Mary Houck, of York County PA, widow of Levi Houck; Lydia Kreidler, wife of Peter Kreidler; Hannah Panabaker, wife of David Panabaker; and Julian Koontz, deceased, died 1857, mother of Mary Koontz, Anna Koontz, and Julian Koontz.
Property situate on Pipe Creek, being part of *Utz's Inheritance*.

Chancery Book 18, pp. 149-189   1868   Equity #1027
Maggie A. Little, and others vs. Jacob Rinehart, and others.   Sale of real estate to satisfy creditors.
John Rinehart died 25 July 1868, intestate, in Westminster, leaving widow, Emily J. Rinehart. Children: Jacob Rinehart, and William G. Rinehart.
Properties situate 2 miles southeast of Westminster on Westminster-Baltimore Turnpike and in Westminster, being parts of *Jordan's Discovery, Charles Mistake, Ellis Folly, Rochester* and Lots 38, 29, 40, 41, 42, 43, and 53 of *Resurvey on Timber Ridge* and *Fisher's Addition to Westminster*.

Chancery Book 18, pp. 190-233   1867   Equity #927
Joshua Brown, and others vs. Belinda Brown, and others.   Sale of real estate to satisfy creditors.

Thomas S. Brown died Jan 1867, intestate, leaving widow, Belinda Brown. Children: Joshua Brown, husband of Ellen M. Brown; Rebecca Gardner, wife of Cyrus M. S. Gardner; Elizabeth Oursler, wife of Curtis E. Oursler; William S. Brown; Sarah J. Manning, of Randolph County IN, wife of John W. Manning; Charity Miller, wife of George W. Miller; and Mary E. Brown.
Property situate in 4th District, on the Reisterstown-Westminster Turnpike, being parts of *Bond's Forrest, James Purchase, Powder's Adventure, Elizabeth's Fancy, Wilson's Intent, Brook's New Adventure* and *Castle Rising*.

Chancery Book 18, pp. 234-246   1867   Equity #938
Chancery Book 18, pp. 293-296
Petition of John Clabaugh. Sale of real estate.
James Clabaugh died 24 Mar 1867 testate, leaving widow, Margaret Clabaugh. Children: James Clabaugh; Mary Ann Baly, wife of James Baly; and John Clabaugh. Mentions grandchildren (probably children of unnamed deceased son, who died about 20 years ago, and his widow, Lilly Clabaugh): Margaret Arnold, wife of John Thomas Arnold; and John F. Clabaugh, deceased, died 4 Nov 1864 in Federal Army at York County PA, intestate, leaving no widow, and no lineal descendants.
Property location not established.

Chancery Book 18, pp. 247-267   1869   Equity #1063
Nathan Crumbacker and Elizabeth Crumbacker vs. Christina Johnson, and others. Sale of real estate to satisfy creditors.
Samuel Johnson died 13 Mar 1869, intestate, leaving widow, Christena Johnson. Children: Christopher Johnson; David Johnson; Jesse Johnson; and Samuel Johnson.
Property being part of *Bedford*.

Chancery Book 18, pp. 268-285   1869   Equity #1061
Daniel Leppo vs. Catharine Leppo. Sale of real estate to satisfy creditors.
Simon P. Leppo died 15 Dec 1868, intestate, leaving widow, Catharine Leppo. Children: David H. Leppo; Ezra A. Leppo; Ira Franklin Leppo; and Elinore Leno Leppo.
Property being part of *Ohio*.

Chancery Book 18, pp. 286-292   1870   Equity #1083
Washington Galt vs. Silas O. Shoemaker and Mary Jane Shoemaker, his wife. Foreclosure.
Silas O. Shoemaker and his wife, Mary Jane Shoemaker.
Property being parts of *Maiden's Point* and *Addition to Brook's Discovery on the Rich Lands*.

Chancery Book 18, pp. 297-316   1870   Equity #1105
David Geiman, and others vs. Lucinda Geiman, and others.   Sale of real estate.
David Cassell died Jan 1861, testate, in Westminster, leaving widow, Elizabeth Cassell. Children: Balinda Geiman, deceased, died Apr 1861, intestate, wife of David Geiman, mother of Jeremiah Geiman, Elizabeth Royer (wife of John Royer), Abraham Geiman, Lucinda Geiman, and William Geiman; Abraham Cassell; Margaret Baile; Mary Engle; Catharine Baile, deceased, wife of Peter Baile; Nancy Nicodemus; Elizabeth Cassell; Susanna Cassell; Lydia Cassell; Deborah Cassell; and Lucinda Cassell.
Property situate in Baltimore City on Mulberry Street.

Chancery Book 18, pp. 317-341   1869   Equity #1076
Sarah Condon vs. David Burdett, and others.   Sale of real estate to satisfy creditors.
Wilton Burdett died 11 Feb 1869, intestate. Children: David Burdett, of Howard County MD; and Mary Fisher, deceased, died 1852, wife of Hugh Fisher, mother of Anna M. Merrell (of Washington D. C., wife of Squire G. Merrell), Lucinda Keefer (of Frederick County, wife of Edward Keefer), William F. Fisher (of Frederick County), Hugh Fisher (of Frederick County), and Wilton Fisher (of Frederick County).
Property formerly situate in Baltimore County, on Frederick Turnpike, being part of *Favor and Ease.*

Chancery Book 18, pp. 342-370   1865   Equity #841
Thomas Coltrider and wife vs. David L. Richards, and others.   Sale of real estate and to satisfy creditors.
Charles Richards died July 1865, intestate, leaving widow, Susannah Richards. Children: Ruth A. E. Coltrider, wife of Thomas Coltrider; David L. Richards; Richard F. Richards; Charles D. Richards; William H. Richards; George E. Richards; and Mary J. Richards.
Properties formerly situate in Baltimore County, near Patapsco Falls, being parts of *Can't You Be Easy, Let Me Alone,* (originally *Starboard,* and *Fingal and Ossian*) *Henry Ebaugh's Resurvey, Ebaugh's Discovery, Corn Hill Resurvey* and *Bite the Biter.*

Chancery Book 18, pp. 371-385   1866   Equity #881
Jacob Shower and Theodore A. Shower vs. Anna Croft and Richard Harris, Admrs.   Sale of real estate to satisfy creditors.
George A. Croft died May 1863, intestate, leaving widow, Anna Croft and only child, Adam A. Croft.
Property being parts of *Henry Ebaugh's Resurvey, Canton Bern* and *Bite the Biter.*

Chancery Book 18, pp. 386-405 1867 Equity #941
Minerva Ritter, next friend, and others vs. Rebecca Ritter, and others. Sale of real estate.
Jacob Ritter, Jr., died Nov 1865, leaving widow, Minerva Ritter. Children: (by former wife, Sarah Kelly Ritter, deceased, died 1863) Rebecca Ritter; and (by widow) Elizabeth M. Ritter.
Properties situate on Nicodemus Road.

Chancery Book 18, pp. 406-423 1868 Equity #1026
Henry A. Young vs. Helen Waltman, Admr. of John E. Waltman, deceased. Sale of real estate to satisfy creditors.
John E. Waltman died 12 July 1868, intestate, leaving widow, Helen Waltman. Children: Margaret Catherine Waltman; Charles W. Waltman; Mary Elizabeth Waltman; William Josiah Waltman; John Thomas Waltman; Martha Ann Waltman; and Richard Franklin Waltman.
Property situate near Wakefield Valley.

Chancery Book 18, pp. 424-429 1870 Equity #1128
Robert M. Jenkins vs. David Nickey and wife. Foreclosure.
David Nickey and his wife, Catherine Nickey.
Property being part of *Shepherd's Retirement*.

Chancery Book 18, pp. 430-445 1870 Equity #1125
David Engle, and others vs. Nancy Engle, and others. Sale of real estate.
John Engle died 21 Jun 1870, intestate, leaving widow, Nancy Engle. Children: David Engle; Mary A. Engle; Hetty Engle; Belinda Stoner, wife of Ephraim Stoner; Jesse C. Engle, of Frederick County; Samuel Engle, of Seneca County OH; Ephraim P. Engle, of CA; and John R. Engle, deceased, of Frederick County, died 1862, father of John D. Engle, Mary A. Engle, and other children who since died as infants and intestate.
Properties being parts of *Resurvey on Good Will*, *Good Will* and (in Frederick County) *Rural Felicity*.

Chancery Book 18, pp. 446-456 1870 Equity #1134
John Myers, and others vs. Catharine Fisher, et als. Sale of real estate.
Abraham Myers died intestate, unmarried, and w/o issue. Brothers and sisters: John Myers; Lewis Myers; Barbara Fisher, deceased, mother of David Fisher, Daniel Lewis Fisher, Elizabeth Walker (wife of Stephen A. Walker), Hannah Foncanmer (wife of Jackson Foncanmer), and Catherine Fisher (all of OH); and Hannah Warner, wife of Henry Warner.
Properties formerly situate in Frederick County, being parts of *High Spring*, *Share's Spring*, *Resurvey on Share's Spring*, *Will's Forest* and *Molly's Fancy*.

Chancery Book 18, pp. 457-476 1867 Equity #972
Clarissa Ann Stoner, mother and next friend, and others vs. Jesse L. Stoner. Sale of real estate to satisfy creditors.
Ezra Stoner died June 1867, intestate, leaving widow, Clarissa Ann Stoner, and only child, Jesse L. Stoner.
Property situate in Union Bridge, being part of *The Rich Indian Garden*.

Chancery Book 18, pp. 477-498 1869 Equity #1038
Elliatta Biehl, mother, and others vs. Lewis M. Biehl, and others. Sale of real estate.
George F. Biehl died c. 1865, intestate, leaving widow, Elliatta Biehl. Children: Lewis M. Biehl; George A. Biehl; Francis M. Biehl; David C. Biehl; Mary L. Biehl; and Edgar S. Biehl.
Property situate on road from Middleburg to Double Pipe Creek, being part of *Resurvey on Mackey's Choice*.

Chancery Book 18, pp. 499-512 1870 Equity #1122
John B. T. Sellman, Mortgagee, vs. Robert T. Smith and wife, Mortgagors. Foreclosure.
Robert T. Smith and his wife, Hester A. Smith.
Property location not established.

Chancery Book 18, pp. 513-529 1870 Equity #1130
Abraham Stoner vs. Alfred Shriner   Sale of real estate to satisfy creditors.
Alfred Shriner.
Property location not established.

Chancery Book 18, pp. 530-543 1870 Equity #1154
John J. Baumgartner and Charles T. Reifsnider, Trustees vs. Jacob N. Houck, and others. Sale of real estate to satisfy creditors.
Jacob N. Houck and his wife, Miriam Houck.
Properties situate on Patapsco Falls, on road from Winchester Mill to Brown's Meeting House, being parts of *Ribble's Folly, Ribble's Meadow, Better Known, Moses Meadow* and *Hazzard*.

Chancery Book 18, pp. 544-552 1870 Equity #1132
to Chancery Book 19, pp. 1-4
Dennis H. Maynard and Daniel Engle vs. Annie M. Townsend, and others. Foreclosure.   Annie M. Townsend.
Property situate 1/4 mile from New Windsor on the road to Libertytown, being part of *Resurvey on Timber Ridge*.

Chancery Book 19, pp. 5-13 1870 Equity #1131
George W. Lamott, Trustee vs. Robert Hunter, and others.
Sale of real estate to satisfy creditors.
Mary Davis died 11 July 1855, intestate, wife of Benjamin Davis. Children: Elizabeth Hunter, wife of Robert Hunter; Margaret A. Beaver, wife of William J. Beaver; and Rebecca Poulson, wife of Levi Poulson.
Benjamin deeded his interest to George Trumbo who died 17 July 1868, intestate, and left sisters: Mary C. Lamott; Hannah Winebrenner, wife of John Winebrenner; and Elizabeth Grove, deceased, mother of Lewis J. Grove (husband of Frances M. Grove), and Augustus G. Grove (husband of Mary Grove).
Property situate on Washington Road, being Lot 8 of *Friendship Completed*.

Chancery Book 19, pp. 14-26 1870 Equity #1113
Josiah Hann vs. Jacob Sentz, and others. Sale of real estate to satisfy creditors.
George Hess died 20 Dec 1869, testate, leaving widow, Susannah, who died 16 Feb 1870, intestate, and w/o issue. Her brothers and sisters: Catharine Sentz, wife of Jacob Sentz; Elizabeth Wilhelm, of OH, wife of George Wilhelm; George Winters, deceased, father of David Winters (of IA), Isaac Winters (of IA), Stephen Winters (of IA), Mary Ann Garner (of IA, wife of George Garner), Susan Crabbs (of IA, wife of George Crabbs), July Ann Lynch (of IA, wife of John V. Lynch), Reuben Winters, George Winters, and Elizabeth Smith (of Howard County MD, wife of Nimrod Smith); Joseph Winters, deceased, father of Deborah Flickinger (wife of Frederick Flickinger), Ephraim Winters, and Mary E. Winters; and Mary Davis, deceased, wife of Jonathan Davis, mother of John W. Davis (of PA), Joseph Davis, William Davis, Anna M. Davis, and Aaron Davis (of Frederick County).
Property siutate on road from Union Bridge to Uniontown, in Middletown, being *Resurvey on Unity*.

Chancery Book 19, pp. 27-43 1869 Equity #1062
George B. Leister vs. Catherine Shipley, and others.
Sale of real estate to satisfy creditors.
Alexander Shipley died 28 Apr 1869, intestate, leaving widow, Catherine Shipley. Children: David Shipley, of parts unknown; Lewis Shipley; Thomas Shipley, of PA; James Shipley; Theodore Shipley; Francis Shipley; and Jabez A. B. Shipley.
Property being parts of *Brook's New Adventure* and *Barbadoes*.

Chancery Book 19, pp. 44-58 1870 Equity #1153
Frances Ecker, et als. vs. Frances Thompson. Sale of real estate.
Jonas Ecker died 22 Aug 1870, testate, in New Windsor, leaving widow, Frances Ecker. Children: Alice Baile, wife of Charles P. Baile; and Margaret E.

Thompson, deceased, died several years prior, intestate, wife of Abel Thompson (of PA), mother of Frances Thompson.
Property situate in New Windsor, on Buffalo Road, being parts of Lots 13 and 14 of *Five Daughters*.

Chancery Book 19, pp. 59-72   1870   Equity #1106
Joshua Bosley vs. Bernard McGinity. Foreclosure.
Bernard McGinity and his wife, Mary McGinity.
Property being part of *Everything Needful Corrected*.

Chancery Book 19, pp. 73-95   1870   Equity #1133
The Manchester Savings Institution vs. Elizabeth Riley, and others. Foreclosure.
Thomas Riley died 2 June 1866, intestate, leaving widow, Elizabeth Riley. Children: James H. Riley, of Fulton County IL, husband of Mary T. Riley; Joseph Riley, husband of Catherine J. Riley; Mary E. Riley; John T. Riley; and Laura V. Riley.
Properties being parts of *Easenburgh* and *Deyes Chance Resurveyed*.

Chancery Book 19, pp. 96-108   1871   Equity #1170
Chancery Book 21, pp. 187-189
Ephraim W. Becker, Trustee vs. Abdiel W. Becker. Sale of real estate to satisfy creditors.
Abdiel W. Becker.
Property situate in or near Manchester.

Chancery Book 19, pp. 109-117   1871   Equity #1178
Hashabiah Haines vs. Francis T. Manahan. Foreclosure.
Francis T. Manahan and his wife, Cinderalla Manahan.
Location of property not established.

Chancery Book 19, pp. 118-127   1871   Equity #1184
Henry E. Beltz and David H. Hoffacker, Trustees vs. Edwin H. Crouse. Sale of real estate to satisfy creditors.
Edwin H. Crouse.
Property situate in Manchester, being parts of Lots 6 and 10 of *The German Church*.

Chancery Book 19, pp. 128-139   1871   Equity #1195
Charles T. Reifsnider, Trustee vs. Henry Drach and wife.
Sale of real estate to satisfy creditors.

Henry Drach, formerly of Baltimore City, and his wife, Rachel Drach.
Property situate in vicinity of New Windsor.

Chancery Book 19, pp. 140-166   1871   Equity #1206
Lucinda Richards, and others vs. Laura V. Richards, and others.   Sale of real estate.
George Richards, Jr., died 26 Nov 1861, intestate, leaving widow, Lucinda Richards. Children: Richard R. Richards, husband of Rebecca Richards; Sarah C. Shaner, wife of Samuel Shaner; William L. Richards, husband of Mary L. Richards; Alice A. Richards; Lucretia E. Abbott, of Baltimore County, wife of John W. Abbott; Laura V. Richards; James B. Richards; and Samuel F. Richards.
Properties being parts of *Pleasant Grove, Brown's Recovery, Brown's Struggle, German Town, The Wee Bit Enlarged, Harriot's Retreat, Hale's Venture Resurveyed* and *Beall's Delight.*

Chancery Book 19, pp. 167-180   1870   Equity #1138
Theo L. Fritchey, Trustee vs. Elijah Fleagle.   Sale of real estate to satisfy creditors.
Elijah Fleagle and his wife, Julia A. Fleagle
Location of property not established.

Chancery Book 19, pp. 181-191   1871   Equity #1205
John J. Baumgartner and Charles T. Reifsnider, Trustees vs. George Houck, of William, and wife.   Sale of real estate to satisfy creditors.
George Houck, of William, and his wife, Elizabeth Houck.
Properties situate on Hanover Pike and on Deep Run, being parts of *Hooker's Meadow Resurvey, Houster's Last Will* and *Wolfe Hill.*

Chancery Book 19, pp. 192-199   1871   Equity #1220
John J. Baumgartner vs. Rufus M. Dell.   Sale of real estate to satisfy creditors.
Rufus M. Dell.
Property being part of *Rochester.*

Chancery Book 19, pp. 200-248   1868   Equity #990
Ann Mayfield vs. Lydia Hoffman, and others.   Sale of real estate to satisfy creditors.
Isaac Hoffman died Apr 1865, intestate, at Relay House in Baltimore County, leaving widow, Lydia Hoffman. Children: Peter B. Hoffman; William J. Hoffman; Octavia Ann Lambert, wife of Andrew J. Lambert; Eliza Jane Richards, wife of John C. Richards; Susannah Davidson, wife of William Asbury David-

son; Isaac Hoffman; James Conrad Hoffman; Lydia Catherine Shafer, wife of William Lewis Shafer; and Sarah Elizabeth Hoffman.
Properties partly situate in Baltimore County, on Patapsco Falls, known as *Fulling Mill Property*, being parts of *Stephen's Defense, Blenheim, New Found Bottom Enlarged, Rockland, Winter's Range, Foxes Denn* and *Wee Bit Enlarged.*

Chancery Book 19, pp. 249-268 1871 Equity #1223
Thomas J. Belts, and others vs. James McFee, and others. Sale of real estate.
Henry Thomas Belts died 1867, testate. Children: Louisa Harker, wife of James Harker, mother of William A. Harker, Purvis Harker, John Harker, Robert Harker (all of Baltimore County), and Alosious Harker (of Washington Territory); Caroline McFee, wife of James M. McFee; Thomas Jefferson Belts, father of Basil Henry Belts, Franklin A. Belts, Julianna Belts, and Mary D. Belts; and Samuel C. Belts.
Location of property in Carroll County not established, but property in Baltimore City was situate at 88 South Eutaw Street and 26 McElderry Street.

Chancery Book 19, pp. 269-289 1868 Equity #1015
David Kneller, and others vs. Abdiel Kneller, and others. Sale of real estate to satisfy creditors.
Godfrey Kneller died 22 Jul 1868, intestate, leaving widow, Keziah Kneller. Children: David Kneller, husband of Emeline Kneller; William G. Kneller, husband of Elizabeth Kneller; Samuel Kneller, husband of Martha Kneller; Daniel Kneller, husband of Rebecca Kneller; Ellenora Kneller; Mary J. Kneller; Eliza A. Loasman, wife of Charles Loasman; Abdiel Kneller; Rachel Kneller; Henry Kneller; and Luther H. Kneller.
Properties being parts of *Everything Needful, Everything Needful Corrected* and *Rock Hill.*

Chancery Book 19, pp. 290-299 1872 Equity 3439
(Frederick County) Solomon Ohler and wife, and others vs. Margaret Ohler, Deliah Ohler, and others. Sale of real estate.
Frederick Ohler, Sr., died, intestate, leaving widow, Margaret Ohler, of Frederick County. Children: Catherine Mort, of Frederick County, wife of William Mort; Elizabeth Houck, of Frederick County, wife of Michael Houck; Solomon Ohler, of Frederick County, husband of Mary Ann Ohler (formerly Mary Ann Chew); Levi N. Ohler, of OH, husband of Catherine Ohler; George A. Ohler, of IA, husband of the former _____ Lynn; Julia Ann Powell, of Frederick County, wife of Daniel C. Powell; Joshua Ohler, of OH, husband of Emeline Ohler (formerly Emeline Chambers); Frederick Ohler, husband of Mary Ohler (formerly Mary Shorb); Delilah Ohler, of Frederick County; and Allie Diehl, of IA, wife of Hann Diehl.

Property formerly situate in Frederick County, on Monocacy River, partly in Frederick County, being part of *Resurvey on Boxes Search*. Woodlot in Frederick County, situate on road from Emmittsburg to Sabillasville, being Lot 3 of *Mountain Lot*.

Chancery Book 19, pp. 300-312   1870   Equity #1107
Moses Parrish vs. William Grimes, and others. Foreclosure.
William Grimes and his wife, Fanny Grimes. Also mentions Amin Grimes and Mary E. Grimes (of Baltimore County), but relationship not established.
Property being part of *Caledonia*.

Chancery Book 19, pp. 313-321   1871   Equity #1238
Charles T. Reifsnider, Trustee vs. Christianna Greenwood, and others. Sale of real estate to satisfy creditors.
Josiah Greenwood died July 1870, intestate, leaving widow, Christianna Greenwood. Children: Lewis H. Greenwood; and Susannah C. Gorsuch, wife of Daniel Gorsuch.
Property partly situate in Frederick County.

Chancery Book 19, pp. 322-338   1867   Equity #918
Leah Seekens, mother and next friend to Eve Seekens vs. Eve Seekens. Sale of real estate to satisfy creditors.
William Seekens (or Segans) died Oct 1866, intestate, leaving widow, Leah Seekens, and only child, Eve Seekens.
Property being part of *York Company Defense*.

Chancery Book 19, pp. 339-354   1869   Equity #1040
John A. Humburgh, and others vs. Joseph Humburgh, and others. Sale of real estate.
Peter Humburgh died c. Feb 1869, intestate, leaving widow, Mary E. Humburgh. Children: John A. Humburgh, of York County PA, husband of Anna M. Humburgh; Francis P. Humburgh, of Franklin County PA, husband of Sarah Humburgh; Jonas W. Humburgh, of LA; and Joseph Humburgh, husband of Helen Humburgh.
Properties being part of *Addition to Brook's Discovery on the Rich Lands*.

Chancery Book 19, pp. 355-380   1865   Equity #843
William C. Duvall, and others vs. Francis L. Duvall, and others. Sale of real estate.
William T. Duvall, of Frederick County, died c. June 1865, intestate, leaving widow, Anna Rebecca Duvall. Children: William C. Duvall; Edward H. Duvall; John F. Duvall; Francis L. Duvall; Mary E. Duvall; Zero E. Duvall; Scott

Elsworth Duvall; Charles T. Duvall; and Kate Duvall (b. 24 Aug 1865), (all of Frederick County).
Property being part of *Shriver's Integrity*.

Chancery Book 19, pp. 381-406   1870   Equity #1109
The Farmers and Mechanics National Bank of Westminster and Samuel S. Linthicum vs. Mary L. B. Williams, Stephen R. Gore and Laura E. Gore, his wife. Foreclosure.
Stephen R. Gore and his wife, Laura E. Gore.
Property situate on road from Baltimore City to Libertytown, being parts of *Windsor Forest Corrected* and *Long Reach*.

Chancery Book 19, pp. 407-444   1870   Equity #1145
John Bentz vs. Mary A. Burns, Admr. of Emanuel Burns, deceased, et als. Sale of real estate to satisfy creditors.
Emanuel Burns died 17 Jul 1870, intestate, leaving widow, Mary A. Burns. Brothers and sisters: George Burns, husband of Eleanora Burns; Amoss Burns, of Bartholomew County IN, husband of Marthela Burns; Edward Burns, of Lycoming County PA; Simon P. Burns, of Champaign County OH, husband of Henrietta Burns; Calvin J. Burns, of Miami County IN, husband of Nancy Burns; Charles Burns, of Montgomery County MD, husband of Mollie Burns; Sophia Carrick, of Anne Arundel County MD, wife of George Carrick; Mary Burns, of York County PA; and John Burns, deceased, died 30 Oct 1863 in IN, father of Sarah E. Burns, Susan A. Burns, and David M. C. Burns (all of Huntington County IN).
Properties being parts of *Everything Needful Corrected, Deyes Adventure, New Market* and *Adam's Contrivance*.

Chancery Book 19, pp. 445-452   1870   Equity #1164
Milton Painter vs. John Morningstar and Harriet Morningstar, his wife. Foreclosure.
John Morningstar and his wife, Harriet Morningstar.
Property situate in Uniontown.

Chancery Book 19, pp. 453-466   1871   Equity #1229
Andrew Bair, and others vs. Catharine Bair, and others. Sale of real estate.
George Bair died Mar 1871, intestate, leaving widow, Catherine Bair. Children: Andrew Bair, husband of Eliza Bair; Jesse Bair, husband of Mary A. Bair; Susan Malchorn, widow of John Malehorn; Jane R. Zile, wife of Jesse N. Zile; Amanda Leister, widow of Josiah Leister; Lucy Henry, of Dark County OH, wife of Daniel Henry; and Elizabeth Shafer, wife of Joshua Shafer.
Property being part of *Baker's Discovery*.

Chancery Book 19, pp. 467-490   1871   Equity #1169
Michael M. Armacost vs. Barbara Holzner, Admrx., and others. Sale of real estate to satisfy creditors.
Francis Holzner died c. 24 Aug 1870, intestate, leaving widow, Barbara Holzner. Children: Francis Holzner; William Holzner; Lewis Holzner; Mary Holzner; George Holzner; Anna Holzner; and Elizabeth Holzner.
Property situate partly in Baltimore County.

Chancery Book 19, pp. 491-500   1871   Equity #1191
Augustus D. Schaeffer, Trustee vs. Daniel Snyder and wife. Sale of real estate to satisfy creditors.
Daniel Snyder and his wife, Mary C. Snyder.
Location of property not established.

Chancery Book 19, pp. 501-514   1871   Equity #1233
David Engle, of P. vs. Robert T. Lindsay. Foreclosure.
Robert T. Lindsay.
Property being parts of *Bachelor's Refuge* and *Dorsey's Prospect*.

Chancery Book 19, pp. 515-525   1871   Equity #1183
John Beiker vs. Jacob Hollenbaugh. Foreclosure.
Jacob Hollenbaugh.
Property location not established.

Chancery Book 19, pp. 526-539   1871   Equity #1247
Nathan J. Gorsuch, Trustee vs. John Bemiller and wife. Sale of real estate to satisfy creditors.
John Bemiller and his wife, Lucinda Bemiller. Mentions Peter Bemiller who died 18 Jan 1871, but relationship not established.
Property being parts of *Africa* and *Ohio*.

Chancery Book 20, pp. 1-35   1868   Equity #1019
Benjamin Reaver, and others vs. Cecelia Crouse, and others. Sale of real estate.
James Crouse died Mar 1868, intestate, leaving widow, Elizabeth Crouse. Children: Margaret Reaver, wife of Benjamin Reaver; John T. Crouse; Richard Crouse, deceased, died 24 Aug 1869, testate, husband of Margaret Crouse, of Adams County PA, father of William Lee Crouse, Marshall Allen Crouse, and Hannah Olivia Idea Crouse; Olivia Crouse; Cecelia Crouse; Jane E. Crouse; William H. Crouse; and Rebecca Crouse.

Properties formerly situate in Frederick County, on Taneytown-Westminster Pike, being parts of *Troy Meadow, Slipe, Runnymede Enlarged* and *Resurvey on Brothers Agreement.*

Chancery Book 20, pp. 36-47   1872   Equity #1269
Andrew McKinney, Trustee vs. Henry A. Shoemaker.
Sale of real estate to satisfy creditors.
Henry A. Shoemaker, son of John Shoemaker.
Property being part of *Addition to Brook's Discovery on the Rich Lands.*

Chancery Book 20, pp. 48-97   1871   Equity #1181
George C. Orendorff, and others vs. John T. Orendorff, and others.   Sale of real estate.
George Orendorff died 1 Nov 1870. Children: George C. Orendorff, husband of Cela Orendorff; Peter F. Orendorff, husband of Elizabeth Orendorff; Josephus Orendorff; John T. Orendorff; Mary Jane Orendorff, lunatic; and William A. Orendorff, deceased, died 29 Dec 1870, unmarried and w/o issue.
Properties formerly situate in Baltimore County and Frederick County. being parts of *Lucky's Enlargement, Resurvey on Bedford, William's Luck, Kellys Range, Daniel's Denn, Addition to Daniel's Denn, Bond's Meadow Enlarged, Rich Meadow, Iron Intention* and *Michael's Chance.*

Chancery Book 20, pp. 98-115   1870   Equity #1098
John Flickinger, and others vs. Jane Humbert.   Sale of real estate.
John Dickensheets died 2 Mar 1870, intestate, and unmarried. Brothers and sisters: Catharine Flickinger, wife of John Flickinger; Frederick Dickensheets; Rachel Dickensheets; Elizabeth Dodderer, wife of Henry Dodderer; Susan Townsend, deceased, widow of John Townsend, mother of Thomas Townsend, Frederick Townsend, Jane Humbert (widow of David Humbert), Nancy Taney (wife of Frederick Taney), Alice Myerly (wife of David Myerly), and Rachel Townsend; and David Dickensheets, deceased, of Dayton OH.
Properties being parts of *Resurvey on Lookabout* and *Ohio.*

Chancery Book 20, pp. 116-125   1869   Equity #1053
Theodore L. Fritchey vs. Joseph Greenwood and wife.   Sale of real estate to satisfy creditors.
Joseph Greenwood and his wife, Margaret Greenwood.
Property situate on Littlestown Turnpike.

Chancery Book 20, pp. 126-142   1869   Equity #1065
Jonathan Hartley, and others vs. George W. Hartley, and others.
Sale of real estate.

Magdalena Hartley died 1862, intestate, leaving husband, George W. Hartley. Children: Jonathan Hartley; William H. Hartley; John D. Hartley, at school in MI; Mary C. Hartley; and Josephine Hartley.
Property situate on Liberty Road, being parts of *John's Industry, Lawrence's Pleasant Vallies* and *Eppington Forest*.

Chancery Book 20, pp. 143-167   1869   Equity #1074
Francis H. Orendorff, Admr. of John Orendorff, deceased vs. Albert Harnickell. Foreclosure.
Albert Harnickell, formerly of Baltimore City, now in NY
Property situate on Baltimore-Reisterstown Turnpike, being parts of *Arnold's Arbour Enlarged, Rochester Resurvey* and *Goneshar*.

Chancery Book 20, pp. 168-178   1871   Equity #1189
Ephraim Cover vs. Joseph Brummel and wife.   Foreclosure.
Joseph Brummel and his wife, Catherine Brummel.
Property being parts of *Hales Venture Resurveyed, Bell's Recovery, Beaver Hall, Addition to Beaver Hall, Bond's Enlargement* and *German Town*.

Chancery Book 20, pp. 179-187   1871   Equity #1174
John T. Orendorff vs. Mary Jane Orendorff.   Sale of real estate to satisfy creditors.
Mary Jane Orendorff, lunatic, was daughter of George Orendorff, and sister to John T. Orendorff and William A. Orendorff, deceased.
Properties in or near Westminster. (See Equity #1181, Chancery Book 20, pp. 48&c).

Chancery Book 20, pp. 188-203   1872   Equity #1281
John M. Smeach, and others vs. Andrew S. Smeach, and others. Sale of real estate.
Andrew Smeach died Mar 1870, intestate, leaving widow, Ann M. Smeach. Children: Mandelia Burgoon, wife of John H. F. Burgoon; Andrew S. Smeach; William W. Smeach; Ellen S. Smeach; David R. Smeach; Barbara A. Smeach; George M. Smeach; and Philip A. Smeach.
Property situate on Westminster-Manchester Road, devised to him by his father-in-law, Jacob Wine, being part of *Dacres Plague*.

Chancery Book 20, pp. 204-212   1871   Equity #1244
Azariah Oursler, Trustee vs. Adam M. Leppo and wife.   Sale of real estate to satisfy creditors.
Adam M. Leppo and his wife, Elizabeth A. Leppo.
Location of property not established.

Chancery Book 20, pp. 213-224   1870   Equity #1144
Chancery Book 22, pp. 268-271
John J. Baumgartner and Charles T. Reifsnider, Trustee vs. Uriah B. Mikesell and wife. Sale of real estate to satisfy creditors.
Uriah B. Mikesell and his wife, Mary Mikesell.
Properties situate in and near Westminster, being parts of *Bonds Meadow Enlarged*.

Chancery Book 20, pp. 225-236   1871   Equity #1190
John E. Smith, Trustee vs. Jacob Campbell, Admr. of John C. Price, deceased. Sale of real estate to satisfy creditors. John C. Price died intestate.
Properties situate in and near Manchester, one being *Washington House Hotel*.

Chancery Book 20, pp. 237-255   1870   Equity #1155
Mary M. Bennett vs. Charles A. Ware, and others. Foreclosure.
Charles A. Ware, formerly of Alexandria VA, and his wife, E. Anna Maria Ware.
Property situate on Westminster-Eldersburg Road, in Freedom District, 1-1/2 miles from Freedom, commonly known as the *Snowden Farm*, being parts of *Stepney's Causeway* and *Colross*.

Chancery Book 20, pp. 256-275   1870   Equity #1088
Chancery Book 66, pp. 380-385
William M. Englar, and others vs. Elizabeth Englar, and others. Sale of real estate.
John Englar died July 1860, intestate, leaving widow, Elizabeth Englar, who died 4 Mar 1912. Children: William M. Englar; Ezra S. Englar; Daniel H. Englar; Alice S. Englar; Ella L. Englar; Ida H. Englar; and John L. Englar.
Properties situate on road from Warfieldsburg to Stone Chapel, being parts of *Poulson's Reserve, Stephensons Garden, Arnold's Chance, Rich Meadow, Poulson's Chance, Strawberry Mead* and *Harbor Hill*.

Chancery Book 20, pp. 276-283   1870   Equity #1116
William A. McKellip, Trustee vs. William H. Lippy, and others. Sale of real estate to satisfy creditors.
William H. Lippy and his wife, Elizabeth Lippy.
Location of property not established.

Chancery Book 20, pp. 284-294   1873   Equity #1349
John J. Baumgartner, Trustee, vs. Absalom H. Bowersox, and others. Sale of real estate to satisfy creditors.

Absalom H. Bowersox, guardian of Jeremiah D. Bowersox.
Location of property not established.

Chancery Book 20, pp. 295-317   1870   Equity #1146
Chancery Book 26, pp. 418-427
Henry C. Bennett vs. Virginia E. Bennett, widow, and others. Sale of real estate. Levi T. Bennett died Dec 1865 testate, leaving widow, Mary M. Bennett. Children: Henry C. Bennett; Nimrod T. Bennett, deceased, died 7 Sept 1870, intestate, husband of Virginia E. Bennett, father of Nimrod T. Bennett; and Charlotte Shipley.
Property situate on Bloom Road, being parts of *Upper Marlborough, Arnold's Desire, Benjamin's Claim, Chance's Luck, Greyhound Forest* and *Ogg's Discovery*.

Chancery Book 20, pp. 318-327   1872   Equity #1327
Chancery Book 52, pp. 105-113, and 346-348.
John T. Orendorff, Trustee vs. Josephus Orendorff. Sale of real estate to satisfy creditors.
Josephus Orendorff.
See Equity #1181, Chancery Book 20, pp. 48&c.

Chancery Book 20, pp. 328-349   1872   Equity #1277
David H. Reindollar, next friend, and others vs. George Samuel Reindollar, and others. Sale of real estate.
George Reindollar died 22 Jan 1872, testate, leaving widow, Catherine Reindollar. Children: Lucinda Ellen Reindollar; George Samuel Reindollar; Alverta Catherine Reindollar; Isaiah Reindollar; Laura Regina Reindollar; and James Henry Reindollar. George had a brother, Samuel Reindollar.
Property being parts of *Shriver's Bottom* and *Ohio*.

Chancery Book 20, pp. 350-376   1871   Equity #1214
Chancery Book 24, pp. 61-64
Tobias Oursler, and others vs. Mary Oursler, and others. Sale of real estate.
Henry Oursler died 20 Jan 1856, intestate, leaving widow, Mary Oursler. Children: David H. Oursler; Sarah E. Shaffer, wife of William H. Shaffer; Tobias Oursler; Gustavus Oursler; Theodore Oursler; John T. Oursler; Mary L. Oursler; and Francis (Frank) Oursler.
Properties being parts of *Cryders Delight, Peter's Lot, Hazard* and *Bond's Meadow Enlarged*.

Chancery Book 20, pp. 376-395 1872 Equity #1268
David H. Rinedollar, next friend, and others vs. Lucinda E. Rinedollar, and others. Sale of real estate.
Samuel Rinedollar died testate. Nephews and nieces (children of brother, George Rinedollar, who died 22 Jan 1872): Lucinda E. Rinedollar; George S. Rinedollar; Isaiah Rinedollar; Laura R. Rinedollar; Alverta C. Rinedollar; and James H. Rinedollar.
Samuel was the son of George Rinedollar and his wife, Mary Rinedollar (she died Aug 1870), and the brother to Rebecca Morter and Lydia Stear.
Property formerly situate in Frederick County, being parts of *Resurvey on the Pines*, *Addition to the Pines* and *The Resurvey on Owings Chance*.

Chancery Book 20, pp. 396-405 1871 Equity #1208
Benjamin Reaver, Trustee vs. William J. Kirkpatrick, and wife. Sale of real estate to satisfy creditors.
William J. Kirkpatrick and his wife, Jane Kirkpatrick.
Location of property not established.

Chancery Book 20, pp. 406-412 1872 Equity #1336
Samuel Lawyer vs. George D. Starner and wife. Foreclosure.
George Starner and his wife, Lucy Ann Starner.
Property being part of *Resurvey on Lookabout*.

Chancery Book 20, pp. 413-426 1872 Equity #1329
Jesse F. Malehorn and Mordecai W. Gist vs. Isaac Belt. Sale of real estate to satisfy creditors.
Leonard Belt died 1871, leaving widow, Rhoda Belt.
Properties being parts of *Colchester* and *Pleasant Spring*.

Chancery Book 20, pp. 427-436 1872 Equity #1325
Frederick Mehring, Trustee vs. Thomas L. Allison and wife. Sale of real estate to satisfy creditors.
Thomas L. Allison and his wife, Mary S. Allison.
Location of property not established.

Chancery Book 20, pp. 437-462 1871 Equity #1210
Alexander McAllister and Andrew McAllister, Exrs. of James McAllister, deceased vs. Margaret Hawk, and others. Sale of real estate to satisfy creditors.
James McAllister died 10 Sept 1867, testate, leaving widow Jane Amanda McAllister and child, John McAllister. James was the son of John McAllister,

and the brother of John W. McAllister, Alexander McAllister, Margaret McAllister, and Elizabeth McAllister.

Joseph Hawk, who bought property from James McAllister, died 28 May 1871, leaving widow, Margaret Hawk, and son, Henry Hawk (he died Jan 1872, intestate, leaving widow, Elizabeth Hawk).

Property being parts of *Resurvey on Owings Chance* and *Exchange*.

Chancery Book 20, pp. 463-479 1871 Equity #1228
George W. Lamotte, Trustee vs. Sarah E. Blizzard, and others. Sale of real estate to satisfy creditors.

Mary Davis died 11 July 1855, intestate, leaving husband, Benjamin Davis. Children: Elizabeth Hunter, wife of Robert Hunter; Margaret A. Beaver, wife of William J. Beaver; and Rebecca Poltson, wife of Levi Poltson.

Benjamin Davis conveyed his interest to George Trumbo who died 17 July 1868, intestate, leaving sisters: Mary C. Lamott; and Elizabeth Grove, deceased, mother of Hannah Winebrenner (of Adams County PA, wife of John Winebrenner), Lewis E. Grove (of Baltimore City, husband of Frances Grove), and Augustus G. Grove (of Sumpter County AL, husband of Mary Grove).

Property situate 2 miles from Westminster on Washington Road.

Chancery Book 20, pp. 480-488 1873 Equity #1344
Theodore L. Fritchey and William B. Thomas, partners trading under the name, firm, and style of Theo L. Fritchey & Co. vs. John B. Hammond. Foreclosure.
John B. Hammond.
Location of property not established.

Chancery Book 20, pp. 489-503 1871 Equity #1211
David Engle, and others vs. John D. Engel, and others. Sale of real estate.
Nancy Engel died 1 May 1871, intestate. Children: David Engel; Mary A. Engel; Hetty Engel; Belinda Stoner, wife of Ephraim Stoner; Jesse C. Stoner, of Frederick County; Samuel Engel, of Seneca County OH; Ephraim P. Engel, of CA; and John R. Engel, deceased, died 1862, in Frederick County, father of John D. Engel and Mary A. Engel.
Properties being parts of *Resurvey on Good Will, Stevenson's Garden* and *Good Will*.

Chancery Book 20, pp. 504-515 1872 Equity #1280
Daniel Bush vs. Daniel Frazier and wife. Foreclosure.
Daniel Frazier and his wife, Prudence Ann Frazier.
Property being part of *Hooker's Meadow Enlarged*.

Chancery Book 20, pp. 516-540   1872   Equity #1305
to Chancery Book 21, pp. 1-7
John Nathaniel Flater, and others vs. Elisha Flater, and others.
Partition of real estate.

John Flater died 15 July 1871, testate. Children: John Nathaniel Flater; Catherine Miller, of Adams County PA, wife of John Miller; Elisha Flater, husband of Sophia Flater, father of John W. Flater (of IN), Francis H. Flater, Mary Flater, and Sarah Flater; Jarusa Manning, deceased, mother of John William Manning and Amanda Manning; Mary Christ, wife of Charles Christ; Isabella Richards, wife of Richard Richards; Jacob Flater, had issue by second wife; Hesekiah Flater, father of two children; and Areanna Algire, wife of Amon Algire, mother of Asbury Algire, John Henry Algire, Rebecca Algire, Ruth Algire, Martha Algire, Amanda Algire, and Ellen Algire. Also mentions negro woman, Ann Eliza Slater.

Properties formerly situate in Baltimore County, on Sandymount Road, being parts of *Stain's Neglect, Bond's Forest, I Will and I Will Not* and *Mount Pleasant*.

INDEX

-A-

ABBOTT, John, 50, 104
  John W., 129
  Lucinda, 104
  Lucretia E., 129
  Margaret, 50
ABLER, Elmira, 111
  William D., 112
ABY, Christian, 55
  Deana, 55
ADAMS, Magdelena, 26
  Mary, 26
  Thomas, 26
ADAM'S CONTRIVANCE, 132
ADAM'S GARDEN, 96
ADDITION, The, 87
ADDITION OF THE TOWN OF WESTMINSTER, 24
ADDITION TO BEAVER HALL, 135
ADDITION TO BROOK'S DISCOVERY ON THE RICH LANDS, 34, 45, 56, 61, 74, 93, 103, 113, 120, 123, 131, 134
ADDITION TO CAROLINA, 33
ADDITION TO CORNWELL, 30
ADDITION TO CURPOY, 44, 111
ADDITION TO DANIEL'S DENN, 134
ADDITION TO GOOD RUN RESURVEYED ON DAIRY, 12
ADDITION TO JOHN'S DELIGHT, 89
ADDITION TO LAND STOOL, 49
ADDITION TO LANDAFF, The, 96
ADDITION TO LOVEALL'S PROSPECT, 89
ADDITION TO MOLLEY'S FANCY, 44
ADDITION TO MOLLY'S FANCY, 69
ADDITION TO PENELOPE AND THOMAS COCKEY'S DEYSBURG, 82, 98
ADDITION TO RICHARD'S LOT, 10
ADDITION TO RICHARDS LOT, 7
ADDITION TO SCHOOL LOT, 75
ADDITION TO THE PINES, 26, 56, 138
ADDITION TO WATER OAK LEVEL, 61, 100
ADDITIONAL PROGRESS, 44, 109
ADELSPERGER, Elizabeth, 21
ADERDS, Elizabeth, 51
  George, 51
ADRAIN, Elizabeth, 86
  George, 86
AFRICA, 133
AGREEMENT, The, 94, 111
AIKIN, Sarah, 27
AIRING, James, 42
Alabama (State), 122
Sumpter County, 139
ALBAUGH, Abraham, 8, 107
  Amelia, 8
  Dallas, 107
  Edmond, 107
  Elizabeth, 107
  Emily Jane, 107
  Jacob, 106, 107
  James A., 109
  John, 8
  William, 107
  William A., 101
  Zachariah, 8
ALBON, Henry, 16
  Mary, 16
ALGIER, Catherine, 49
  George, 49
  Henry, 49
  Mary, 49
  Matilda, 47
  Nicholas, 47
ALGIRE, Amanda, 140
  Amon, 140
  Areanna, 140
  Asbury, 140
  Ellen, 140
  George, 22
  Jane K., 22
  John Henry, 140
  Martha, 140
  Rebecca, 140
  Ruth, 140
ALLGIRE, Julian, 104
  Melchor, 104
ALLISON, Mary S., 138
  Thomas L., 138
ALLTOGETHER, 22
ALLTOGETHER TOO LATE, 57, 91
AMES, Joseph, 14
  Leah, 14
ANDERS, Elizabeth, 8

INDEX

ANDERS, Elizabeth, 8
  Henry, 8
ANGEL, Abraham, 26, 31
  Adam, 59
  Barbara, 31
  David, 91
  Eliza, 26
  Ephriam, 26
  Hannah, 59
  John, 26
  Mary, 26, 91
  Michael, 26
  Samuel, 42, 98
  Thomas, 26
ANTRIM, 110
ANXIETY REMOVED, 48
APPLER, Abraham, 54
  Jacob, 38
  Mary, 38
ARABIA PETRIA ENLARGED, 3
ARBAUGH, Margaret, 89
  Mary, 25
  Peter, 25
ARMACOST, Barbary, 41
  Catherine, 104
  Christopher, 104
  Elizabeth, 41, 55
  Ellen, 104
  George, 104
  John, 55
  Joseph, 104
  Julia A., 104
  Lynda, 55
  Mary E., 104
  Melchor, 104, 115
  Michael M, 133
  Susan, 115
  William, 104

ARMSTRONG, Abraham, 53
  Rachel, 53
ARNOLD, Ann, 73
  Anthony, 60
  Barbara, 37, 46
  Basil, 60
  Caleb, 37, 60
  Catherine, 37
  Charles, 60
  Charles W., 60
  Henry, 60
  James, 37, 60
  John, 37, 46, 60
  John Thomas, 123
  Joseph, 1, 60, 73
  Margaret, 1, 60, 123
  Mary, 1, 37
  Prudence, 60
  Sarah, 60
  Susanna, 1
  Susannah, 60
ARNOLD'S ARBOUR ENLARGED, 135
ARNOLD'S CHANCE, 136
ARNOLD'S DESIRE, 72, 137
ARNOLD'S DESIRE RESURVEY, 72
ARTER, Edwin A., 76
  Magdalena, 20
  Philip, 20
ARTHER, Elizabeth, 69
  Joseph, 69
ASHBURNERS DISAPPOINTMENT, 32
ASPEN HILL, 89, 119
AULD, James, 34
  Mary, 34
AUSDING, Ferdinand, 48

  Mary, 48

-B-

BABYLON, Andrew, 101
  Caroline, 101
  Catherine, 101
  Emanuel, 101
  Jacob, 85
  Jeremiah, 89
  John, 101
  Margaret, 89
  Rachel, 101
  Rachel A., 101
  Samuel, 101
  Sarah, 101
  Sarah L., 101
  Uriah J., 101
BACHELOR'S PROSPECT, 112
BACHELORS REFUGE, 72, 121, 133
BACHMAN, Catherine, 119
  David, 58, 119
  Henry, 1
  Mary, 1
  William, 48
BAGDAD, 41
BAIGHTEL, Emmet, 30
  Isaiah, 30
  Jonas, 30
  Mary Ann, 30
  Noah, 30
  Samuel, 30
  Uriah, 30
BAIL, Ludwick, 52
  Peter, 52
BAILE, Abraham, 29
  Alice, 127
  Catharine, 124
  Charles P., 127

INDEX

David, 29, 56
Eliza, 115
Isaac C., 77, 115
John, 22, 29
Ludwick, 29
Margaret, 124
Mary, 20
Mary A., 29
Michael, 20, 29
Nathan K., 115
Peter, 29, 56, 124
Peter W., 56
Reuben, 29
Sarah V., 115
Sophia, 29
Susan, 56
Susanna, 29, 102
William, 29
BAILEY, Catharine, 11
Daniel, 11
BAIR, Andrew, 132
Catherine, 132
Eliza, 132
George, 132
Jesse, 132
Mary A., 132
BAKER, Ann Rebecca, 86
Barbara E., 101
Jacob, 32
Levi, 86
Meshak, 71
Salomi, 71
Samuel, 101
Susannah, 32
BAKER'S DISCOVERY, 59, 132
BALY, James, 123
Mary Ann, 123
BANGUE, Elizabeth, 11
George, 11

BANK OF WESTMINSTER, The, 24, 58, 68, 80
BANKER, Abdiel, 31
David, 31
Elizabeth, 31
Ephraim L., 31
Lydia, 31
Peter, Jr., 31
Peter, Sr., 31
Sabilla, 31
William, 31
BANKERT, Abraham, 62, 63, 80
Christina, 79
Henry, 78, 79
James, 78, 79
John of Jacob, 79
John Peter, 63
Rebecca, 80
Sarah, 79
Susan, 63
BANKERT'S AMENDMENT, 95, 106, 116
BANK'S FOLLY, 65
BANSEMER, Augustus, 92
Elizabeth, 92
Susan, 92
William G., 92
BARBADOES, 84, 127
BARBOUR, Amelia, 14
James, 14
BARE, Daniel, 27
David, 27
Elizabeth, 27
Lydia, 27
Maria, 27
Samuel, 27
Susanna, 27
BARKLEY, Frederick, 9
Rachel, 9

BARNES, Alfred, 16, 18, 28
Ann, 69
Anna, 15
Aquilla G., 41
Archibald, 28
Arey, 28
Belinda, 12, 24, 57
Cordelia, 69
Eliza J. E., 113
Elizabeth, 16, 18, 109
Elizabeth Ann, 18
Elizabeth Dorsey, 118
Ellen, 81
Esther Ann, 41
Eurith, 41
Francis, 57
George, 57
George H., 69
Ira Nathaniel, 119
James, 17
James A., 15
James H., 54
Jehu, 57
John, 57
John T., 113
Joseph D., 118
Joshua, 54, 109
Joshua Tevis, 109
Julia Ann Rebecca, 41
Keziah, 55
Mary Ann, 17
Mary Hall, 57
Miranda, 118
Moses, 55
Nathaniel, 119
Providence, 2
Robert E., 119
Sally Elizabeth, 28
Sarah A., 119
Silas, 57
Solomon, 2, 109
Thomas, 28, 54, 118

INDEX

Violette E., 28
Washington, 81
Wesley F., 119
William, 12, 24, 69, 109
BARNES LEVEL RESURVEYED, 75
BARNHART, Ann Rebecca, 46, 71
Elizabeth, 47
Sarah, 22
William, 47
BARRICK, Elizabeth, 34
John, 34
BARTHOLOW, Cornelia, 30
Hanson F., 35
Hanson T., 30, 82
Margaret A. R., 35
Rebecca, 35
Thomas, 30, 35
BATCHELOR'S PROSPECT, 11, 43
BATCHELOR'S REFUGE, 54, 77
BATCHELOR'S REFUGE RESURVEYED, 36
BATSON, Daniel, 9
George, 101
Mary, 101
BAUBLITS, Catherine, 16
Ephraim, 16
Henry, 16
Jacob, 16
Michael, 16
Rachel, 16
Samuel, 16
BAUBLITZ, John J., 103
BAUGHER, Alexius, 80
Joseph, 80

BAUM, Catherine, 62, 67
George, 62, 67
BAUMGARDNER, Barbara, 21
Francis J., 60
Helen, 60
John F., 60
Lenah, 21
Margaret, 21
Mary L., 60
Samuel, 21
BAUMGARTNER, Caroline, 120
Catherine, 120
Eliza, 112
Elizabeth, 121
Francis A., 120
Francis J., 120
Harriet A., 121
John, 120
John J., 120, 121, 126, 129, 136
Margaret, 120, 121
Margaret H., 120
Margaret O., 121
Mary L., 120
Samuel, 112
William H., 120
BAUSEMER, Elizabeth, 72
William G., 72
BAUST, Cornelius, 31
Elizabeth, 74
Isabelle, 75
John, 74
Joseph, 74
Mary Jane, 75
Samuel, 75
Sarah, 75
Sidney, 74
Valentine, 74
William, 74

BEALL'S DELIGHT, 129
BEAN, Ezra, 54
George, 54
Joseph, 54
Margaret, 54
Samuel, 54
Savilla, 54
Tabitha, 54
BEASMAN'S DISCOVERY CORRECTED, 96
BEAVER, Margaret A., 127, 139
William J., 127, 139
BEAVER HALL, 135
BEAVER TRAP, 99
BECHTEL, Samuel, 30
BECKER, Abdiel W., 128
Abdol, 113
Edmond, 113
Elizabeth, 113
Ephraim, 113
Ephraim W., 128
George, 113
Jeremiah, 113
John, 113
Michael, 113
BECRAFT, Benjamin, 69
James, 69
John, 69
Louisa, 69
Nancy, 69
Peter, 69
BEDFORD, 28, 32, 46, 57, 83, 91, 123
BEECHER, Anna Mary Elizabeth, 105
Elias, 105
Eve, 105
Henry, 111
Juliann, 111, 112

INDEX

Levi, 105
Matilda, 112
Noah, 105
William, 111
William Henry, 105
William V., 112
BEGGS, Catherine, 118
  Richard, 118
BEIGHTEL, Henry, 89
  Mandilla, 88
BEIKER, John, 133
BELL'S RECOVERY, 20, 135
BELLS VENTURE, 17
BELT, Isaac, 138
  Leonard, 138
  Rhoda, 138
BELTS, Basil Henry, 130
  Franklin A., 130
  Henry Thomas, 130
  Julianna, 130
  Mary D., 130
  Samuel C., 130
  Thomas J., 130
  Thomas Jefferson, 130
BELTZ, Henry E., 21, 128
BEMILLER, John, 133
  Lucinda, 133
  Peter, 133
BENJAMIN'S CLAIM, 137
BENNER, Daniel, 69
BENNETT, Adaline, 35
  Arabella, 65
  Asberry F., 87
  Benjamin, 35, 65, 77, 87
  Benjamin W., 87
  Catherine, 77, 82
  Catherine A., 27
  Charles W., 65

Charles W., Jr., 65
Edward L., 87
Eli, 77
Eli R., 77
Eli T., 35
Elisha, 65, 77
Elizabeth, 65
Elmira DeMerville, 87
Eurith Ann, 65
Harriet, 77
Henry C., 137
Henry M., 65
Jesse, 65
Jesse L., 77
John W., 87
Joshua, 77
Larkin, 35
Larkin Samuel, 35
Levi T., 35, 77, 137
Maria, 65
Mary, 18
Mary A., 87
Mary Ann, 65
Mary E., 35
Mary M., 136, 137
Mary Wilson, 18
Nimrod T., 137
Perry, 65
Polly, 35
Rachel, 77
Ruth E., 35
Samuel, 18, 77
Samuel M., 77
Thomas, 77
Virginia E., 137
Wesley, 65
BENNETTS CHANCE, 64
BENNETTS PARK, 64
BEN'S FANCY, 72
BENSON, Elijah, 49
  James, 55
  Margaret, 49, 73

Reuben, 73
Susannah, 55
BENTZ, John, 121, 132
BENZEL, Ann Mary, 19
  Catharine, 19
  David, 19
  Elizabeth, 19
  Emeline, 19
  Ephraim, 19
  Jacob, 19
  John, 19
  William, 19
BENZER, John, 20
  Matilda, 20
  Susanah, 20
BEST, David, 60
  George, 60
  Jacob, 60
  John, 60
BETHEL, 43, 77, 98
BETTER KNOWN, 126
BEVARD, Christiana, 51, 115
  William, 115
BEVARDE, Christian, 86
BIDEN, Ann, 37
  John, 37
BIEHL, David C., 126
  Edgar S., 126
  Elliatta, 126
  Francis M., 126
  George A., 126
  George F., 126
  Lewis M., 126
  Mary L., 126
BIGGOTH, Judah, 6
BIGHAM, Joseph, 20
  Lydia, 20
BILLMYER, Daniel, 64
  Emily, 64
BIRELY, David, 107

Elizabeth, 22, 107
Francis Thomas, 107
Jacob, 107
Lewis, 107
Mary Catharine, 107
Sarah Ellen, 107
Thomas, 22
William, 107
BISH, Catherine, 89
  Jacob, 63, 89
  Michael, 62
  Susan, 62
BISHOP, Catherine, 67
  Elizabeth, 60
  Jacob, 60
  John, 60
  Philip, 67
  Rachel, 60
BITE HIM SOFTLY, 4, 19
BITE THE BITER, 25, 124
BIXLER, Barbara, 11, 122
  Benjamin, 62
  Catherine, 88
  Daniel, 122
  Elias, 81
  Elizabeth, 11
  Ellen, 74
  George, 74
  Henry, 74
  Jacob, 10, 11, 62, 74
  Jacob, Sr., 11
  Jesse, 74, 88
  John, 10, 11
  Lydia, 74
  Mary, 62, 74
  Mary A., 81
  Nancy, 62
  Peter, 122
  Priscilla, 122
BLACK, Adam, 43

Catherine, 21
Frederick, 43
John, 43
Joseph, 43
Magdalena, 43
Rebecca, 43
Ulrick, 43
BLACK FLINT, 108
BLANKERT, Catherine, 70
  Joseph, 70
BLENHEIM, 87, 130
BLINDFOLD, 4
BLIZZARD, Ann Rebecca, 84
  Belinda Virginia, 84
  Catherine Ellen, 84
  Elias, 102
  Elias Nelson, 102
  George, 102
  Hiram C., 102
  Hyanthe, 102
  John, 102
  John Lewis, 84
  Martha E., 102
  Ruth E., 102
  Samuel, 84
  Samuel H., 102
  Sarah E., 139
  William H., 102
BLOOM, David, 89
  George W., 89
  Isaac, 89
  Jacob, 89
  Josiah, 89
  Martha Jane, 89
  Mary, 89
  Mary C., 89
  Philip H., 89
  Wesley, 89
  William H., 89

BLOOMING PLAINS RESURVEYED, The, 109
BOLLINGER, Daniel, 25
BOND, Ann E., 3
  Benjamin, 3
  Cornelius, 52
  Thomsey, 52
BOND'S ENLARGEMENT, 135
BOND'S FORREST, 123, 140
BOND'S MEADOW ENLARGED, 10, 18, 24, 59, 70, 134, 136, 137
BONSACK, Daniel, 83
  Susanna, 83
BOOT, 22
BOREING, Elizabeth, 55
  Rachel, 55
BORING, Caroline, 68
  Ezekiel, 48, 80
  Jacob W., 68, 80
BORNS, Amos, 53
  Calvin J., 53
  Charles S., 53
  Daniel, 53
  David, 53
  Edmond, 53
  Elizabeth, 53
  Emanuel, 53
  George, 53
  Jacob, 53
  John, 53
  Lydia, 53
  Margaret, 53
  Mary, 53
  Mary A., 53
  Simon P., 53
  Sophia, 53

INDEX

BOSLEY, Ann, 7
David, 88
Edward W., 88
James, 90
John W., 88
Joshua, 7, 88, 128
Joshua W., 88
Mary Ann, 88
Mary J., 88
Ruth A., 88
BOWERS, Jacob, 111
Joel, 86
Lydia Levinia, 86
William Ellsworth, 86
BOWER'S CHANCE, 96
BOWERSOX,
Absalom, 88, 89, 95, 97
Absalom H., 97, 136, 137
Catherine, 89, 95, 97
Daniel, 27, 88
Elizabeth, 89, 95, 97
Ezekiah D., 88, 95, 97
George A. W., 89
Isabella, 89, 95, 97
Jeremiah, 88, 89, 95, 97
Jeremiah D., 137
Jeremiah R., 89, 95, 97
John T., 89
John Thomas, 97
Margaret Ann, 113
Mary, 27, 88, 89
Susan, 88
BOWMAN, George, 11
John, 25
Magdalena, 11
Mary Ann, 10, 11
BOWSER, Andrew L., 105
Charlotte, 105
Joseph, 105, 113

Solomon, 105
BOYERS, David, 44
Elizabeth, 44
Henry, 44
John, 44
Margaret, 44
Peter, 44
Susan, 44
BOYLES, Eliza, 52
James, 52
BRAMWELL,
Amanda, 34
George, 34
BRANCH ENLARGED, The, 32
BRANDENBURG, William, 54
BRASHEARS, John, 74
Susan Ann, 74
BRENGLE, Catherine, 32, 36
Eliza, 33, 36
Elizabeth, 32, 36
Lawrence, 36
Lawrence T., 33
Olivia, 32, 36
BRICK MILLS, 26
BRILHART,
Catherine, 113
Isaac, 113
BRISON, Andrew, 105, 106
Mary, 106
BROAD MEADOW, 1
BROMWELL, Joseph, 94
BROOK'S DISCOVERY ON THE RICH LAND, 39, 43
BROOK'S NEW ADVENTURE, 123, 127

BROTHERS,
Benjamin, 2
Elias, 2, 11
Elizabeth, 3, 11, 12
Francis, 2
Joshua, 2, 3, 12
Nancy, 3
Rebecca, 3
Thomas, 3
William, 3
BROTHER'S AGREEMENT, 4, 28
BROTHER'S DISCOVERY, 41
BROTHER'S INHERITANCE, 38, 56
BROWN, Andrew J., 24, 61
Andrew Jackson, 12
Ann Virginia, 8
Ann W., 8
Barney, 34
Basil Perry, 8
Belinda, 122, 123
Benjamin F., 8
Bethsheba, 87
Catherine, 100
Charity, 12, 24
Charles W., 24
Charles Westley, 12
Charlotte, 4
Darius, 48
David, 2
Davious, 2
Elias, 100
Elijah, 16
Elizabeth, 24, 38, 48
Ellen M., 123
Ephraim, 15, 16
Ezra Jacob, 48
George, 12, 24, 77
George W., 29

INDEX

Hannah, 31
Henry, 16, 48
Hester Ann, 4
Honor, 77
Jacob, 94
James, 16
Jamima E., 8
Jane, 16
Jesse, 77
Joel, 4
John, 2
Joshua, 122, 123
Lloyd, 77
Lucinda R. I., 8
Lydia, 28
Magdalena, 94
Margaret, 4, 77
Martha Ann, 58
Mary, 34, 94, 102
Mary Ann, 8, 118
Mary E., 123
Miles A., 60
N.A., 87
Nelson, 12, 24
Nicholas H., 24
Nicholas Hall, 12
Peter, 118
Peter, Jr., 31
Rachel, 4
Rebecca M. W., 8
Rezin, 20, 77
Richard, 30
Ruth, 12, 24
Susan, 12, 30
Susanna D., 8
Susannah, 2
Thomas C., 8
Thomas S., 123
William, 2, 8
William A. T., 8
William H., 58
William S., 24, 123

William Stansbury, 12
BROWN'S CONTRIVANCE, 108
BROWN'S FIRST ATTEMPT, 87
BROWN'S FREE AND INDEPENDENT PROSPECT, 8
BROWN'S LOT, 108
BROWN'S PLAGUE, 12
BROWN'S PLAGUE RESURVEY, 79
BROWN'S RECOVERY, 129
BROWN'S STRUGGLE, 129
BROWN'S VEXATION, 72
BRUCE, Ann Elizabeth, 107
  Isaac, 107
  Isaac E. M., 107
  Susan L., 107
BRUMMEL, Catherine, 135
  Joseph, 135
BRUNGART, Barbara, 11
  George, 11
  Jacob, 11
  John, 11
  Mary, 11
BRUNICORD, John, 11
BUCHANAN, Jane, 18
  John, 18
BUCHEN, David, 55
  Elizabeth, 55
  George, 55
  John, 55
  John Z., 55
  Rachel, 55

  William, 55
BUCHER, Adam, 76
  Elizabeth, 76
BUCK, Elizabeth, 114, 117
  Solomon, 114, 117
BUCK BOTTOM, 116
BUCK FOREST, 71
BUCK LODGE, 23
BUCKEN, Henry Z., 22
  Sarah I., 22
BUCKINGHAM, Amelia, 16
  Beal, 16
  Benjamin, 17, 35
  Benjamin W., 17, 69, 80
  Caroline, 118
  Caroline E., 80
  Eleanor E., 27
  Elias, 17
  Elisha, 37
  Elizabeth, 35, 118
  Ephraim, 16, 118
  George E., 66, 118
  George H., 17
  George W., 17
  John, 118
  Laban, 17
  Leonard, 17
  Louisa, 28
  Lucinda, 17
  Maranda, 27
  Margaret Ruth, 17
  Mary, 47, 80, 118
  Mary A., 37
  Mary Jane, 66
  Nancy, 17
  Nancy M., 80
  Nicholas, 17
  Nimrod, 16, 18
  Nora Jane, 17
  Obediah, 17, 27

INDEX

Owen F., 17
Rachel, 16
Rachel E., 16, 18
Richard P., 79
Silas, 17
Thomas B., 80
Thomas V., 27
Westly, 17
William, 69, 80
William B., 17
BUCKINGHAM'S GOOD WILL, 16, 17, 75
BUCKINGHAMS VENTURE, 17
BUCK'S FOREST, 107
BUCK'S PARK, 17, 110
BUCKS RANGE RESURVEYED, 9
BUFFINGTON, Elizabeth, 83
Jacob, 49
John F., 76
William A., 83
BUMMOND, Elisha, 112
Lydia A., 112
BUNKER HILL FORTIFIED, 121
BUNKER'S HILL FORTIFIED, 27
BURDETT, David, 124
Wilton, 124
BURGOON, Aaron, 95
David N., 95
Edith, 95
Francis N., 95
John, 95
John H.F., 135
Mandelia, 135
Sarah, 95
Susannah, 95
William, 95
William N., 95

BURKE, Catherine, 84
John, 84
BURNS, Amoss, 132
Calvin J., 132
Charles, 132
David M.C., 132
Edward, 132
Eleanora, 132
Emanuel, 132
George, 132
Henrietta, 132
John, 132
Marthela, 132
Mary, 132
Mary A., 132
Mollie, 132
Nancy, 132
Sarah E., 132
Simon P., 132
Susan A., 132
BUSE, Catherine, 19
Peter, 19
BUSH, Daniel, 139
BUSHMAN, Andrew, 9
Catherine, 9
Eli, 111
George, 111
Henry, 9, 111
Jacob, 9
John, 9
Magdalena, 9
Margaret, 9
Mary, 9
Molly, 111
BUSSEY, Mary, 103
BYERS, Amanda, 92
Andrew Jackson, 85
Caroline, 27
Catherine, 81
Daniel, 15, 72, 92
David, 29, 75
David H., 27

Elizabeth, 15, 29, 79, 85
Elizabeth C., 27
Elizabeth Jane, 85
Ellen, 72
Ellen C., 92
Ellen R., 85
Ezra David, 85
Francina, 27
Frederick Washington, 85
George M., 27
George S., 92
Helena, 1, 15, 92
Henry, 79
Jacob, 27
John, 79, 85
John A., 1, 15, 72, 92
John F., 15
John Franklin, 72, 92
John G., 27
John Henry, 85
Joseph, 27
Joshua, 27
Margaret, 27, 37
Mary, 79
Michael, 27
Noah, 81
Noah A., 27
Peter, 37, 79
Rachel Ann, 85
Sidney, 75
Susan, 79
Susannah, 15, 72
William G., 15, 72, 92

-C-

CAIN, Rebecca, 47
William, 47
CALEB'S DELIGHT ENLARGED, 4
CALEDONIA, 6, 37, 38, 60, 100, 122, 131

INDEX

CALEDONIA SINCE RESURVEY, 4
California (State), 60, 63, 69, 125
CALTRIDER, Anna M., 94
  Jacob, 94
CALTRIDER'S LOT, 99
CAMBRIDGE, 9
CAMPBELL, Edward, 71
  Jacob, 136
  Margaret, 71
CAMPBELL'S SEARCH, 75
CANOUFF, Catherine, 6
  William, 6
CAN'T YOU BE EASY, 124
CANTON BERN, 124
CAPLE, Susan, 2
  William of William, 2
CARMACK'S CHANCE, 89
CAROLINA, 33
CARPENTER, Hoesa, 111
  Jane E., 111
  Solomon, 111
  Theodore, 111
  William H., 111
CARRICK, George, 132
  Sophia, 132
CARROLL'S RANGE, 70
CARSON, Abarilla, 116
  Caroline, 116
  Elias, 116
  Elizabeth, 116
  George, 116
  Mary E., 116
  Sarah A., 116
  Wesley, 116
CASH, Lewis, 107
  Maggie Ann, 107
CASHMAN, Elizabeth, 31
  John, 31
CASSATT, David, 93
  Sarah, 93
CASSELL, Abagail, 102
  Abraham, 52, 115, 120, 124
  Charles E., 115
  Charles Ellsworth, 120
  David, 120, 124
  Deborah, 124
  Elizabeth, 62, 90, 124
  John, 62
  John T., 90
  Lucinda, 124
  Lydia, 124
  Margaret, 62, 90
  Mary, 62, 90
  Mary J., 115
  Reuben, 62, 90
  Susanna, 124
CASTLE HANNAH, 49
CASTLE RISING, 123
CATEY'S DELIGHT, 61
CAYLOR, Abraham, 68
  Amos, 68
  Joel, 68
  Levi, 46, 68
  Margaret, 46, 68
  Martha Jane, 68
CHAMBERS, Emeline, 130
  Helena, 3
  Mary, 3
  Sarah, 3
CHANCE, 16
CHANCE'S LUCK, 137
CHARLES MISTAKE, 122
CHASES FORREST, 39
CHENOWETH, John B., 52
  John B., 55
  Kiturah, 55
  Sarah, 55
  William, 55
CHESTNUT RIDGE, 35, 95
CHEW, Elizabeth, 14
  Mary Ann, 130
  William H., 14
CHRIST, Charles, 140
  Elizabeth, 67
  Jacob H., 79
  Mary, 140
  Peter, 67
CHRISTOPHER'S LOT, 13
CHRISTOPHER'S LUCK, 58
CIRCLE, Ann, 66
  David, 66
  Lucinda, 66
  Lydia, 66
  Lydia A., 66
  William, 66
CLABAUGH, Anna M., 61
  E. A., 70
  James, 12, 123
  John, 61, 123
  John F., 123
  Lilly, 123
  Margaret, 123
  Monacai, 12
CLARK, Francis, 115
  Margaret J., 115
CLARY, 36, 42
CLASSON, Ann M., 84
  John, 84

INDEX

CLEAR MEADOW, 83
CLEARY'S NEW HOLLAND, 2, 58
CLEMSON, Hanson G., 111
CLIFFS, 42
CLINGAL, Mary Jane, 90
  William, 90
CLINGING, Catharine, 88
CLOVER VALLEY, 72
COALE, Richard, 7
COCKEY, Ann, 103
  Dr. J.F.C., 103
  Elizabeth, 49
  Joshua F., 49
  Joshua T., 82
  Rachel R., 103
  Sally, 103
  Susan G., 103
  Thomas, 103
COLCHESTER, 138
COLE, Elizabeth, 55
  Samuel, 55
COLHOON, Ann Philips, 9
  Benjamin C., 9
  John, 9
  Mary C., 9
COLROSS, 74, 136
COLTRIDER, Daniel, 118
  Elizabeth Ann, 115
  James, 115
  Joshua, 115
  Keziah, 115
  Matilda, 118
  Ruth A. E., 124
  Thomas, 115, 124
COLTRIDER'S LOT, 119
COMMISSIONERS OF PRIMARY SCHOOLS FOR CARROLL COUNTY, The, 63
COMPLICATION CORRECTED, 113
COMYNS, Henry, 67
  Mary, 67
CONAWAY, Amelia, 13, 85, 88
  Amelia P., 13
  Charles, 88
  Charles V., 85
  Charles W., 13, 85
  Columbus H., 85
  Cornelius, 13
  Cornelius H., 85
  Corrilla, 16
  Corrilla Ann, 18
  Hail Columbus, 13
  Hale C., 16, 18
  John, 13, 85
  John C., 85
  John H., 85, 88
  John O., 13
  John W., 13
  Lloyd N., 13, 85
  Louisa C., 13
  Louisa G., 85, 88
  Louisa N, 13
  Lucinda, 85
  Mary J., 85
  Mary Jane, 88
  Reuben, 13, 85, 88
  Reuben N., 85, 88
  Sarah Ann, 13
  Thomas, 27
  William P., 85, 88
CONAWAY'S IMPROVEMENT, 96
CONAWAY'S VENTURE IMPROVED, 96
CONCORD, 71, 117
CONDO, Catharine, 11
  George, 11
CONDON, Arey, 16
  Eliza E., 18
  Ellen, 16
  Levi Z., 16, 18
  Mary Jane, 16, 18
  Prudence A., 18
  Prudence Amelia, 16
  Richard, 16
  Richard U., 16
  Richard W., 16, 18, 54
  Sarah, 124
  Thomas, 16, 18
  Thomas E., 18
CONNAND, George, 10
CONNOR, Hannah L., 6
  James, 6
COOK, Elisha J., 44, 90
  Elizabeth, 29
  Ephraim, 35
  Ruth, 35
COOKSON, Frances, 108
  Frances E., 121
  Joseph, 108
  Levi, 108, 121
  Mary E., 108
  Robert L., 108
COOL SPRING, 72, 79
COPENHAVER, Anna, 31
  Catherine, 15, 31
  Elizabeth, 31
  John, 31
  Mathias, 31
  Rebecca, 31
  Susannah, 31

INDEX

William, 31
CORBAN, Catherine, 5
  William, 5
CORN HILL RESURVEY, 124
CORNELL, Sarah, 15
CORNWALL'S DESIRE, 10
CORNWELL, 30, 44, 61, 115, 120
COSTLY, 24
COUTTER, James, 20, 21
  Polly, 20, 21
COUTZ LOT, 77
COVER, Charles, 121
  Columbus, 121
  David, 14
  Elizabeth, 121
  Ellen, 50
  Ephraim, 50, 121, 135
  Hannah, 14
  Henry, 121
  James B., 121
  John, 121
  John of T., 116
  Josiah J., 119
  Josiah T., 59
  Maria Ann Margaret, 37, 43
  Mary C., 121
  Samuel, 37, 43, 121
  Susan, 59
  Thomas B., 121
  Tobias, 121
COVER'S ADVENTURE, 1
COX, Mary, 55
CRABBS, Andrew J., 83
  Ann, 110
  Catherine, 34
  Charles E., 83
  Frederick, 34, 83, 110
  George, 110, 127
  George W., 83
  John, 110
  John W., 83
  Mary, 110
  Matilda, 83
  Rachel, 83
  Susan, 110, 127
  William, 110
  William J., 83
CRABS, Mary, 31
CRAFT, John B., 69
CRAMER, Andrew, 10
CRAWFORD, Ann, 78
  Eve, 6
  John S., 78
  Robert, 6
  Ruth E., 77
  Sarah, 78
CRAWMER, Christiana Neidig, 19
  Elias, 86
  Helpher, 19
  Henry, 19, 81
  Henry W., 81
  Jacob W., 82
  John W., 82
  Lewis W., 81
  Lucinda, 81, 82
  Lydia, 81
  Philip, 19
  Rebecca, 81
  Sophia N., 19
CREAGER, Elizabeth, 48
  George, 38
  Jonathan P., 48
  Mary, 38
CRESWELL, Cornelia, 88
  James V., 88
CRICHTON, William, 110
CRISE, Elizabeth, 67
CRISTWELL, Cordelia, 85
  James V., 85
CRISWELL, Ann, 37
  Elijah, 37, 45
  George C., 37
  Mary, 45
  William Wagus, 45
CROCKET, James, 12
CROCKETT, James, 45
CROFT, Adam A., 124
  Anna, 47, 124
  Benjamin, 47
  George, 47
  George A., 124
  John, 47
  John, Jr., 47
  Martha, 47
  Mary, 47
  Matilda, 47
  Nancy, 47
CROOKED ROUNDS, The, 83
CROOKS, Alexander W., 100
  Caroline, 99, 100
  Florida, 100
  Henry, 99
  John, 100
  John H., 100
  Mary E., 100
  Nelson M, 100
  Rachel M., 99
  Richard S. T., 100
  Samuel, 99
  Samuel A., 100
  Samuel W., 99
  Sarah, 99
  Sarah E., 100
  Susannah, 99
CROPSEY, Francis J., 14

INDEX

Miranda, 14
CROUSE, Cecelia, 133
  David, 35
  Edwin H., 128
  Elizabeth, 28, 35, 52, 133
  George, 28
  Hannah Olivia Idea, 133
  Jacob, 24
  James, 26, 52, 133
  Jane E., 133
  John T., 133
  Margaret, 133
  Marshall Allen, 133
  Mary, 4
  Olivia, 133
  Rebecca, 133
  Richard, 133
  William H., 133
  William Lee, 133
CROUT, Hezekiah, 22
CROWL, Elias, 77
  Elizabeth, 77
  George, 77
  Henry, 83
  John, 77
  Lavina, 77
  Leah, 77
  Nancy, 83
CROWNOVER, Ellen C., 97
  Samuel, 97
CRUMBACKER, Abraham, 52
  Ann, 89
  Catherine, 39
  David, 52, 89
  Elizabeth, 52, 89, 123
  Ephraim, 52
  Jacob, 52
  Jesse, 52
  John, 52
  Jonas, 52
  Lydia, 89
  Mary, 52
  Nathan, 52, 89, 123
  Peter, 52
  William, 52, 89
CRUMP, John H., 2
  Mary Jane, 2
CRUMRIN, Daniel, 5
  Mary, 5
CRUMRINE, Daniel, 105
  Edwin J., 120
  Laura K., 120
  Lydia, 10, 120
  Mary, 75, 105
  Mary F., 120
  William, 10, 75
  William J., 120
CRYDERS DELIGHT, 137
Connecticut (State), 68
CULLIMORE, David, 20
  Sarah, 20
CULLISON, Lydia, 108
  Rebecca, 104
  Wesley, 104
CUMBERLAND, 84
CUMMINGS, Henry, 62
  Mary, 62
CUNNINGHAM, Mary L., 110
  William A., 110
CURGAFORGUS, 37
CURPOY, 91
CURRANS, Upton, 74
CURRY, Frances, 50
  Francis, 13
  Martha, 13, 50
  Martha G., 13
  Martha Grizelda, 50
  Theodore, 13
  Theodore E., 50
  William, 13
  William R., 117

-D-

DACRES PLAGUE, 135
DAGUE, George, 112
  Harriet, 112
DAIRY, 68
DANIEL'S DENN, 134
DANNER, Adam, 93
  David W., 81
  Elizabeth, 81
  Elizabeth R., 93
  John, 8
  Martin, 10
  Thomsey, 8
DAVIDSON, James, 50
  John, 87
  Julia Ann, 50
  Susannah, 129
  William Asbury, 129
DAVIS, Aaron, 23, 127
  Amelia C., 39
  Ann Marie, 23
  Anna M., 127
  Benjamin, 127, 139
  Catherine Mary, 40
  George, 23
  Hanna A., 40
  Hanna G., 40
  John W., 23, 121, 127
  Jonathan, 23, 127
  Jonathan C., 23
  Joseph, 23, 127
  Mary, 23, 127, 139
  Mary E., 39
  Mary Jane, 23, 121
  Rachel, 40
  Samuel, 40

INDEX

Samuel G., 40
Silas W., 39
Susan J., 39
Thomas, 39
Thomas of Zachariah, 39
William, 23, 127
DAYHOFF, Ann, 53
Elias, 53, 73
Hannah, 73
Jacob, 53
James A., 73
John T., 73
Joseph, 53
Josiah, 73
Margaret A., 73
Polly, 53
Susan, 53
William H., 73
DE, New Castle, 10
DEAL, Catherine, 25
David P., 25
John, 25
Jonas, 15, 25
Rachel, 25
DEALEYS DELIGHT, 22
DEAMUTH, Barbara, 59
David, 59
DEAN'S COMFORT, 51, 85, 93
DEAR BOUGHT, 69
DEARHOFF, Anna Mary, 19
Henry, 19
DEAVER'S FORREST, 8
DEEP VALLEY RESURVEYED, 51
DEHOOF'S PLEASURE, 39, 86
DELAPLANE, Cornelia R., 70

DELL, Harriet, 109
Henry, 2
Jerome, 109
John, 109
John K., 108, 109
Martha, 109
Mathilda, 109
Rufus M., 129
Sarah, 2
DEMMITT, Henry, 59
James, 59
Nelly, 59
William, 59
DEMOSS, Eurith, 109
Jane, 109
Jehu, 109
John, 109
Lewis D., 109
Nimrod, 109
Thomas, 109
DERN, Ann E., 114
Eliza, 114
Elizabeth, 114
Frederick, 114
George, 114
Isaac, 84, 114
Jane, 114
Sophia, 114
Washington, 114
William, 114
DERR, Amanda J., 103
George W., 103
Jacob F., 103
John, 103
Mary, 43, 103
Noah, 103
Samuel, 103
William, 103
DEVILBISS, Adam A., 96
Ann Maria, 96
Frederick A., 68
Levi, 27, 52

Margaret, 68
DEWEES, Andrew, 21
DEYES ADVENTURE, 132
DEYES CHANCES RESURVEYED, 128
DEY'S ADVENTURE, 28, 105, 120
DICKENSHEETS, David, 134
Frederick, 134
John, 134
Rachel, 134
DIEHL, Allie, 130
Hann, 130
DIFFENBAUGH, John H., 83
DIFFENDALL, Margaret, 46
Samuel, 46
DISAPPOINTMENT, 14, 47
DIXON, Doratha, 81
Haines, 81
DODDERER, Elizabeth, 134
Henry, 134
DODS, George, 78
Margaret, 78
DODSON'S TENT, 28
DORSEY, Benjamin, 41
Catherine, 41
Eliza O., 23
Fanny, 94
Ferdinand, 23
Hannah E., 41
Isabella H., 41
Joshua, 41
Nicholas, 73
Rachel, 41
Samuel T., 41
Susan J., 41

INDEX

DORSEY'S CLAIM, 20
DORSEY'S DELAMA, 44, 109
DORSEY'S INDUSTRY, 13, 18, 20, 85, 88
DORSEY'S INTEREST, 33
DORSEY'S MILL FROGG, 84, 87
DORSEY'S NEGLECT, 33
DORSEY'S PROSPECT, 133
DORSEY'S THICKET, 41
DORSEY'S THICKET RESURVEYED, 118
DOTTERER, Conrad, 47
  Emma C., 71
  Hezekiah, 46, 47
  John, 47
  John W., 47, 71
  Joshua, 47
  Josiah, 47
  Juliann, 71
  Lemuel H., 71
  Mary, 47
  Mary J., 71
  William H., 47
DOUGHTERTY, John, 26
DRACH, Daniel L., 57
  Elizabeth, 57
  Hanson M, 57
  Henry, 57, 64, 128, 129
  Henry L., 57
  John P., 57
  Mary L., 57
  Peter E., 57
  Rachel, 129
  Rachel S., 64
  Winfield S., 57

DRESSLER, Anna Mary, 39
  George, 39
  John, 39
  Mary Magdelina, 39
DRY LODGING, 75
DUDERER, Andrew, 27
  Conrad, 27
  George, 27
  Henry, 27
  John, 27
DUNBLANE, 72
DUNN, Rebecca, 18
  William, 18
DURBIN, Anna, 5
  Benjamin, 1
  Catherine, 1
  Comfort, 1
  Daniel, 5
  John, 87
  Margaret, 1
  Mary Ann, 87
  Susannah, 1
DURBIN'S MISTAKE, 31, 51, 76
DUTTERER, John, 27
DUTTEROW, John, 47
DUVALL, Ann Rebecca, 131
  Benjamin, 69
  Charles T., 132
  Edward H., 131
  Emma, 103
  Francis L., 131
  John F., 131
  Kate, 132
  Mary E., 131
  Sarah, 69
  Scott Elsworth, 132
  William C., 131
  William T., 131

  Zero E., 131
DYER'S MILL FOREST, 27, 96, 112

-E-

EARHART, Daniel, 32
  David B., 23, 62
  Edward, 32
  Horatio, 32
  J. William, 97
  Martha E., 32
  Mary, 32
  Priscilla R., 32
EASENBURG, 128
EASTERN BRANCH RESURVEYED, 23
EBAUGH, Adam, 38
  Amos, 38
  Andrew, 38
  Benjamin, 38
  Catherine, 48
  Conrad, 38, 48
  David, 38
  Elias K., 38
  Elisha, 38
  Elizabeth, 38, 104
  Emanuel, 48
  George, 38
  Henry, 38
  Jacob, 38
  Jerome, 48
  Jesse, 38, 116
  John, 104
  John K., 38
  Joseph, 15, 38, 55
  Matilda, 47
  Rachel, 48, 116
  Sabina, 48
  William, 38, 122
EBAUGH'S DISCOVERY, 124
ECK, Ann Rebecca, 72

INDEX

Barbara, 48
Barbary, 72
Harriet E., 72
Henry T., 72
John P., 48
Joseph, 72
Joseph A., 72
Lewis, 48
Mary, 48
Samuel T., 72
William, 48
William J., 72
ECKARD, George, 32
  Henry, 32
  Jacob, 32
  Jesse, 32
  Mary, 32
  Rebecca, 32
  Sarah Ann, 32
  Susanna Jane, 32
  Thomas, 32
  William, 32
ECKER, Albert, 66
  David, 39, 107
  Deborah, 39
  Elizabeth A., 66
  Ellsworth, 66
  Eugene, 113
  Frances, 127
  Hannah, 39, 59
  Harrison, 39
  Hettie A., 91
  Jacob, 39
  James M., 113
  John, 39, 59
  Jonas, 39, 64, 127
  Martha E., 66
  Mary, 59, 107
  Mary A., 113
  Mary Catherine, 39
  Peter, 39
  Rachel L., 66
  Samuel, 39, 66
  Sarah, 39
  Solomon S., 66, 91
  Susannah, 66
  William, 39, 59, 113
ECKERT, Levi, 112
EDINBURGH, 4, 6, 17, 100
EDWARDS, Catherine, 87
  Moses, 87
EGE, Andrew G., 110
EIGHT SISTERS, 44, 111
ELDER, Ann, 12
  Catherine, 12
  Eleanora, 12
  Elizabeth, 12
  Francis, 12
  Henry, 12
  Hilary, 12
  Lucy Ann, 12
  Margaret, 12
  Mary Ann, 12
  Susan, 12
ELINE, Helen, 60
ELIZABETH'S FANCY, 24, 123
ELLIS, Catherine, 53
  John, 53
ELLIS FOLLY, 122
ELSON, Joseph, 54
  Lelitia, 54
EMPTY CUPBOARD, 36
ENGEL, Abraham, 59
  Ann Maria, 59
  Daniel, 59, 113
  David, 59, 87
  David of P., 63
  Ephraim P., 139
  John, 59
  John R., 139
  Peter, 59, 78
  Samuel, 139
  Theresa Ann, 113
ENGLAND, Orrel, 61
ENGLAR, Alice S., 136
  Daniel H., 136
  David, 18
  Elizabeth, 136
  Ella L., 136
  Ezra S., 136
  Hannah, 52
  Ida H., 136
  John, 136
  John L., 136
  Joseph of David, 4
  Louisa, 18, 102
  Mary J., 115
  Philip, 52
  Susanna, 113
  Uriah, 113
  William M., 115, 136
ENGLE, Daniel, 27, 36, 38, 126
  David, 125, 139
  David of P., 133
  Ephraim P., 125
  Hetty, 125, 139
  Jesse C., 125
  John, 125
  John D., 125, 139
  John R., 125
  Mary, 124
  Mary A., 125, 139
  Michael, 26
  Nancy, 125, 139
  Samuel, 125
ENGLEMAN, Elizabeth, 30
  Emaline, 30
  Harriett, 30
  John, Jr., 30
  Julia Ann, 30
  Julian, 30

INDEX

Mary, 30
Palmer, 30
Varden, 30
William H., 30
ENSEY, Mary Jane, 63
　Richard L., 63
EPING FOREST, 115
EPPINGTON FOREST, 16, 28, 80, 119, 135
ERB, Abraham, 3
　Abraham E., 112
　Eli, 3
　Elizabeth, 112
　Jacob, 3, 112
　John, 112
　Levi, 3
　Mary, 112
　Mary G., 112
　Peter, 3, 112
　Peter, Jr., 3
ERBAUGH, Conrad, 13
　Elizabeth, 13
　George, 13
　Henry, 13
　Jacob, 13
　John, 13
　Margaret, 13
　Peter, 13
　William, 13
ERB'S PLEASURE, 96
ERROR'S CORRECTED, 75
ESCAPE, 14
ETZLER'S CONTENTMENT, 43
EVANS, David, 15
　John, 73
　Joseph, 73
　Joshua, 15
　Kinzy, 119
　Levi, 18, 73

Lewis, 73
Lucinda A., 119
Samuel, 19
Susannah, 73
William, 73
EVANS SEARCH, 20
EVAN'S VENTURE, 59
EVERET PROGRESS, 69
EVERHART, George, 28, 29
　George, Jr., 25
EVERLY, Alice A., 117
　Ann, 52
　David, 49, 54, 59
　Elizabeth, 49, 54, 59
　John L., 52
　Joseph, 117
　Levi D., 117
　Mary, 117
EVERYBODY'S LAND, 35, 114
EVERYTHING NEEDFUL, 1, 130
EVERYTHING NEEDFUL CORRECTED, 1, 7, 11, 21, 29, 45, 80, 107, 120, 128, 130, 132
EWING, William, 18
EXCHANGE, (The) 29, 97, 139
EYLER, Ann S., 89
　Samuel, 89

-F-

FACE, Elizabeth, 20
　Frederick, 20
FAIRVIEW, 64
FANNY'S MEADOW, 2, 12, 14, 16, 22, 62, 90, 103

FARMERS AND MECHANICS BANK OF CARROLL COUNTY, The, 66
FARMERS AND MECHANICS NATIONAL BANK OF WESTMINSTER, The, 132
FARMERS MECHANICS BANK OF CARROLL COUNTY, The, 104
FARQUHAR, George A., 46
　John H., 46
　Mary, 46
　William L., 46
FATHER'S ADVICE, 44, 69
FATHER'S CHOICE, 22
FAVOR AND EASE, 72, 124
FEESER, Adam W., 42
　Catherine, 73, 111, 112
　Catherine Susan, 42
　Eliza A., 42
　George W., 73, 112
　Jacob, 111
　John, 42
　Mary E., 42
　Sarah A., 42
　Susan, 42
FEISER, Sarah Ann, 54
　Susan, 49
　Susannah, 54
FELL'S RETIREMENT, 56
FETTERLING, Catherine, 114
FIESER, Adam, 116
　David, 116

INDEX

David H., 116
Eliza, 116
Elizabeth, 116
Ellen J., 116
Jacob, 116
John, 116
John Jacob, 116
Mandella, 116
Margaret, 116
Rebecca, 116
Samuel, 116
Sevilla, 116
FINCH, Matilda, 77
FINE SOIL FORREST, 8
FINGAL AND OSSIAN, 124
FINK, Adam, 21
Catherine, 21
Elizabeth, 21
Samuel, 21
Sarah, 11, 21
Solomon, 11
FIREFROCK, Andrew, 19
Barbara N., 19
FIRST TRAPEZINM, The, 43
FISHBURN, Lydia, 62
FISHER, Barbara, 125
Catharine, 125
Daniel Lewis, 125
David, 125
Elizabeth, 11
George, 11
Hugh, 124
Jacob, 6, 19
Jeremiah, 80
John, 17, 24
Magdalena, 6
Mary, 124
Sophia, 6
Thomas, 6
William F., 124
Wilton, 124
FISHER'S ADDITION TO WESTMINSTER, 122
FITEZ, Andrew, 38
Mary, 38
FITZE, Amos, 118
Elizabeth, 118
Elizabeth C., 118
Ellen M., 118
George, 118
Jacob, 118
Joseph, 118
Mary Ann, 118
Mary J., 118
Samuel, 118
Susannah R., 118
FIVE DAUGHTERS, 66, 76, 108, 128
FLAGG'S MEADOW, 4, 21, 41
FLATER, Elisha, 140
Francis H., 140
Hesekiah, 140
Jacob, 140
John, 140
John Nathaniel, 140
John W., 140
Mary, 140
Sarah, 140
Sophia, 140
FLEAGLE, Ann Elizabeth, 48
Elijah, 48, 129
Julia A., 129
Mary Jane, 48
FLEGEL, Magdalena, 54
Samuel, 54
FLEMMING, Elizabeth A., 39
Otho, 39
FLETCHER, James, 106
Julia A., 106
FLETTER, Jacob, 24
Ruth, 24
FLICKINGER, Catharine, 134
Deborah, 127
Frederick, 127
John, 134
Maria, 112
Mary A., 112
Thomas, 112
William, 112
FOGG, Charles H., 103
Susan L., 103
FOGLE, David, 95
Elizabeth, 38
Hiram, 38
John, 95
Joseph, 95
Mary Alice, 95
Michael, 95
FOGLESON'S HOTT, 79
FONCANMER, Hannah, 125
Jackson, 125
FORD, Adazillah, 17
Adedzelah, 17
Isaac, 17
FOREMAN, Absalom, 51
Absolom, 49
Henry, 62, 67
John, 11
Rachel, 11
Sarah, 51, 62, 67
Sarah Jane, 49, 54
Susannah, 62
FOREST LEVEL, 9
FORESTER, John, 114
Margaret Ann, 114

INDEX

FORMWALT, John, 2
FORREST'S VENTURE, 33
FORT ROYAL, 37
FOSTER'S HUNTING GROUND, 53, 98
FOSTER'S PLEASANT MEADOWS, 115
FOUTZ, David, 27
FOWBLE, Andrew, 55
  Anna, 96
  Catherine, 87
  Charlotte, 55
  Elizabeth, 55
  Francis, 104
  Frederick, 96
  Jacob, 48
  John, 49
  John of Jacob, 10
  John T., 55
  Joshua, 49
  Julian, 104
  Kenney, 49
  M. Julian, 33
  Maria, 55
  Melchor, 48, 49
  Melchour, 48
  Peter, 49
  Richard, 49, 55
  Ruth, 55
  Sabina, 48
  Stephen M., 55
  Thomas, 33
  William, 87
FOWBLE'S BARREN HILLS, 101
FOWBLE'S LOT, 23
FOWLER, Benjamin, 1, 24
  Catherine, 24
  Edward, 1
  Ellenor, 1
  Rachel, 60
  Rebecca, 1
FOX RANGE, 57
FOXES DENN, 47, 130
FOXES FOREST, 87
FRANK, George K., 116
  Jacob K., 116
  John, 88
  Violet, 88
FRANKFORT, 122
FRANKFORTER, Anna M., 68
  Conrad, 68
  Daniel, 68
  David C., 68
  Elizabeth, 68
  Frederick, 121
  Jacob, 21, 29, 41
  Lavina, 68
  Louisa, 121
  Regina, 68
  Sarah, 29
FRANKLIN, Amaretta, 15
  Charles, 15
  Charles Washington, 15
  Cordelia, 16
  Eliza, 15
  Elizabeth, 15
  Helen M. E. V., 15
  James, 15
  Jesse W., 26
  John, 15, 26
  Joshua, 15, 26
  Mary Virginia, 26
  Resin, 15
  Rezin, 26
  Sarah Ann, 26
  Thomas, 16
FRAZIER, Daniel, 139
  Prudence Ann, 139
FREDERICK TOWN SAVINGS INSTITUTION, 2
FREDERICKSBURG, 70
FREDERICKSBURGH, 43
FREEZE, Alfred, 50
  Jefferson, 50
  Mary, 50
  Mary Ann, 50
FRENCHMAN'S PURCHASE, 56, 120
FRIENDSHIP, 53, 108
FRIENDSHIP COMPLETED, 5, 61, 86, 93, 122, 127
FRIER, Elizabeth, 70
  Philip, 70
FRIERMOND, Elizabeth, 63
  William, 63
FRINGER, Alice, 26, 40
  Caroline V., 114
  Elmira, 40
  Emily J. C., 114
  Ephraim, 26, 40
  George, 26, 40, 43, 114
  George N., 114
  Harman, 40
  Henry L., 106
  Jacob, 26, 40, 114
  Margaret, 40
  Michael, 26, 40
  Nicholas, 26, 40
  Sarah, 114
  Susan, 26
  Susannah, 43
  Theodore, 40
  Washington, 26
  Winfield K., 114
  Worthington, 40

INDEX

FRITCHEY, Theo. L., 129
  Theodore L., 134, 139
FRIZELL, Ann, 50
  Hannah E., 50
  John C., 50
  Nimrod, 50
  William, 50
FRIZZEL, Anne, 62
  William, 62
FRIZZELL, Ann, 90
  William, 90
FRIZZLE, Catharine, 29
  William, 29
FROCK, Catherine, 37
  Elizabeth, 37, 42
  Isaah, 42
  Jacob, 42
  John, 42
  Mary, 42
  Michael, Jr., 37
  Peter, 37
  Sarah, 42
FROGG'S FOREST, 86
FRONTFELTER, Henry, 69
  John, 69
  Mary, 69
  Rachel, 69
  Sarah, 69
FROUNFELTER, Catherine, 61
  David, 61
FROWNFELTER, John, 98
  Mary E., 98
FUHRMAN, Amelia, 99
  Catherine, 99
  Conrad, 99
  Eli, 99
  Elizabeth, 99
  Frederick, 11

George, 99
Henry, 99
John, 99
Lewis, 99
Malinda, 99
Polly, 99
Rachel, 99
Rebecca, 99
Salonous, 99
Sarah, 11
Urias, 99
FULLER, Angelico, 17
  Ann Rebecca, 17
  Azariah, 17
  Emily, 17
  Leander, 17
  Mary Elizabeth, 17
  Nicholas, 17
  Oliver P., 17
FUSS, Catherine, 64
  Henry, 64
  Henry D., 47
  John A., 47
  John Adam, 47, 77
  John Henry, 98
  Lavinia, 98
  Mary Ann, 47
  Samuel, 47
  Sarah C., 47
  William, 98
  William Edward, 98
FUSS PURCHASE, 76

-G-

GA, Lafayette, 119
GAITHER, Elvira, 117
  George, 91
  James W., 117
  John E., 117
  Sarah C., 91
  Warner, 117

GALT, Washington, 123
GALT'S FANCY, 56
GAMBRILL, Horatio N., 110
GARDNER, Catherine, 17
  Cyrus M. S., 123
  Freeborn, 17
  Nimrod, 17
  Rebecca, 123
  Ruth, 17
GARNER, Elizabeth, 32, 74
  Ephraim, 54
  George, 127
  Harriet, 55
  John, 32
  Mary Ann, 127
  Wesley W., 55
GARNETT, Catherine, 81
  Harriett, 81
  Henry, 81
  William, 81
GARTRELL, Edward, 72
  Rachel R., 72
GASSHIDE, Charity, 101
  James, 101
GEARHART, Elenora, 58
  George, 58
  Lydia, 58
  Mary J., 58
GEIGER, Charlotte, 64
  Peter, 4, 64
GEIMAN, Abraham, 124
  Balinda, 124
  David, 124
  Jeremiah, 124
  John, 24

INDEX

Lucinda, 124
Mary, 24
William, 124
GEISER, Daniel, 35
GELSTON, Hugh, 39
GEORGE'S LOT, 37
GERMAN CHURCH, 10, 120
  The, 45, 128
GERMAN TOWN, 87, 129, 135
GERMAND, Henry, 111
GESELMAN, John, 23
GETTY, Catherine, 4
  James, 4
GIBSON, Charles Allen, 92
  Jane Ann, 92
  Samuel, 92
  Samuel Owings, 92
GILBERT, Lewis, 121
  Magdalena, 121
GILES, Aquilla, 91
  Lucretia, 91
GILL, John T., 22
  Rose A., 22
GILLISS, Alexander, 72
  Elijah, 72
  Elizabeth, 72
  Francis, 72
  Gassaway, 72
  George W., 72
  Porcius, 76
  Rebecca E., 72
  Thomas H., 72
GILL'S PROSPECT, 65
GIST, Ann, 78
  Branford Porcher, 109
  Elizabeth Sarah, 109
  Independence, 109
  John, 78
  Joseph Mordecai, 109

Mary, 109
Mordecai, 109
Mordecai W., 138
Richard Joshua, 109
States L., 109
GIST'S AMBITION, 81
GIST'S FORREST, 76
GITTIER, Jacob, 1
  Margaret, 1
GITTINGER, Jacob, Jr., 25
  Mary, 25
GITTINGER'S GLADE, 94
GIVENS, Airey Ann, 7
  Elizabeth, 7
  James, 7
  Moses, 7
GLADE SPRINGS, 41
GLASE, Henry, 35
  Leah, 35
GLENDOICK, 3, 5, 12, 56, 102
GONESHAR, 135
GOOD, Jacob, 4
GOOD FELLOWSHIP, 36
GOOD INTENT, 46, 76
GOOD LUCK, 53, 81, 120, 121
GOOD WILL, 72, 125, 139
GOODWIN, Ellen, 84
  Thomas, 84
GOOSE QUARTER, Josephine, 61
GORE, Ann Rebecca, 96
  Henry H., 96
  Laura E., 132
  Stephen R., 132
GORSUCH, Ann, 17
  Benjamin, 84
  Corrilla, 37

Daniel, 131
Dennis H., 84
Eleanor, 65
Elizabeth Ann, 33, 65
Ellen M., 65
Ellen Maria, 65
George R., 65
George W., 82
Henrietta S., 65
Henry C., 65
James, 65
James M., 65
Jane, 84
John L., 65
John Thomas, 33
Joshua, 65
Joshua M., 65
Lovelace M., 17
Martha L., 65
Mary, 65, 84
Mary L., 65
Matilda, 35
Nathan, 17, 33, 37
Nathan I., 17
Nathan J., 133
Petitia, 33
Robert D., 84
Sarah, 84
Sarah A., 65
Stephen, 33
Susan, 38
Susannah C., 131
Susannah H., 65
Thomas, 35, 84
Thomas F., 65
Thomas T., 65
William McHenry, 65
William P., 33
GOSNELL, Isabella, 63
  Jesse, 6
  John, 63
  Lemuel W., 78

INDEX

Lydia, 63
Rebecca, 6
Susan Price, 63
GOTHAM, 55, 62, 67
GRABIL, Peter, 12
Sarah, 12
GRABILL, Peter, 106
Sarah, 106
GRACE, Jonas, 71
Michael, 71
GRAMMER, Andrew, 81
Dorothy, 81
Henry, 81
Henry B., 81
Rebecca, 81
Simon J., 81
GRANDFATHER'S GIFT, 116
GRANDFATHER'S GIFTS, 53
GRAVE YARD, 1
GREEN, Eleanor, 78
John, 78
Joshua, 7
Joshua B., 7
Lewis, 87
Rachel, 7
Shadrack, 7
Thomas, 7
GREEN VEISENBURG, 115
GREENHOLTZ, Ann, 74
Jacob, 6
James W., 74
GREENWOOD, Abraham, 96
Ann Maria, 96
Caroline V., 96
Christianna, 131
John, 96
Joseph, 134
Josiah, 131

Lewis H., 131
Margaret, 134
Mary, 29, 96
Minerva A., 96
Peter, 96
Philip, 27
William, 96
GRESFELD, Caroline, 120
GREYHOUND FOREST, 137
GREY'S MEADOW, 37
GRIFFIE, Louisa, 82
Mary Elizabeth, 82
William, 82
William, Sr., 82
GRIMES, Amin, 131
Eliza, 54
Fanny, 131
Joshua, 54
Mary E., 131
William, 131
GROFF, George, 51
Margaret, 78
Susanna, 51
GROGG, David, 60
Mary Ann, 60
GROSS, Francis, 41
Henry, 7, 21
John, 7, 20, 21, 41
John, Jr., 21, 41
Lydia, 41
Mary, 41
William, 41
GROUND OAK HILL, 33
GROUND OAK THICKET, 33
GROVE, Augustus G., 122, 127, 139
Elizabeth, 127, 139
Frances, 139
Frances M., 127

Hannah, 122
Israel, 91
Israel Ann, 91
Jacob, 14, 122
Julian, 91
Lewis E., 139
Lewis J., 122, 127
Mary, 127, 139
Mary S., 122
GRUMBINE, John, 61
Seranda A., 61
GUGEL, Henry, 76
Mary, 76
Wilhemina, 76
GUMMEL, Amanda E., 112
Elizabeth, 112
George, 112
Jacob, 112
GUSHARA, Henry, 23
Pamela, 23
GWINN, Ellen M., 4
John, 4
Mary E., 4
Washington, 4
William B., 4

-H-

HAHN, Benjamin, 111
Elizabeth, 88
Isaiah, 88
Jacob, Jr., 112
Jesse, 112
Joseph E., 50, 112
Josiah, 127
Lucy, 12
Margaret, 112
Mary A., 111
Philipinia Louisa, 94
Rebecca, 112
Sarah, 38, 88
Susannah, 50

INDEX

William, 38
HAIFLEIGH,
   Catherine, 41
Catherine A., 41
George, 41
Levi, 41
HAIFLEY, Catherine, 80
David, 80
HAINES, Abraham, 20, 71
   Augustus Ann, 44
   Caroline, 71
   Edward, 64
   Eli, 44
   Elinora, 46
   Elizabeth, 64
   Ellen M., 33
   Eurith E., 100
   Francis, 11
   George Washington, 71
   Hashabiah, 128
   Isaac, 44, 115
   Jacob, 33
   Job, 44
   Joel, 44
   Joel Lewis, 20
   John, 20, 46
   John T., 33
   Joseph, 44
   Levi U., 100
   Margarette C., 33
   Martha N., 100
   Mary, 20, 115
   Mary E., 33
   Michael, 20
   Nathan, 44
   Nelly, 64
   Rachel, 44
   Reuben, 44, 64
   Samuel, 44
   Samuel A., 33
   Sophia, 71
   Tabitha, 100
   Thomas Vinton, 82
   William, 100
   William H., 33
   William Henry, 44
HALE'S VENTURE, 20
HALE'S VENTURE RESURVEY, 89
HALE'S VENTURE RESURVEYED, 86, 87, 115, 129, 135
HALL, Dr. Elisha, 65
HALLS RANGE, 26
HALVERSTADT, Eli, 50
   Rebecca, 50
HAMILTON'S RECOVERY, 47
HAMMOND, Allen C., 52
   Caroline A., 52
   George W., 52
   John B., 139
   Judy, 8
   Mary, 52
   Phillip, 8
   Thomas J., 52
   Virginia A., 50
   William M., 50
HAMMOND MEADOWS, 3
HAMMOND'S CHOICE, 12
HAMMONDS FINE SOIL FORREST, 9
HAMPTON COURT, 39, 40
HAND, Harry, 12
   Lucy, 12
HANN, Abraham, 76
   Daniel, 76
   Elizabeth, 94
   Elizabeth Ann, 39
   Jesse, 31, 76
   Mathias, 84
   Phillip, 39
   Phillip W., 39
   Sabrina L., 94
   Samuel, 76
   Sarah, 84
   Susanna, 39, 88
HANNA, Nathan, 64
HAPE, David, 75
   James Madison, 75
   Louisa, 75
HARBOR HILL, 136
HARDEN, Amanda C., 110
   Helena, 3
   Joseph, 3
   Joseph W., 110
   Louisa R., 110
   Nicholas, 110
   Samuel G., 110
   William H., 110
HARE, Catherine, 58
   George H., 58
   Henry, 58
   Jacob, 58
   John, 58
   Samuel, 58
   Sarah, 58
HARKER, Alosious, 130
   James, 130
   John, 130
   Louisa, 130
   Purvis, 130
   Robert, 130
   William A., 130
HARMAN, Elizabeth, 61
   Uriah, 61
HARNER, Abraham, 33, 34
   Ann Maria, 117

INDEX

Anna, 112
Augustus, 117
Augustus Jacob, 117
Barbara, 33, 34
Catherine, 117
Charles, 92
Clara Ellen, 117
David W., 92
Eli, 92
Elizabeth, 92, 117
Ellen, 117
Jacob, 117
James, 112
Joanna, 92
Levi, 117
Lydia, 117
Michael, 92
Michael, Jr., 117
Michael, Sr., 117
Noah, 92
Suzen, 117
Sylvester, 117
HARNICKELL,
  Albert, 135
HARP, James, 38
  Margaret, 38
HARPS, Mary, 34
  Michael, 34
HARRIOT'S
  RETREAT, 129
HARRIS, Eliza J., 6
  Emeline, 100
  Henrietta, 6
  John, 6
  Louisa C., 6
  Maria Wharfe, 6
  Mary J., 6
  Nancy, 6
  Richard, 124
  William, 6
HARRISBURG, 6
HARRISON,
  Benjamin, 6

Mary, 6
HARRY, Sarah, 25
  Tobias, 25
HARRYFORDE, 75
HART, Ann E., 6
  William A., 6
HARTLEY, George
  W., 134, 135
  John D., 135
  Jonathan, 134, 135
  Josephine, 135
  Magdalena, 135
  Mary C., 135
  William H., 135
HARTZELL, Eliza, 44
  John, 44
  Samuel, 44
  Susanna, 44
HARVEY, Charles W.,
  110
  Jacob A., 110
  John E., 110
  Lovinia C., 110
HATTERMAN, Isaac,
  111
  Mary A., 111
HAUGH, Ann E., 46
  Catherine, 44
  David, 46
  Elijah, 46
  John, 46, 75
  Paul, Jr., 46
  Susan W., 75
  William, 44, 46
HAWK, Catherine, 70
  Daniel, 70
  Elizabeth, 139
  Emanuel, 70
  Frederick, 70
  George, 43, 70
  George Peter, 70
  Henry, 139
  Joseph, 139

Margaret, 43, 138, 139
Mary, 70
Mary Jane, 70
Peter, 70
Rebecca, 43, 70
Samuel, 70
HAWKINS FANCY, 59
HAWK'S FANCY, 84
HAWN, Jesse, 51
  Maria, 51
HAX, Caroline, 80
  Peter, 80
HAYDEN, Ambrose, 5
  Appulla, 17
  Basil, 5, 17
  Catherine, 5
  Dennis, 5
  James, 5
  John, 5
  Richard, 5
  Theresa Ann, 5
  William, 5
HAYS, Daniel F., 47
  Deborah, 47
  Elizabeth, 47
  Joseph, 47
  Joseph T., 47
  Thomas H., 47
HAZARD, 137
HAZZARD, 126
HEADS GOOD
  LUCK, 74
HEAGY, Andrew, 34
  Hannah M., 34
  Margaret E., 34
  Matilda, 34
  William, 34
HEATH, David, 26
  Sarah Ann, 26
HECK, Nicholas, 70
  Sophia, 70
HEDDINGTON,
  Andrew Jackson, 30

INDEX

James O., 14
Jarrett, 30
Jesse, 30
Laban, 30
Lebbeus, 14
Margaret, 30
Martin Van Buren, 30
Murray Barrow, 30
Oliver, 30
Sarah, 30
Thompson P., 30
HEDNOR, Honor, 15
HEIDELBURG, 117
HEINER, Catherine, 32
  Emily, 32
  Hannah, 32
  Henrietta, 28
  Henry, 32
  John, 27
  Levi, 32
  Samuel, 32
  William, 28, 32
HEIRD, James, 23
HEISER, Catherine, 62
  Daniel, 62, 67
  David, 62, 67
  Frederick, 62, 67
  George, 62
  Jacob, 62, 67
  John, 62, 67
  Lewis, 62, 67
  Peter, 62, 67, 117
  Rebecca, 62, 117
  Sally, 62
  Sarah Ann, 62, 67
  Susan, 62
  Susannah, 62
HELM, Anna Mary, 19
  Francis, 19
HELTERBRICK, Araminta M., 120
  Henry, 120

HENDRICKS, Adam, 55
  Isabella J., 55
  John, 55
  Rebecca, 55
HENRY, Catherine, 77
  Catherine E., 77
  Catherine M., 77
  Daniel, 77, 132
  David, 77
  Elizabeth, 77
  Jacob, 77
  Joseph, 21
  Louisa, 77
  Lucy, 132
  Lydia A. R., 77
  Mary C., 77
  Matilda, 77
  Michael, 77
  Michael M., 77
  Nicholas, 77
  Nicholas I., 77
  Samuel I., 77
  Sarah A., 77
  Theresa, 21
  William D., 77
HENRY EBAUGH'S RESURVEY, 33, 124
HENRY'S MILLS, 82
HERGESHEIMER, David I., 50
  Sarah E., 50
  Virginia A., 50
HERRING, Angelina A., 63
  Daniel S., 114
  George D., 63
  John, 63
  Joshua W., 114
  Julia Ann, 80
  Mary, 62, 63
  Samuel W., 63

  Susannah, 63
  Thomas M., 63
  Tilghman R., 63
  William J., 63
HERSCH'S SECOND PURCHASE, 42
HERSH, Elizabeth, 80
  George Adam, 80
  Sophia, 80
HERSPERGER, James, 106
  Sarah, 106
HESS, Abraham N., 43
  George, 127
  John, Jr., 72
  Mary, 43
  Susannah, 127
HESSON, Abraham, 51, 103
  Balser, 51
  Balzer, 70
  Catherine, 41, 59, 60
  Daniel, 51
  Eleanor, 51
  Elizabeth, 51
  Isaac, 59
  Jacob, 70
  James, 41, 60
  Joseph of Peter, 59
  Lovis, 51
  Magdalena, 51
  Margaret, 51
  Mary, 103
  Peter, 51
  Philip, 70
  Rachel, 70
  Rebecca, 59
  Samuel, 70
  Susannah, 49
  William, 49
HEWITT, Rachel P., 117
  Septemius, 117

INDEX

HIBBARD'S ADDITION, 91
HIBBERD, Elizabeth, 44
  Silas, 44
HICKORY RIDGE, 51
HICKORY RIDGE RESURVEYED, 81, 85, 93
HIDE, Isaac, 64
  Polly, 64
HIGH GERMANY, 27, 31
HIGH SPRING, 85, 125
HILBETTS, Mary J., 87
HILL, Elizabeth, 61
HILL SPRING, 33, 95
HILLS AND VALLEYS, 57, 111
HILTEBRIDLE, Barbara, 37
  Jacob, 37
HILTERBRICK, Catherine, 56
  George, 97
  Margaret E., 97
  Peter, 56
HINER, Ann, 44
  Elizabeth, 44
  Harrison B., 44
  Jesse, 44
  John, 44
  Mary, 44
  Peter, 44
  Sophia, 44
HINES, Anthony, 16
  Elizabeth, 16
  Mary, 73
  Philip, 73
HINKLE, Barbara, 5, 105
  George, 5, 105
HIPSLEY, John, 43
  Joshua, 43
  Solomon, 43
HITESHEW, Ephraim, 31
  Mary, 31
HITESHUE, Louisa, 62, 90
  William, 57, 62, 90
HIVELY, Jacob, 101
  Mary C., 101
HOBB, Ellen, 43
  Gustavious, 43
HOFF, Deborah, 64
  William L., 64
HOFFACKER, David, 53
  David H., 128
  Henry Jacob, 98
  Jeremiah, 119
  Jeremiah H., 98
  Lydia, 98
  Margaret, 119
  Mary Cordelia, 53
HOFFMAN, Elizabeth, 59, 104
  George, 96
  Henry, 96
  Isaac, 129, 130
  James Conrad, 130
  Lydia, 129
  Mary C., 96
  Peter B., 129
  Sarah Elizabeth, 130
  William, 59
  William D., 104
  William J., 129
HOLBY, Anaretta, 85
  Angelina, 85
  Naomi Mary, 85
HOLLENBAUGH, Jacob, 133
HOLLINGSWORTH, Jesse, 9
HOLLY, Albert, 93
  Angelina, 51, 93
  Ann Aretta, 93
  Ann Onetta, 51
  Naomi Mary, 51, 93
HOLMES, Adam, 69
  Mary, 99
  Sarah E., 57
  Susan, 69
  William, 99
  William T., 57
HOLZNER, Anna, 133
  Barbara, 133
  Elizabeth, 133
  Francis, 133
  George, 133
  Lewis, 133
  Mary, 133
  William, 133
HONOR DELIGHT, 5
HOOD, Henry, 71
  James, 72
  John, 71
  Thomas, 71
HOODS FINE SOIL FOREST, 71
HOOK, James, 14
  Mary T., 116
  Thomas, 63
  William H., 116
HOOKER, Amos, 4
  Jacob, 4
  James, 109
  James S., 4
  Jesse, 4
  John, 4
  Laura, 109
  Lloyd, 4
  Mary, 4
  Rachel, 25
  Samuel, 25
  Susanne, 4
HOOKER'S MEADOW, 21, 34

INDEX

HOOKER'S MEADOW ENLARGED, 17, 64, 139
HOOKER'S MEADOW RESURVEY, 129
HOOKER'S MEADOW RESURVEYED, 25, 106
HOOVER, Adam, 21
　Adam L., 100, 101, 104
　Barbara, 21
　Benton, 104
　Catherine, 22, 100, 105
　Conrad, 100, 101, 104
　Daniel, 21, 22, 100, 101, 104, 105
　Daniel L., 100, 101, 104, 105
　David B., 100, 101, 104, 105
　Edward, 104
　Edward R., 100, 101
　Eliza H., 101, 104, 105
　Eugene B., 100, 101
　Francis, 100, 101, 104
　James B., 100, 101, 104, 105
　John L., 100
　Mary Ann, 100
　Polly, 101, 104
　Robert, 105
　Robert H., 100, 101, 104
　Thomas W., 100, 101, 104
HOPEWELL, 116
HOPPE, J. Henry, 2, 64, 111
　John Henry, 60
　Leah, 46
HORN, George M., 110
　John S., 110
　Louisa R., 110
　Mary, 110
　Philip C., 110
HORNER, Alexander H., 34
　Charles W., 34
　David, 34
　Eaton G., 34
　Eli R., 34
　Elizabeth, 34
　Franklin T., 34
　George W., 34
　James L., 34
　John A., 34
　William, Jr., 34
　William, Sr., 34
HORN'S MEADOWS, 32
HOUCK, Amelia, 119
　Annastatia, 3
　Belinda, 87
　David, 119
　Eli, 119
　Elias, 104
　Elizabeth, 119, 129, 130
　George, 87, 104
　George of William, 129
　Henry, 119
　Jacob, 104, 119
　Jacob H., 112, 119
　Jacob N., 126
　John, 119
　Joshua, 3
　Larkin, 2
　Levi, 122
　Lucy, 104
　Mary, 122
　Michael, 130
　Miriam, 126
　Rebecca, 119
　Ruth, 2
　Sarah, 112
　William, 104
HOUSEFEL, Andrew, 114, 117
　Louisa, 114, 117
HOUSTER'S LAST WILL, 129
HOWARD'S DISCOVERY, 57, 98
HOWARD'S RESOLUTION, 61, 66
HUCKLEBERRY BOTTOM, 51
HUFF, Hester Ann, 69
　Mary A., 69
　Owen, 69
HUGHES, Patrick, 26
　Susannah, 26
HULL, David, 37, 43
　Eli, 46, 113
　Fanny, 37, 43
　Hezekiah, 36, 37, 43
　Isaac, 36, 37, 43, 112
　John, 51
　Martha, 113
　Peter, 37, 43
　Rebecca, 36, 37, 43, 46
　Sarah, 112
　William, 37
　William H., 43
HULL'S NEGLECT, 96
HUMBERT, Aaron, 6
　Adam, 95
　Catherine, 6
　Daniel, 6
　David, 134
　Elizabeth, 95
　Eve, 83
　Frederick, 6
　George, 6
　Henry, 6
　Jane, 134
　John, 6

INDEX

Michael, 6
Peter, 6
Sarah, 6
Susanna, 6
William, 83
HUMBURG, Catherine, 5, 105
George, 5, 105
HUMBURGH, Anna M., 131
Francis P., 131
Helen, 131
John A., 131
Jonas W., 131
Joseph, 131
Mary E., 131
Peter, 131
Sarah, 131
HUNT, Lindy, 92
HUNTER, Elizabeth, 127, 139
Robert, 127, 139
HUNTER'S CHANCE, 8, 33
HUNTER'S RIDGE, 47
HYDE, Elizabeth A., 58
Isaac, 58
Joshua L, 58

-I-

I WILL AND I WILL NOT, 140
ILL NEIGHBORHOOD, 25
Illinois (State), 46, 47, 53, 59, 64, 95, 99, 104
Clark County, 82
Fulton County, 92, 94, 117, 128
Galena, 14
INCLOSURE, 25
INDIAN TOWN, 75

The, 16
Indiana (State), 13, 25, 27, 37, 44, 45, 46, 47, 55, 58, 92, 140
Bartholomew County, 132
Huntington County, 132
Miami County, 111, 112, 132
Montgomery County, 83
Parke County, 97
Randolph County, 111, 123
INGELLS, Hanson T., 90
Julia Ann, 90
INGELS, John, 38
Margaret, 38
Thomas, 38
INGLEMAN, Cecelia, 109
Palmer, 109
INGLES, Hanson T., 38
Jane, 38
John, 38
Rachel, 38
Susannah Polk, 38
Iowa (State), 55, 59, 104, 127, 130
Johnson County, 115
IRELAND (Country), Donegal County, 18
IRELAND, Edward, 9
Elizabeth H., 9
IRON INTENTION, 7, 11, 13, 50, 74, 81, 91, 105, 112, 134
IRON INTENTION RESURVEYED, 1
IRONS, Andrew, 78
Edward D., 78
Isaac, 78
Isaac, Jr., 78

James, 78
John, 78
John B., 78
Joshua, 78
Washington, 78
IRVING, Mary E., 100
William H., 100

-J-

JACKSON, Anthony J., 107
JACOBS, George, 75
John, 75
Richard, 75
Thomas S., 75
JACOB'S BEGINNING, 86, 87
JACOB'S LOT, 61, 95
JACOB'S VENTURE, 75
JAMES, Sarah, 15
JAMES DELIGHT, 51
JAMES' PURCHASE, 84, 123
JAMESON, Catherine, 40
Robert J., 40
JANE, John, 58
Julian, 58
JARVIS, Leonard, 22
JEMISON, Benjamin, 71
Robert, 71
Robert J., 71, 78
JENKINS, Cecelia, 72
David, 69
Elizabeth, 69
John, 69
Margaret, 69
Nancy, 69
Rezin T., 72
Robert, 69
Robert M., 125

INDEX

JERUSALEM, 25
JEWETT, Isaac W., 116
JOHN FANCY ENLARGED, 7
JOHN PLEASANT MEADOW, 3
JOHN'S BEGINNING, 112
JOHN'S CHANCE, 41, 118
JOHN'S CHOICE, 9
JOHN'S DELIGHT, 89
JOHN'S DESIRE, 89, 119
JOHN'S INDUSTRY, 18, 20, 28, 135
JOHN'S LOT ENLARGED, 108
JOHN'S LOTT, 89
JOHN'S PLEASURE, 11
JOHNSON, Christina, 123
  Christopher, 123
  David, 93, 123
  Eliza Ann, 45
  Elizabeth W., 65
  Henrietta, 93
  Jeremiah, 45
  Jesse, 123
  John N., 122
  Mary N., 122
  Samuel, 123
JONES, Ephraim, 92
  Henry B., 25
  John, 24
  Rebecca, 92
  Thomas, 56
JONES FANCY, 68
JORDAN, Alice A., 51
  Edward, 16
  Elias, 37, 51
  Elias F., 51
  George W., 37

  Hanson P., 37
  Hellen, 37
  Hezekiah, 37
  Isabella, 16
  James W., 37, 51, 84, 104
  John W., 121
  Lovelace, 16
  Margaret Ann, 121
  Mary, 37, 51
  Mortica W., 51
  Robert H., 16
  Samuel, 4
  Samuel I., 37
  William, 37
  William N., 16
  William R., 16
  William Robert, 16
  Zacheriah, 16
JORDAN'S DISCOVERY, 122
JOSEPH'S CHANCE, 60

-K-

KAGEL, Elizabeth, 40
  John C., 40
KAKE, Christiana, 80
  Philip, 80
KALKMAN, Alexander E., 97
  Frederick W., 97
  Maria L., 97
  Susan E., 97
Kansas Territory, 74
  Leavenworth, 73
Kansas (State), 76
KAUFFMAN, David, 9
  Fanny, 9
KAUFMAN, George, 71
  John P., 71, 79
  Julia Ann, 79

  Margaret, 71
  Mary Ann, 71
KAUTZ, Elizabeth, 10
  Henry, 10
  Joshua, 10
  Michael, 10
  Nancy, 10
KEALBAUGH, Christian, 16
  Conrad, 16
  Jacob, 16
  John, 16
  William, 16
KEARNES, Henry, 52
  Rebecca, 52
KEEFER, Anna Barbara, 51
  Edward, 124
  George, 51
  Henry, 39, 88
  Isaac, 70
  Jacob, 39, 88
  Lucinda, 124
  Mary, 70
  Rebecca, 77
  Sarah, 39, 88
  Thomas, 39, 88
  William, 77
KEEFER'S RANGE, 37, 92
KEEFFER, Daniel, 8
  Elizabeth, 8
  Ferdinand, 8
  John, 8
  Magadalina, 8
  Susannah, 8
KEITH, Kinsey, 13
  Mary, 13
KELBAUGH, Christian, 16
KELLEAD, Thomas, 2
KELLER, Philip, 35
  Rachael, 35

INDEX

KELLEY, James N., 85
KELLY, David, 69
John, 69
John A., 9, 19, 22
Lydia, 9, 19
Nelly, 59
Prudence, 29
Rachel, 69
Thomas S., 59
William, 30
KELLY'S RANGE, 15, 134
KEMP, Harriet, 1
Honorah, 1
Margaret, 53
Peter, 53
KENELL, Andrew, 78
Elizabeth, 78
Nathan, 78
KENTUCKY (Tract), 22
Kentucky (State), 6, 7, 79, 113
KEPHART, David, 50
George, 26
Hannah, 26
Mahala, 50
Sarah, 26
KERCHNER,
Elizabeth A., 94
George W., 94
Joel, 94
Peter, 94
KERR, Francis J., 121
Mary L., 121
KESLINGER, Eliza, 55
Samuel, 55
KESSELRING, John, 70
Mary Jane, 40
Samuel, 40
Susanna, 70
KEY, Jeremiah, 102

Stephen A., 102
KEYS, David, 5
Elizabeth, 5
Samuel, 5
Stephen, 5
KEY'S INDUSTRY, 1
KILER, David, 6
Simon, 6
KIN FAUNES, 109
KIN FAUNS, 100
KINDALL'S DELIGHT, 41
KING, Nancy, 93
William, 93
KIRKPATRICK, Jane, 138
William J., 138
KLINCK'S BEGINNING, 10
KNELLER, Abdiel, 130
Daniel, 130
David, 113, 130
Elizabeth, 130
Ellenora, 130
Emeline, 113, 130
Godfrey, 130
Henry, 130
Keziah, 130
Luther H., 130
Martha, 130
Mary J., 130
Rachel, 130
Rebecca, 130
Samuel, 130
William G., 130
KNOTE, Rachel, 22
KNOX, Barbara, 34
Col. William, 34
KONTZ, Henry, 35
KOONS, Albert, 83
Andrew, 21
Catherine A., 75
Eliza, 75

Elizabeth, 104
Emily I., 75
Henry, 75
Jacob H., 75
James H., 75
John, 83
Margaret, 83
Mary Ann, 21
Paul, 21
Peter, 21
Upton, 75
KOONTZ, Anna, 122
Elias, 103
Elias G., 103
Eliza, 3
Emanuel, 102
George, 3
Jacob, 75, 83
Jacob M., 103
Julian, 122
Louisa C., 102
Margaret A., 102, 103
Mary, 122
Mary E., 103
Rachel, 83
Sarah A., 103
William, 102
KOPP, Alfred, 45
Amanda, 104
Francis Thomas, 45
J. Alfred, 104
Joseph, 45
Joshua F., 45
Julia Frances, 45
Lysander, 45
Sarah, 45
Theodore, 45
KOUTZ, Henry, 99
John, 99
Lydia, 99
Nathan, 99
KRANTZ, Catherine, 107

INDEX

Edward H., 107
Edward T., 104
Lavinia, 104
William, 107
KRAUSE, Eliza, 24
Jacob, 24
James, 24
James L., 24
Jesse W., 24
John, 24
William, 24
KREGLOW, Barbara, 47
Frederick, 47
George, 47
John, 47
Lydia Ann, 47
KREIDLER, Edward, 119
Elizabeth, 119
Lydia, 122
Peter, 119, 122
KRESLER, Frederick, 62
Sarah, 62
KRISE, Elias, 47
Mary Ann, 47
KROH, Elizabeth, 10
John, 10
Julia Ann, 10
Lewis, 10
KRUMRINE, Eliza, 67, 73
Elizabeth, 73
Emanuel, 67
Henry, 67, 73
Isaiah, 67, 73
Jacob, 67
John, 67
Judith, 67
William S., 67
William S. of Henry, 73
KUHN, John, 9, 19, 40

Lovice, 40
Sarah A., 19
Sarah Ann, 9
KUHNS, Mary Ann, 72
Paul, 72
KUMP, Josiah, 116
Mary E., 116
Peter, 92
Rachel, 92
KURTZ, Caroline, 62
Israel, 62
Jesse, 62
Magdalena, 62
Maria, 62
Noah, 62

-L-

LAFF, Elias F., 99
Jane, 99
LAMBERD, John, 69
Lydia, 69
LAMBERT, Abraham, 90
Abraham Augustus, 90
Andrew J., 129
Ann, 64
Elizabeth, 64
Ellen, 64
Esther, 64
George W., 90
Isaac, 64
Jesse, 64
John, 64
Jonathan, 64
Mary, 64
Octavia Ann, 129
Samuel, 64
Sarah, 90
Sarah A., 90
Sarah Ellen, 90
Uriah P., 90
LAMB'S PLAGUE, 62

LAMMOTT, Anna Maria, 57
Benjamin, 57
Daniel, 57
George W., 82, 107
Henry, 22
Jacob, 22, 57
John, 22, 113
John H., 77
Joseph, 57
Josephine, 22, 31
Margaret, 31
Polly, 77
Priscilla, 57
Samuel, 22, 31
Sarah, 22, 31
LAMMOTTE, John H., 105
LAMMOTT'S DELIGHT, 57
LAMMOTT'S MIDDLE OF THE WORLD, 57, 91
LAMOTT, Abraham, 122
George W., 122, 127
Mary C., 122, 127, 139
LAMOTTE, George W., 139
LAMPERT, Andrew I., 5
George, 5
Michael, 5
William, 5
LAND STOOL, 49
LANDAFF, 98, 104
LANDAW, 105
LANDERS, James, 78
Robert, 78
William, 78
LANE, Caleb, 23
Elizabeth, 64
LANE'S DELIGHT, 93
LANTZ, Elizabeth, 68

Elizabeth A., 43
George, 81
James W., 43
John, 43
John T., 43
Joseph, 2
Rachel, 2, 81
Sally, 98
Sarah, 43
Theodore A., 43
William L., 43
William S., 68
LAPLAND, 72
LARKIN THE SECOND, 109, 121
LAST RESURVEY ON SHEREDINES RANGE, The, 16, 80
LATHAM, Elizabeth, 34
Joseph, 34
Louisa, 34
LAUREL BANK, 112
LAUVER, Frances, 50
Samuel A., 50, 70
LAWRENCE'S DISAPPOINTMENT, 84
LAWRENCE'S INDUSTRY, 84
LAWRENCES PLEASANT HILLS, 35
LAWRENCE'S PLEASANT VALLEY, 18, 28
LAWRENCE'S PLEASANT VALLIES, 20, 135
LAWSON, Edward, 28
Elizabeth, 28
Jacob, 28
John, 28
Moses, 28
Moses R., 28

Sarah A., 28
Thomas, 28
LAWYER, Samuel, 138
LEARCH, Eliza A., 57
Joseph, 57
LEAS, Philip, 53
Sophia, 53
LEATHERWOOD, Ana, 54
Hanson, 54
LEE, Catherine, 120
LEGORE, Elizabeth, 50
Ezra, 50
Jacob, 50
Jesse H., 51
John, 50
Rachel, 50
William H., 50
LEIGH CASTLE, 20, 38, 57, 59, 98
LEIPOLT, Nicholas, 111
LEISTER, Amanda, 132
Ann Mary, 81
David, 31
George B., 127
Henry, 81
Josiah, 132
Polly, 31
LEMON'S CHOICE, 27, 43
LEMON'S VINEYARD, 47
LENOX, John, 3
Polly, 3
LEONARD'S LOT(T), 33, 95
LEOPARD, Jacob, 111
Louisa, 111
LEPPO, Adam M., 135
Catharine, 123
Daniel, 123

David H., 123
Elinore Leno, 123
Elizabeth A., 135
Ezra A., 123
Ira Franklin, 123
Rebecca, 116
Simon, 116
Simon P., 123
LESCALEET, Susannah, 71
LET ME ALONE, 124
LEVEL GROUND, 25
LEVERING, Decatur, 27
LEWIS LUCK, 112
LIGHTNER, Jacob, 117
Joseph, 43
Lydia, 116
Mary, 43
LIME STONE RIDGE, 116
LIMESTONE RIDGE, 72
LINAWEAVER, George, 1
Ruth, 1
LINDLEY, Abra, 101
Amanda, 101
Hannah Jane, 102
James Franklin, 101
Jared L., 101
John, 102
Mary E., 101
Stephen Douglas, 102
Susan E., 101
LIND'S BOTTOM, 71
LINDSAY, John, 29
Lewis G., 68
Robert T., 133
Sally, 29
Susannah, 68
LINTHICUM, Samuel S., 132

INDEX

LIPPY, Ann, 49
  Barbara, 49, 55, 59
  Catherine, 49, 55
  David, 49, 55
  Elizabeth, 49, 136
  Elizabeth Ann, 55
  George, 59
  George L., 58
  Jacob, 81
  John, 49, 55, 59
  Joseph, 49, 55
  Magdalena, 49, 55
  Mary, 49, 55, 59
  Rebecca, 49, 55
  Samuel, 49
  Sarah, 81
  Susan, 55
  William, 49, 55
  William H., 136
LIPPY'S ADDITION, 10
LITTLE, Catherine, 73
  George Lewis, 46
  Henry, 73
  Maggie A., 122
  Polly, 46
LITTLE ADDITION, 101, 105
LITTLE BRITTON ENLARGED, 80
LITTLE CHANCE, 89
LITTLE PROFIT, 81
LITTLE ROCK, 57
LITTY, Robert, 24, 28
  Ruth, 24, 28
LIVER, Susanna, 6
LOASMAN, Charles, 130
  Eliza A., 130
LOCKARD, Eliza A., 56
  Eliza C., 119
  John, 56, 58

Margaret, 56
William H., 119
LOCUST NECK, 112
LOG CABIN, 89
LOGSDEN, Anna, 10
  Eleanor, 5
  Honor, 10
  James, 10
  John, 10
  John, Sr., 10
  Joseph, 5
  Mary Ellen, 10
  Prudence, 10
  Rebecca, 1
  William, 10
LOGSDON, Prudence A., 10
LOGSDON'S AMENDMENT, 46
LOHR, Andrew, 23
  Catherine, 23
  Levi, 23
  Margaret Josephine, 23
LONG, Angeline V., 119
  Catherine, 60, 89
  Christian, 67, 89, 118
  Conrad, 19, 89
  Daniel, 118, 119
  Elizabeth, 119
  Emeline C., 119
  George, 19, 89
  Henry, 89
  Jacob, 89
  Jacob, Jr., 89
  Lenah, 118
  Lucy, 89
  Ludwick, 19, 89
  Lydia A., 119
  Margaret, 19, 89
  Peter, 19, 89
  Sarah A., 119

William, 60
William L., 119
LONG HILL, 114
LONG MEADOW, 4
LONG REACH, 132
LONG TRUSTED RESURVEYED, 118
LONGWELL, John K., 68
LOOKABOUT, 22, 41, 44, 50, 85
Louisiana (State), 131
  New Orleans, 10
LOVEALL, Charity, 15
  Elizabeth, 108
  Enoch, 15
  Greensbury, 15
  John, 15, 108
  John Thomas, 108
  Lucinda, 108
  Luther, 15
  Margaret Ann, 108
  Rebecca, 15
  Solomon, 15
  Stephen, 15
LOVEALL'S ENLARGEMENT, 92, 117
LOVEALL'S PROSPECT, 89, 119
LOWE, Andrew, 112
  Clarence Willie, 109
  Jesse M., 109
  Jesse Marion, 109
  Margaret M. E., 109
  Mary, 112
  Silas Conn, 109
LOWER, Ellen, 119
  Levi, 119
LOWER SLIPE, 23
LOWERY, Susannah, 1
LOYD, Helen, 64
  John L., 64

INDEX

LUCAS, Basil, 60
  James, Jr., 56
  Mary, 56, 60
LUCKY'S ENLARGEMENT, 134
LYNCH, George, 87
  John V., 127
  July Ann, 127
  Sarah, 87
LYNN, David, 92
  Sarah, 92

-M-

MCALLISTER,
  Alexander, 138, 139
  Andrew, 138
  Elizabeth, 139
  James, 138, 139
  Jane Amanda, 138
  John, 138
  John W., 139
  Margaret, 139
MCCLAIN, Harriet, 16
  William, 16
MCCLEARY, John, 118
  Margaret, 118
MCCLELLAN,
  Elizabeth, 2
  Samuel, 2
MCCORMICK,
  Elizabeth, 20
  James, Jr., 20
  John P., 20
MCFEE, Caroline, 130
  James, 130
  James M., 130
MCGINITY, Bernard, 128
  Mary, 128

MCGUIGAN, James, 21
  Salley, 21
MCILHENNY,
  Alexander, 93
  Eliza M., 93
  Elizabeth, 93
  Elmira, 93
  James, 93
  Jane Maria, 93
  John, 93
  Mary, 93
  Samuel, 93
MCKAIN, Alexander, 14
  Rachel, 14
MCKELLIP, Anna, 74
  James, 74
  James H., 74
  John, 74
  Joseph A., 74
  Maggie C., 74
  Mary Elizabeth, 74
  William A., 74, 136
MCKINNEY, Andrew, 134
  Ann, 73
  John, 73
MCKINSTRY, Samuel, 45
MACKLEY, Bridget, 70
  David, 70
  Emanuel, 70
  Jacob, 70
  Jacob S., 84
  James, 70
  John, 70
  Lucinda, 84
  Mary C., 84
  Michael, 70
  Milton O., 84
  Samuel D., 84
  Samuel F., 70

William H. Harrison, 70
MCLANE, Eliza Jane, 33, 36
  George, 33, 36
MCMASTER, Mary, 54
MCMASTERS, Eliza Jane, 49
  Mary, 49
  Rachel Frances, 49
  Samuel, 49
MCQUAY, David N., 88
  Levina, 88
MCQUEEN'S CHOICE, 87
MAGORS, Eliza, 60
MAHANNY, Elmira, 60
  George, 60
MAIDEN'S POINT, 39, 123
MALEHORN,
  Amanda C., 99
  Andrew J., 99
  Catherine, 99
  Elizabeth, 99
  Ella B., 99
  Franklin P., 99
  George W., 99
  Jacob, 99
  Jeremiah, 99
  Jesse F., 138
  John, 99, 132
  Lucinda, 99
  Mary, 99
  Mary J., 99
  Oliver P., 99
  Samuel, 99
  Sarah, 99
  Susan, 132
  Susannah, 99
MANAHAN,
  Cinderalla, 128

INDEX

Francis T., 128
Levi, 59
MANALLA, Amelia, 61
Reuben, 61
MANCHESTER SAVINGS INSTITUTE, The, 80
MANCHESTER SAVINGS INSTITUTION, The, 128
MANHEIME TOWN, 25
MANN, Mathias, 79
MANNING, Amanda, 140
Jarusa, 140
John W., 123
John William, 140
Richard, 60, 116
Sarah J., 123
MANRO, Catherine, 3
David, 3
James, 3
Sarah, 3
Squire, 3
Thomas, 3
MARGARET'S DELIGHT, 68
MARING, Abraham Buffington, 49
Alice Catherine, 49
Amy, 49
Ann Eliza, 49
Anny, 49
Caroline Otelia, 49
Catherine, 49
Daniel, 49
David, 49
David Albert, 49
Esther, 49
John, 49
Mary Louisa, 49

Susanna Rebecca, 49
MARKER, Christina, 51
David, 37, 61
Elias, 61
Henry, 61
Jacob, 37
John, 37, 51, 61
Mary, 61
Rachel, 61
Susannah, 37
MARKEY, Amos, 22
Christian, 22
Jane, 22
John Henry, 22
Joseph, 22
Nathaniel, 22
Samuel, 22
Susannah, 22
MARKS, Catherine, 47
John, 47
MARTIN, Barbara, 22
Mary, 22
William, 50
MARTIN'S MISTAKE, 68
MARYLAND COPPER COMPANY OF CARROLL AND BALTIMORE COUNTIES, The, 110
MARY'S VICTORY, 18, 20, 35
MASEMER, Yoder, 39
MASEMORE, Jacob, 119
John, 119
Susannah, 119
MASONHEIMER, Abagail, 106
Alfred, 106
Catherine, 106
Frederick, 105, 106

Henry E., 105
Jacob, 106
Jane, 106
Mary, 63
Nathaniel, 106
Peter, 42, 59
Susan, 62
William, 106
Massachusetts, Boston, 6, 68
MATHIAS, Barbara, 62, 67
Benjamin, 46
Daniel, 46
Edward, 62, 67
Elizabeth, 62
Henry, 62, 67
Jacob, 22, 49
John, 46
Joseph, 46
Leah, 46
Leander, 46
Lewis, 62, 67
Lydia, 62
Mary, 46, 62, 67
Reuben, 46
Silvester, 46
Urias, 62, 67
MATTER'S CHOICE, 75
MATTINGAN, 11
MATTINGLY, Benjamin, 1
Charles, 1
Dominic, 1
Eliza, 1
Ellen, 1
Hannah, 1
Henry, 1
John, 1
Nancy, 1
Samuel, 1
Susannah, 1

INDEX

William, 1
MAURER, Paul, 57
MAUS, John, Jr., 37, 43
  Savilla, 37, 43
MAYFIELD, Ann, 129
MAYNARD, Dennis H., 126
MAYS, John, Jr., 7
  John, Sr., 7
  Temperance, 7
  Thomas, 7
MEADOW BRANCH, 32
MEHRING, Alverta M., 97
  Amy, 97
  Catherine, 102
  Elizabeth, 102
  Emma M., 97
  Frederick, 138
  George, 102
  Harriet, 97
  Harriet R., 97
  Isaiah E., 97
  Jacob, 102
  John, 102
  John O., 97
  John of John, 97
  Jonathan F., 97
  Josiah E., 97
  Lydia, 102
  Lydia A., 97
  Mary, 102
  Sarah J., 97
  Solomon D., 97
  Susan, 102
MENCHA, Julia Ann, 99
  Martin, 99
MENTZER, Francis, 72
  Jacob, 72
  John, 72
  Lewis, 72

  Rachel, 72
  Samuel, 72
  Thomas, 72
  William, 72
MERCER, Amanda, 82
  Amanda E., 82
  Andrew, 82
  Andrew of Richard, 65
  Elizabeth M., 82
  Emily R., 82
  Gustavus, 82
  Isabella A., 82
  John, 82
  Joseph F., 82
  Joshua, 82
  Littlewood S., 82
  Lydia, 82
  Mary C., 82
  Richard, 82
  Ruth, 82
  Salome A., 82
  Serena H., 82
  Susan M., 82
  Thomas B., 82
  Virginia B., 82
  William, 82
  William H., 82
MERING, Clementine, 90
  Frederick, 76
  George, 76
  George T., 90
  Joanna, 76
  Luther, 76
  Margaret, 76
  William Marshall, 76
MERRELL, Anna M., 124
  Squire G., 124
MERRICK, Emma, 78
  Joseph, 78
MERRING, Jacob, 18
  Mary, 18

MERRYMAN'S MEADOWS, 98
MESSINGER, Ephraim, 92, 112
  John, 112
  Martin, 112
  Mary, 92
  Samuel, 112
  Susanna, 112
METCALF, Elinor, 64
  Joshua, 30, 64
MICHAEL'S CHANCE, 134
Michigan (State), 62, 67, 135
  Eaton County, 117
MIHM, John George, 80
MIKESELL, Anna M., 95
  Elizabeth, 95, 122
  Mary, 136
  Peter B., 122
  Rebecca, 122
  Uriah B., 95, 136
  William B., 95, 122
MILES, Abraham, 7
  Mathilda, 7
MILL LOT, The, 33
MILLER, Amelia, 56
  Amon, 8
  Catherine, 114, 117, 140
  Charity, 123
  Christian, 103
  David, 56
  David E., 81
  Elizabeth, 7, 76, 87
  George, 114, 117
  George W., 123
  Henry, 9, 13
  Henry H., 98
  Jacob, 7, 21, 87
  John, 60, 95, 140

INDEX

Lewis, 76
Lydia, 8
Margaret, 13
Mary, 21, 60
Mary A., 88
Mary M., 7
Rachel, 7, 95
Robert, 7
Sarah, 81
Stephen, 7
Thomas, 11
William D., 64
MILLERS CHANCE, 26
MINER COURSES, 57
Minnesota (State), 91
MINOR'S BEGINNING, 66
MINTER, William, 91
Mississippi (State), 15, 78
MISSLER, Ann, 46
  Benjamin, 46
  David, 46
  Elinora, 46
  Grenelda, 46
  John, 46
  John T., 46
  Joseph, 45, 46
  Mahlon, 46
  Martha, 46
  Reuben, 46
  Ulrick, 46
  William, 46
Missouri (State), 3, 55, 60
  Johnson County, 115
  St. Joseph, 81
  St. Louis, 101, 120
MITCHELL, Gideon, 35
MITTEN, Christena, 60
  Daniel, 60

Dulsina, 61
George A., 61
James, 61
John, 61
John, Jr., 61
Martha Ann, 60
Miles, 60
Noah, 60
Rachel, 60, 61
Rosina, 61
Thomas, 61
William, 61
MOALS, Asbury, 52
  Lloyd, 52
MOLLY'S DELIGHT, 13, 81
MOLLY'S FANCY, 3, 30, 41, 48, 50, 69, 75, 83, 85, 97, 102, 125
MOLLY'S INDUSTRY, 59
MONOCACY, 47
MONZIE, 13, 85, 88
MOORE, David, 92
  Elizabeth, 92
MORELOCK, Daniel, 101
  David E., 90
  David Ezra, 36
  Dennis Abraham, 36
  Elizabeth, 101
  Elizabeth Amy, 36
  Henry E., 68
  Jacob, 2, 10, 36
  Jeremiah Andrew, 36
  Joseph, 36
  Louisa, 36
  Mary, 10
  Mary Ann Rebecca, 36
  Michael, 79
  Michael, Jr., 10
  Michael, Sr., 36
  Samuel, 101

Sarah, 68
Susan, 101
Susanah, 10
Susannah, 2
Uriah J., 83
Uriah James, 36
MORGAN'S TENT, 100
MORNINGSTAR, Harriet, 132
  John, 132
MORRIS, Mary, 98
MORRISON, Harriet, 78
  Henry Clay, 68
  John, 68
  Louisa G., 68
  Lydia, 103
  Robert, 68
  Samuel, 103
MORROW, Frances E., 50
  John, 50
MORT, Catherine, 130
  George, 63
  William, 130
MORTER, Rebecca, 138
MORTON, Kesiah, 64
  Samuel, Jr., 64
MOSER, Daniel, 111
  Eliza, 111
MOSES MEADOW, 126
MOSS, Adeline, 99
  James, 99
  Rebecca, 77
MOTTER, Alice, 12, 106
  George, 1
  Henry, 29, 45
  Lewis, 12, 106
  Rebecca Ann, 29
  Sarah, 1

INDEX

MOUNT PLEASANT, 96, 140
MOUNT PLEASANT ENLARGED, 86, 98, 117
MOUNT PROSPECT, 117
MOUNT SAFETY, 16
MOUNTAIN LOT, 131
MOUNTAIN PROSPECT, 67
MULBERRY BOTTOM, 38, 59
MURPHY, Michael, 86
MURRAY, Catherine, 55
  Catherine A., 57
  Catherine Ann, 98
  Charles, 55
  Charles Milton, 98
  Columbus, 55
  Eleanora, 55
  Elenora, 98
  Elizabeth, 55
  Hanson, 55
  Jabez, 55
  Jacob, 55
  James, 118
  John, 55, 98
  John P., 55
  John Paul, 98
  John W., 55
  John, Jr., 55
  Joshua, 55
  Joshua S., 55
  Mary, 77
  Sarah, 55, 118
  Thomas, 55
  Thomas B., 57, 98
  Thomas P., 55
  Whitfield, 55, 98
  William, 55
  William Columbus, 98

MURRAY'S RIDGE, 105, 115
MYERLY, Alice, 134
  David, 134
  Elias, 29, 104
  Jacob, 24
  Margaret, 104
  Mary, 29
  Susan, 24
MYERS, Abraham, 125
  Alford, 80
  Ann E., 96
  Ann Eliza, 46
  Ann Louisa, 80
  Catherine, 62, 80
  Charles, 80
  Charles F., 46
  David, 73, 80, 112
  Eliza C., 46
  Elizabeth, 73, 80, 83, 96
  Emanuel, 80
  Frederick H., 73, 112
  Henry, 80
  Huttle, 62, 67
  Jacob, 80
  Jesse T., 83
  Joel, 80
  John, 2, 62, 73, 80, 112, 125
  John D., 46
  John of Jacob, 96
  John of Joseph, 85
  Josephus, 96
  Lewis, 125
  Noah, 80
  Reuben, 96
  Samuel, 46, 80, 83
  Samuel J., 46
  Samuel of Jacob, 96
  Saranda, 62
  Seranda, 67
  Susan Alice, 96
  Susan Catherine, 83
  William, 73, 112
MYERS GOOD LUCK, 68
MYER'S RESURVEY, 108

-N-

NACE, Amanda, 112
  Augustus D., 1
  Charles L., 106
  Dellatha, 1
  Drusill, 55
  Eli, 112
  Emanuel, 55
  George, 1, 53
  Independence, 1
  Indiana, 1
  Jacob, 1
  Jane, 106
  Jeremiah, 1
  John, 1
  Keziah, 55
  Loreney, 1
  Margaret, 53
  Murray, 55
  Noah, 1
  Peter, 1, 52, 106
  Peter, the Elder, 1
  Rachel, 106
  Sarah, 78
NACE'S TAVERN, 90, 94, 114
NAIL, Susannah, 57
NAILL, David W., 57, 121
  Henry C., 121
  Mary A., 121
  Sophia A., 121
  William, 121
NANKIVIL, John, 26
  Mary, 26
NARROW SLIPE, 47

INDEX

NATHAN'S DESIRE, 16
Nebraska, Territory of, Otoe County, 97
NEFF, Mary, 8
  Samuel, 8
NEIGHBOR, 117
NEIGHBORHOOD CONTENTION, 43
NELSON, Hamilton, 111
  Mary E., 111
  Thomas, 111
  Thomas C., 111
NEW FARM, 81
NEW FOUND BOTTOM ENLARGED, 130
NEW GERMANY, 95
NEW LONDON, 86, 93
NEW MARKET, 132
NEW WINDSOR, 52, 106
NEW YORK, 12, 74
New York (State or city), 135
  Brooklyn, 14
NEWCOMER, Catherine, 71
  Henry, 71
  Isaac, 95
  John, 11
  Margaret, 11
  Mary Ann, 11
  Nancy, 95
NEWFOUND BOTTOM ENLARGED, 63
NEWFOUNDLAND, 101
NEWMAN, Mary, 76
  William, 76
NEWPORT, 81
NICHOLAS, Catherine, 66

Lewis, 66
NICHOLS, Rachel, 78
  Samuel, 78
NICKEY, Catherine, 125
  David, 125
NICODEMUS, Abraham, 102
  David, 56
  Eliza, 56
  Elizabeth, 56, 102
  Isaac, 102
  Jacob, 102
  Mary, 102
  Mary Catherine, 56
  Nancy, 124
  Philip, 102
  Sophia, 102
  Valentine, 102
  Washington, 102
NORRIS, Edward Oliver, 63
  Elizabeth, 107
  Maria Elizabeth, 63
  Martha Emma, 63
  Nicholas D., 73
  Nimrod, 107
  Rebecca Lee, 63
  Sarah, 63
  William A., 58
NORTH CANTON, 81
NOTTENSTOT, 117
NULL, Abraham, 40, 43, 56
  Abraham E., 56
  Absalom, 96
  Caroline, 96
  Catherine, 56
  Daniel, 96
  Elizabeth, 43
  Emily J., 43
  Francis C., 56
  George, 40, 56

Henry, 40
Isaiah, 56
Jacob, 43
Jane L., 56
John, 43
John H., 43
Joshua, 56
Levi, 56
Lewis, 56
Lydia, 40
Margaret, 40
Margaret E., 43
Mary, 21, 40
Mary Agnes, 96
Mary C., 56
Mary E., 43
Michael, Jr., 43
Rebecca, 40
Samuel, 43, 56
Susannah, 56
Susannah E., 56
William H., 43
NUNEMAKER, Catherine, 57
  Samuel, 57
NUSBAUM, John, 101

-O-

OCKER, Ann Elisa, 14
  Barbara, 14
  Barbara Fleagle, 14
  Henrietta, 14
  Jacob, 14
  John Henry, 14
  Josiah, 14
  Samuel, 14
  Thomas, 14
OGG, Benjamin, 37
  Catherine, 2
  Elias, 2
  George, 37
  Hellen, 37

INDEX

Henrietta, 37
James, 37
John, 37
Laben, 37
Mary, 37
Moses, 37
Nicholas, 37
Rachel, 37
Richard, 37
Susan, 37
William, 37
William Hamilton, 37
OGG'S DISCOVERY, 137
O'HARA, Margaret, 15
OHIO (Tract), 9, 27, 29, 33, 37, 42, 49, 66, 67, 73, 80, 92, 95, 97, 106, 112, 116, 123, 133, 134, 137
Ohio (State), 3, 4, 5, 9, 10, 11, 13, 14, 15, 16, 19, 25, 29, 30, 34, 35, 37, 43, 45, 46, 47, 50, 53, 54, 55, 57, 59, 60, 62, 63, 66, 67, 69, 71, 78, 89, 92, 93, 95, 114, 125, 127, 130
Ashland County, 57
Champaign County, 132
Clark County, 11
Columbiana County, 11
Dark County, 34, 101, 132
Dayton, 101, 134
Erie County, 66
Franklin County, 112
Knox County, 34, 87
Monroe County, 115
Montgomery County, 77
Muskingham County, 57
Pickaway County, 81

Preble County, 22, 77, 79
Seneca County, 125, 139
Wood County, 102
OHLER, Abraham, 34
Ann, 93
Catherine, 130
Deliah, 130
Edward, 93
Eliza, 33, 34
Emeline, 130
Frederick, 34, 130
Frederick, Sr., 130
Gassaway, 34
George, 22, 34
George A., 130
George Adam, 34
Jacob, 34
James, 34
John, 33, 34
John Thomas, 93
Joshua, 130
Levi N., 130
Margaret, 34, 130
Mary, 130
Mary Ann, 130
Solomon, 130
Thomas, 34
Washington, 93
OLD FORT, 10, 29
OLD GERMANY, 82
OLIVER, James, 17
Julian, 17
Rebecca, 17
Thomas, 17
ORCHARD, 14
ORENDORF, Francis H., 92
ORENDORFF, Cela, 134
David, 81
Elizabeth, 134

Francis H., 135
George, 134, 135
George C., 134
John, 14, 135
John T., 134, 135, 137
Josephus, 134, 137
Mary Jane, 134, 135
Peter F., 134
Rebecca, 81
William A., 134, 135
ORMLEY, 81
OTT, Eli, 47
Michael, 113
Sophia, 47
OTTER, Elizabeth, 34
William, 34
OTTO, Catherine, 39, 88
Elizabeth Ann, 90
Evan, 90
George, 70
Hebert, 53
Jacob, 39
Louisa A., 43
Margaret, 70
Peter, 43
Sophia, 53
OURSLER, Azariah, 107, 135
Curtis E., 123
David H., 137
Elizabeth, 123
Francis, 137
Frank, 137
Gustavus, 137
Henry, 137
John T., 137
Mary, 137
Mary L., 137
Theodore, 137
Tobias, 137
OVALL, The, 70
OVERPRONN, 35

INDEX

OWENS, Charles, 36
  Sarah, 36
OWENS OUTLAND PLAINS, 9
OWINGS, Celius W., 3
  Cordelia, 3
  Cordelia E., 3
  Dr. Thomas B., 3
  Elizabeth, 22
  George W., 100
  James, 65
  Onellana, 3
  Richard, 22
  Susannah, 100
  Thomas B., 3
OWINGS SECOND CHANCE, 19, 111, 121
OXMOORE, 68, 89, 119

-P-

PAINTER, Milton, 132
PALMER, David, 91
  Mary, 91
PANABAKER, David, 122
  Hannah, 122
PARIS, 106
PARIS RANGE, 4
PARKER, Elizabeth, 105
  James E., 106
  Joseph, 45
PARKS, Amelia, 8
PARRISH, Charles Albert, 79
  Mary Virginia, 79
  Moses, 131
  Richard, 79
  Sarah E., 79
PARRISH'S CHANCE, 41
PARTNERSHIP, 81
PATIENCE CARE, 112
PATTERSON, Joseph J., 78
  Sarah I., 78
PAYNE, Ann Elizabeth, 68
  Elisha D., 19, 45, 68
  Fanny Olive, 68
  George Washington, 68
  Julia Olivia, 68
  Samuel Sanford, 68
  Sarah, 68
PEACE AND GOODWILL, 36
PEACH BRANDY FOR(R)EST, 30, 35, 45, 104, 122
PEARRE, Deborah, 102
PEDDICORD, Elizabeth, 4
  Humphrey, 4
  Mary Ann, 4
PENELOPE AND THOMAS COCKEY'S DEYSBURG, 82, 98
PENN, Elizabeth, 118
  James, 118
  Lucy A., 118
PENNIGTON, Obid, 45
  Owen, 45
PENNINGTON, Ann, 45
Pennsylvania (State), 3, 12, 14, 15, 21, 24, 25, 28, 29, 34, 35, 44, 48, 53, 56, 60, 62, 67, 75, 78, 86, 89, 91, 93, 99, 127, 128
  Adams County, 9, 11, 28, 31, 44, 50, 60, 67, 70, 72, 79, 84, 85, 89, 92, 93, 97, 111, 112, 117, 122, 133, 139, 140
  Alleghany County, 50, 105, 106
  Allegheny County, 9
  Bedford County, 9
  Carlisle, 111
  Cumberland County, 59, 62, 93, 105, 111
  Dauphin County, 93
  Fayetteville, 34
  Franklin County, 9, 47, 62, 75, 131
  Gettysburg, 49, 54
  Hanover, 114
  Lancaster County, 75, 104
  Laurence County, 106
  Lycoming County, 132
  Percy County, 113
  Philadelphia, 6, 59, 114, 117
  Pittsburgh, 7
  Westmoreland County, 6, 14
  York County, 11, 19, 25, 39, 76, 77, 80, 81, 82, 99, 105, 112, 114, 122, 123, 131, 132
PERSERVERANCE, 69
PERTH, 24
PETER TRASHEL'S MANAGEMENT, 44
PETERMAN, Ann, 77
  Benjamin, 77
PETERS, Jacob, 56
  Lewis, 56
PETER'S DISCOVERY ENLARGED, 9
PETER'S GARDEN ENLARGED, 4
PETER'S LOT, 137
PETERSBURG, 1, 105

INDEX

PETERSBURG RESURVEYED, 1, 10, 23
PETERSBURGH, 38
PETERSBURGH RESURVEYED, 86
PETRE, Catherine, 77
  Michael F., 77
PHILIPS, Alexander, 100
  Asbury, 100
  Basil T., 32
  Edwin J., 100
  Elias, 100
  Eliza, 32
  George W., 100
  Harriet, 32
  Jesse, 100
  John, 32
  John T., 32
  Julian, 32
  Lemuel McAlister, 32
  Lewis H., 100
  Matilda, 32
  Milkey, 100
  Susan, 32
  Thomas, 100
PHILIPSBURGH, 60
PHILLIPS, Ann M., 67
  George H., 67
  Julia A., 67
  Margaret, 3
  Thomas, 3
  Uriel Clark, 67
  William W., 67
  Winfield S., 67
PHILLIPSBURGH, 95
PICKET, Susan E., 88
  Susannah, 85
  Wesley, 85, 88
PICKETT, Amelia, 15, 66
  Charles W., 66
  George, 66, 118
  James Wesley, 66
  Jesse, 66, 118
  Levin, 66
  Lucy Ann, 66
  Mary Rosanna, 66
  Teresa, 118
  Thomas, 66
  William Henry, 66
PILSON, George W., 117
PIPER, James, 110
PLAINE, Daniel, 114
  Jonathan, 72
  Samuel, 114
PLANK, Mary, 93
  Peter, 93
PLEASANT GROVE, 129
PLEASANT HILLS, 21, 41, 53
PLEASANT MEADOW CONCLUDED, 55
PLEASANT MOUNTAIN, 68
PLEASANT SPRING, 82, 138
PLEASANT VALLEY, 18
PLOWMAN, Noah, 91
PLYMOUTH, 57
POINT ESPRITE, 104
POINT PATIENCE, 106
POLTSON, Levi, 139
  Rebecca, 139
POOLE, Charles, 8
  Dennis, 8
  Ellen, 8
  Esther, 91
  Frances, 8
  Jesse H., 91
  John, 8
  Joseph I., 91
  Margaret, 8
  Margaret E., 91
  Matilda, 91
  Rachel R., 3
  Thomas, 8
  Thornton, 3
  Upton S., 91
  William, 8
  William, Jr., 8
POOL'S DESIRE, 39
POPLAR SPRING, 96
PORK HALL, 38
PORTER, Amanda, 59
  Ann Rebecca, 59
  Eliza A., 30
  George, 57, 59
  Harriet, 57
  Harry, 30
  John H., 59
  Maria, 59
  Sarah, 59
  Susannah, 59
PORTER'S DESIRE, 34
PORTERS PLEASANT LEVEL, 18
PORTERS TREBLE PURCHASE, 18
PORTS, Henry W., 52
POULSON, Cornelius L., 19
  Cornelius S., 19
  Lee, 19
  Levi, 127
  Mary Ann, 19
  Rebecca, 127
POULSON'S CHANCE, 19, 136
POULSON'S RESERVE, 136
POWDER, Andrew, 48, 68

INDEX

Eveline L., 65, 68
Isaac, 68
John, 65, 68
Margaret, 68
Rachel, 25
POWDER'S ADVENTURE, 123
POWEL, David, 92
Eliza, 92
Elizabeth, 92
Ephraim, 92
Hannah, 92
Jacob, 92
Jacob, Sr., 92
John, 92
Nancy, 92
POWELL, Caroline B., 79
Daniel C., 130
Ellenor, 38
Esther, 79
Jacob, 79
Jacob H., 79
John, 79
Julia Ann, 130
Matilda, 79
Moses, 79
PRICE, Amon, 88
Catherine, 7, 88
Elizabeth, 24, 88
Elizabeth Ann, 12
George, 7
James, 7
Jeremiah, 88
John, 88
John C., 136
John Coltrider, 88
Keziah, 88
Leah, 88
Ruth, 23, 88
Samuel, 88
Susan, 88
Thomas, 12, 24

PROGRESS, 44, 109
PROSPECT, 10
PRUGH, Catherine, 29
Charlotte, 35
Honor, 77
Peter, 35
PUSEY, George, Jr., 40
Sarah, 40
Thomas, 40

-R-

RANDALL, Catherine, 78
Vachel, 78
RATHFON, John, 29
Lydia, 29
RATTLESNAKE DENN, 72
RAY, Benjamin, 108
Josephine C., 108
RAYMOND, Ann E., 100
Calvin C., 100
Caroline R., 100
James, 100
REAVER, Benjamin, 133, 138
George, 113
Hamilton, 113
Isabella C., 113
Margaret, 133
Mary, 113
Samuel, 113
Sarah, 113
Ulrich, 113
RECK, Adam, 31
Ann, 31
Catharine, 31
Catherine, 31
Charles, 30, 31, 83
Charles Franklin, 83
Eleanore, 83
Elias, 31

Henry, 30, 31, 83
Hester Ann, 31
James Calvin, 83
John, 31
Lucretia, 83
Margaret Lucretia, 83
RECOVERY UNEXPECTED, 43, 77, 98
RED OAK RIGDE, 119
REECE'S INDUSTRY RESURVEYED, 81
REED, Elias G., 110
Eliza, 110
REESE, Absalom, 81
Andrew, 110
Ann Marie, 81
David, 85
Jacob, 17, 100
Jacob G., 81
John, 1, 81
Laura C., 110
Mary, 1
Noah, 81
Simon Jonas, 81
Sophia, 81
Susan, 81
Washington, 81
REICHART, Elizabeth, 8
John, 8
John, Sr., 8
REID, Alexander H., 93
Hugh F., 93
John, 93
Margaret, 93
REIFSNIDER, Appolonia, 1
Charles T., 126, 128, 129, 131, 136
Jesse, 1
REIKEL, John, 70
John E., 70

INDEX

Susannah, 70
REINDOLLAR,
  Alverta Catherine, 137
  Catherine, 137
  David H., 137
  George, 137
  George Samuel, 137
  Isaiah, 137
  James Henry, 137
  Laura Regina, 137
  Lucinda Ellen, 137
  Samuel, 137
REINECKER, Anna, 116
  Anna Maria, 116
  Paul, 116
REISTER, Peter, 15
REISTER'S LAST SHIFT, 24
RENOULL, Jacob, 13
  Mary, 13
RENSHAW, John Alexander, 33, 36
  Rebecca, 33, 36
REPP, Ephraim R., 115
  Susan, 115
RESOLUTION, 81
RESURVEY, The, 51
RESURVEY OF BEDFORD, The, 2
RESURVEY ON BAILES INDUSTRY, The, 56
RESURVEY ON BEDFORD, 18, 134
RESURVEY ON BLACK OAK HILL, 43, 64, 108
RESURVEY ON BOXES SEARCH, 131
RESURVEY ON BRIERWOOD, 43
RESURVEY ON BROTHER'S AGREEMENT, 12, 26, 43, 54, 75, 89, 95, 121, 134
RESURVEY ON CLARK'S DISCOVERY, 108
RESURVEY ON DAIRY, 51
RESURVEY ON DIGG'S LOT, 47
RESURVEY ON DYER'S MILL FOREST, 112
RESURVEY ON FATHER'S GIFT, 33, 56, 102
  The, 84
RESURVEY ON FRIENDSHIP, 36, 42
RESURVEY ON GILBOA, 4, 40
RESURVEY ON GOOD FELLOWSHIP, 36, 62
RESURVEY ON GOOD WILL, 4, 40, 77, 125, 139
  The, 98
RESURVEY ON HALFER STADT, The, 95
RESURVEY ON HARD BARGAIN, 87
RESURVEY ON HIBERNIA, The, 111
RESURVEY ON HIGH GERMANY, 89
RESURVEY ON JOHN'S LOT, 66, 116
RESURVEY ON LOCUST NECK, The, 83
RESURVEY ON LONG TRUSTED, 40
RESURVEY ON LOOKABOUT, 1, 36, 62, 69, 79, 92, 102, 118, 134, 138
  The, 27
RESURVEY ON MACKEY'S CHOICE, 42, 126
RESURVEY ON MILL LOT, 30
RESURVEY ON MOUNT PLEASANT, 71, 78
RESURVEY ON OWING'S CHANCE (The), 26, 49, 56, 97, 139
  The, 138
RESURVEY ON PATIENCE CARE, The, 80
RESURVEY ON PINES, 56
RESURVEY ON POULSON'S CHANCE, 19
RESURVEY ON RETIREMENT, 32
RESURVEY ON SHARE SPRING, The, 48
RESURVEY ON SHARE'S SPRING, 125
RESURVEY ON SMITH'S LOT, 26
RESURVEY ON STEPHEN'S PURCHASE, 121
RESURVEY ON STONEY BATTER, 19

INDEX

RESURVEY ON SUSAN'S FANCY, 87
RESURVEY ON TEN TRACTS, 23
RESURVEY ON TERRA RUBRA, 99, 114
RESURVEY ON THE ADDITION TO STOCKSDALE'S HILL, 36
RESURVEY ON THE DEEPS, 53, 96, 114, 117
RESURVEY ON THE PINES, 26, 138
RESURVEY ON THREE SPRINGS, 42
RESURVEY ON TIMBER HILLS, 113
RESURVEY ON TIMBER RIDGE, 18, 122, 126
  The, 114
RESURVEY ON UNITY, 65, 91, 127
RESURVEY ON WALNUT BOTTOM, 96, 117
  The, 111
RESURVEY ON WEAVER'S LOT, 90
RESURVEY ON WORMAN'S CONTENT, 113
RETIREMENT CORRECTED, 23, 28, 31, 32, 44, 121
RHODES, Caroline L., 40
  Henry C., 40
  Samuel, 27
  Sophia, 107
RIBBLE'S FOLLY, 126
RIBBLE'S MEADOW, 126
RICH INDIAN GARDEN, The, 126
RICH LAND, 93
RICH MEADOW, 6, 101, 134, 136
RICH MEADOWS, 22
RICHARDS, Alice, 87
  Alice A., 129
  Ann, 47, 87
  Catherine, 87
  Charles, 124
  Charles D., 124
  Daniel, 47, 87
  David L., 124
  Eliza Jane, 129
  Elizabeth, 47
  George, 47, 87
  George E., 124
  George, Jr., 129
  George, Sr., 87
  Isabella, 140
  Jacob, 87
  James, 87
  James B., 129
  John C., 129
  Laura, 87
  Laura V., 129
  Lucinda, 129
  Lucretia, 87
  Mary J., 124
  Mary L., 129
  Rebecca, 129
  Richard, 55, 140
  Richard F., 124
  Richard R., 87, 129
  Samuel, 87
  Samuel F., 129
  Susannah, 124
  William, 87
  William H., 124
  William L., 129
RICHARD'S HUNTING GROUND, 88
RICHARDS HUNTING GROUND, 8
RICHARD'S LOT, 10
RICHARDS LOT, 7
RICHARD'S THIRD CHANCE, 39
RICHART, Catherine Yingling, 11
  David, 11
RIGGLER, George, 79
  Savilla, 79
RILEY, Catherine J., 128
  Elizabeth, 128
  James H., 128
  John T., 128
  Joseph, 128
  Laura V., 128
  Mary E., 128
  Mary T., 128
  Thomas, 128
RINEDOLLAR, Alverta C., 138
  David H., 138
  George, 138
  George S., 138
  Isaiah, 138
  James H., 138
  Laura R., 138
  Lucinda E., 138
  Margaret, 106
  Mary, 138
  Samuel, 138
  William, 106
RINEHART, Amelia, 114, 117
  Ann M., 42
  Ann M. M., 49, 54
  Catherine, 114, 117
  Eli, 114

INDEX

Elias, 117
Elizabeth, 49
Elizabeth R., 42, 54
Emily J., 122
George, 49, 54, 59, 114, 117
Jacob, 122
Jeremiah, 49, 54, 59
John, 42, 49, 51, 54, 59, 74, 122
Joseph, 114, 117
Magadelena, 62
Magdalena, 42, 49, 51, 54, 59, 105
Margaret, 42, 54, 59
Margaret A., 49, 54
Maria, 42, 49, 54, 59
Martha J., 42, 49, 54
Mary, 59, 114, 117
Mary Ann, 54
Peter S., 42, 49, 54, 59
Rachel A., 42
Rachel A. L., 49, 54
Rebecca, 59
Sarah A., 42, 49, 54
Susan C., 42, 49, 54
Susanna, 22, 114
Susannah, 117
William G., 122
William Henry, 114, 117
RINEHART'S FOLLY RESURVEYED, 121
RINGER, Catherine, 80
RIPPLE, Catherine J., 66
  Clorida, 66
  Francis M., 66
  Mary, 66
  Samuel, 66
  Samuel L., 66
RIPPLES, Cobb, 121
  Emma R., 121

Francis M., 121
Mary C., 121
S. Marian, 121
RITES, Frederick, Sr., 19
Rosina N., 19
RITNER, Susan G., 103
RITTENHOUSE, Catherine, 14
  Christian, 14
  Daniel, 14
  Hannah, 14
  Henry, 14
  Jesse, 14
  Joseph, 14
  Mathias, 14
  Samuel, 14
RITTER, Ann, 105
  Catherine, 58
  Catherine E., 58
  Elizabeth M., 125
  Frederick, 5, 104, 105
  Jacob, 5, 104, 105
  Jacob, Jr., 125
  John, 5, 58, 104, 105
  John, Jr., 5
  Joseph, 58
  Lewis, 5, 105
  Magdalena, 105
  Mary Ann, 5
  Michael, 5, 105
  Minerva, 125
  Polly, 5, 105
  Rebecca, 125
  Sarah Kelly, 125
ROACH, Caleb, 45
  Rachel, 45
ROBBISON, Richard David, 92
ROBENSTIEN, Amelia, 112
  Eli M., 112
  Elias, 112

George, 112
John, 112
Peter, 112
ROBERTS, Ann, 8, 32
  Catherine Ann, 83
  Francis N., 83
  Henry H., 83
  Henry S., 84
  John, 54
  Kate A., 84
  Mary, 50
  Mary Elizabeth, 84
  San Salvador, 84
  Virginia S., 84
  Walter C., 83
  William, 54
ROBERTSON, John, 14
ROCHESTER, 2, 12, 14, 22, 58, 61, 65, 68, 99, 104, 122, 129
ROCHESTER ENLARGED, 61
ROCHESTER RESURVEY, 135
ROCHESTER RESURVEYED, 65
ROCK HILL, 130
ROCKEY POINT, 87
ROCKLAND, 130
RODKEY, Catherine, 35
  Daniel, 35
  Elizabeth, 35
  Esther, 35
  George, 35
  John, 35
  Jonathan, 35
  Leah, 35
  Mary, 35
  Michael, 35
ROELKY, Sarah, 64
  William L., 64

INDEX

ROHRBAUGH,
  Margaret, 11
  Solomon, 11
ROME, 57
ROOP, David, 85
  John, 59
  John of Joseph, 4
  John, Jr., 85
  John, Sr., 85
  Joseph, 59
  Lydia, 56, 59
  Samuel, 56
  Susannah, 59
ROOT, Basil, 22
ROSENBERGER,
  Lenhart, 17
ROSENSTEEL,
  Charles, 26
  Maria, 26
  Mary, 26
ROSS'S RANGE, 72
ROUTZON, Barbara, 31
  Henry, 31
ROW, Hannah, 53
  Isaac, 87
  Nancy, 87
  Samuel, 53
ROWE, Isaac, 65
ROYER, Amos
  Mehring, 102
  Ann, 18
  Christian, 18, 102
  Elizabeth, 124
  Emanuel, 45
  Jacob B., 45
  Jehu, 18, 102
  Jesse, 18, 45, 102
  John, 124
  Joseph D., 45
  Peter, 18
  Rebecca, 45
  Samuel, 45

Sarah I., 45
Susan A., 45
Uriah, 45
RUBY, Anna, 47
RUDISEL, Ann, 106
  Anna, 12
  Ludwick, 12, 106
  Margaret, 12
  Mary E., 106
  Mary Jane, 106
  Nancy, 12, 106
  Thomas, 12, 106, 121
  Tobias, 12, 106
  Tobias, Jr., 106
  William, 12, 106
RUDOLPH, Anna
  Mary, 76
  Daniel, 76
RUMBY, Martha E., 103
  Thomas Benton, 103
RUMLER, Perry, 46
  Rachel, 46
RUNKELS, Basil, 72
RUNKLES, Catherine, 72
  Mary E., 72
RUNNYMEDE, 36
RUNNYMEDE
  ENLARGED, 42, 54, 134
RUOFF, George, 114, 117
  Jacob, 114, 117
  Mary, 114, 117
RURAL FELICITY, 125

-S-

SAFFELL, Mary Ann, 39
  William T. R., 39

SALLY'S CHANCE
  RESURVEY, 39
SANTZ, Adam, 13
  Andrew, 13
  Catherine, 13
  David, 13
  Eliza, 13
  George, 13
  John, 13
  Mary, 13
  Peter, 13
  Salone, 13
  Sarah, 13
SAPLING GROUND, 81
SARAH'S
  PLEASURE, 13
SATER, Anna, 22
  Elizabeth, 22
  John, 22
  Mariah, 22
  Samuel, 22
  Sarah, 22
SCANBORN, Michael, 121
SCHAEFFER,
  Augustus D., 133
  David, 122
  Susanna, 122
SCHEAMING
  DEFEATED, 1
SCHLOPER,
  Catherine, 60
  George, 60
SCHOOL
  COMMISSIONERS
  OF CARROLL
  COUNTY, The, 110
SCHWEIGART,
  Christian, 62
  Clementine, 62
  Cyrus, 62, 90
  Jesse, 62, 90
  John, 62, 90
  Lewis, 62, 90

INDEX

Mary, 62, 90
Rufus, 62, 90
Sarah, 62, 90
Sevilla, 90
Scotland (Country), 78
SCOTT, Thomas Parker, 103
SEABROOKS, Henry, 15
SECOND ADDITION TO ACORN HILL, 55
SECOND ADDITION TO BROOK'S DISCOVERY ON THE RICH LANDS, 71, 78, 103
SECOND AMENDMENT, 72
SECOND RESURVEY ON BRIERWOODS, 30
SECOND TRAPEZINM, The, 43
SEEKENS, Eve, 131
  Leah, 131
  William, 131
SEGANS, William, 131
SEIF, Louisa, 121
  Martin, 121
SELL, Daniel, 22
  Jacob, 35
  Mary, 35
SELLERS, Amanda E., 94
  Ann Mary, 94
  Belinda Ann, 94
  Catherine, 10
  George, 94
  George, Sr., 94
  Jacob, 94
  John, 10, 94
  Mary, 94
  Peter, 94

Rachel, 94
Ruth, 94
Sallie, 94
Samuel, 94
Serepta, 94
SELLMAN, Barbara, 10
  Beall, 10
  Caroline Louise, 71
  Catherine, 71
  Emily Jane, 71
  Henry A., 108
  John B.T., 126
  Mary Catherine, 71
SELMON PURCHASE, 69
SENSE, Peter, 13, 15
  Rachel, 15
SENSENEY, Anna, 67
  Elizabeth, 67
  Jacob, 67
  Jacob, Sr., 67
  James, 67
  Peter, 67
  Washington, 68
SENTZ, Andrew, 49, 54, 59
  Asa, 50
  Catharine, 127
  Catherine, 7, 31
  Catherine Ellen, 49, 51, 54
  Charles, 50
  Isabella, 49, 50, 54
  Jacob, 127
  Joseph, 31
  Joshua, 49, 54
  Mahala, 50
  Margaret, 80
  Mary, 7, 49
  Peter, 50
  Philip, 7
  Rachel, 7

Sally, 49, 54, 59
Salome, 59
Urias, 50
SETTLED IN PEACE, 47
SHADE, Catherine, 1
  John, 1
SHADRACK'S LAST SHIFT, 35
SHADRACK'S LAST SHIFT RESURVEYED, 113
SHAEFFER, Elizabeth, 112
  Jacob, 41
  Joseph, 1, 24, 101
  Lewis, 112
  Mary, 41
  Susan, 1
SHAFER, Elizabeth, 132
  Joshua, 132
  Lydia Catherine, 130
  William Lewis, 130
SHAFFER, Adam, 87
  Andrew, 8
  Barbara, 11
  Benjamin, 8
  Catherine, 62, 67
  David, 62, 67
  Eliza, 74
  Elizabeth, 8, 29
  Ellen, 29
  Emanuel, 29
  Harriet, 87
  Henry, 29, 88
  Henry A., 87
  James, 29
  Jesse, 11
  John, 29
  John R., 13
  Margaret, 29
  Mary A., 88

INDEX

Nancy, 87
Nicholas, 29
Samuel, 29, 74
Sarah, 88
Sarah E., 137
Susanna, 13
Susannah, 8
William, 29
William H., 137
SHANER, Elizabeth, 98
Samuel, 129
Sarah C., 129
SHARER, Jacob, 8, 107
Margaret, 107
Ruth, 8
SHARE'S SPRING, 125
SHARRER, Catherine, 38
David, 21
Elizabeth, 21
Jacob, 21
Mary, 21
SHARRETTS, William, 117
SHAW, Catherine, 12
Erasmus, 12
Moses, 50, 94, 102
William, 50
SHEALER, Anthony, 6
Mary, 6
SHEARER, Elizabeth, 7
Jacob, 7
SHEELER, Jessiah, 112
Lucinda, 112
SHEETS, George, 24
Rachel, 24
SHEPHERD'S RETIREMENT, 102, 125
SHERFY, Abraham, 97
Christopher Columbus, 97

John Thomas, 97
SHERMAN, Conrad, 18
Elizabeth, 17
George S., 2, 18
Jacob, 17
SHEW, Elizabeth, 87
Henry, 87
SHILT, Mary, 111
Samuel, 111
SHIPLEY, Absolom, 48
Alexander, 127
Catherine, 37, 127
Charles H., 20
Charlotte, 137
Cordelia, 13, 80, 85
Cornelius H., 20
David, 127
Edwin, 107
Elizabeth, 109
Francis, 127
Francis L., 20
Frederick, 109
George W., 37
Grove, 13
Grove, Jr., 85
Henry H., 20
Jabez A.B., 127
James, 127
John, 85
John F., 13
John R., 37
Joshua, 43
Juliana B. H., 20
Lewis, 127
Lloyd, 37
Louisa, 13, 85
Nancy, 43
Nathaniel, 102
Peter, 43
Rachel H., 20
Robert H., 20
Ruth, 20

Ruth E., 20
Sarah, 48
Theodore, 127
Thomas, 80, 127
William G., 27
William of Robert, 20
SHIRICK, Barbara, 105
SHIVERS INTEGRITY, 4
SHOCKEY, Jacob, 57
SHOCKNEY, Charles, 37
Sarah, 37
SHOE, Catherine N., 19
Zachariah, 19
SHOEMAKER, Abraham, 115
Alice J., 115
Amanda, 54
Americus, 54, 110
Anna F., 120
Araminta M., 120
Barney, 28
Catherine E., 115
Clara E., 115
David M., 115
Edward E., 120
Elizabeth, 21
Emma C., 115
George, 28
George A., 120
Henrietta, 54
Henry, 28
Henry A., 115, 134
Hester, 28
Jacob, 21
Jacob L., 120
John, 21, 28, 54, 115, 134
John Ezra, 120
Joseph, 28
Lydia, 54
Maria R., 120

INDEX

Mary, 21, 110
Mary Jane, 123
Oliver B., 120
Peter, 22
Samuel, 21, 28
Samuel C., 120
Silas O., 123
Solomon S., 120
Thomas, 28
William, 28, 120
William Albert, 120
SHOEMAKER'S LOT, 112
SHOLL, Barbara, 31
Peter, 31
SHORB, Abraham, 93
Catherine, 93
Conrad, 93
James, 93
John, 93
Mary, 130
Samuel, 93
William Thomas, 93
SHORT, Abraham, 44
Mary Ann, 44
SHOWER, Jacob, 124
Theodore A., 124
SHREEVE, David, 55
Nimrod, 77
Sarah, 55
SHRINER, Alfred, 126
Christian, 73
Eliza J., 108
Elizabeth, 73
Ezra, 108
Hannah, 73
Isaac, 86
James, 53
John, 53
Levi, 53
Louisa, 53
Mary, 73
Mary Ellen, 86
Philip, 73
Samuel, 53
Sarah, 53
William, 53
SHRIVER, Andrew, 32, 36
Andrew K., 32, 36
Eliza H., 17
Elizabeth, 17, 18
Eve, 17
Isaac, 14
Jacob Sherman, 17
James, 33, 36
John S., 32, 36
Joseph, 32, 36
Samuel S., 33, 36
Thomas, 32, 36
William, 33, 36
William Waggoner, 17
SHRIVER'S BOTTOM, 9, 137
SHRIVER'S INTEGRITY, 132
SHROEDER, Harry B., 76
SHUE, Catherine, 20, 25, 119
David, 20
George, 67
Jeremiah, 119
Rebecca, 8
Susan M., 67
SHUEY, Debora, 87
Elizabeth, 87
John, 87
Lucinda C., 87
Monro, 87
Nancy, 87
Sarah, 87
Susannah, 87
SHULE, Henry, 88
SHULER, Henry, 111
John, 112
Sarah, 112
SHULL, Amanda, 57
Catherine A., 57
Daniel C., 57
Daniel L., 57
John H., 57
Kesiah, 57
Mary A., 57
Samuel P., 57
Sarah, 57
SHULTZ, John, 80
Rebecca, 80
SHUMAN, Emanuel, 53
George, 53
George H., 53
Israel, 53
Julia A., 53
Nathaniel, 53
Serepta, 53
SHUNK, Benjamin, 91
Daniel, 91
Elizabeth, 91
George, 91
John, 91, 115
Michael, 112
Rebecca, 115
Samuel, 91
Susan, 112
SIAS, Ann, 64
Jeremiah, 64
Nicodemus, 64
Noah, 64
SIDELING HILL, 31
SIKINS, David, 92
SIM, Dr. Thomas, 40
Lucy Ann, 40
SIMON'S DELIGHT, 4
SIMPERS, Benjamin, 42
Henry, 41
Mary Ann, 41

SINGERY CHANCE RESURVEYED, 98
SINGERY'S CHANCE RESURVEY, 82
SIX BROTHERS, 47
SKIDMORE, James, 80
  Minerva A., 80
SLATER, Ann Eliza, 140
SLICK, David, 46
  Elin, 46
  James, 46
  Mary A., 46
SLIPE, 134
SLUSS, Michael, 42
SLYDER, Mary, 95
  Peter, 95
SMALL, James, 64
  Jane, 64
SMALL BIT, 10
SMEACH, Andrew, 91, 135
  Andrew S., 135
  Ann M., 135
  Barbara A., 135
  David R., 135
  Ellen S., 135
  George M., 135
  John M., 135
  Philip A., 135
  William W., 135
SMELSER, Anna Mary, 57
  David, 57, 98
  David P., 98
  George, 98
  John P., 98
  Mary, 98
  Michael, 98
  Susannah, 61
  Virginia C., 98
  William A., 61
  William W., 98

SMELTZER, Carolina Louisana, 4
  George, 4, 40
  Isaac W., 40
  Isaac Washington, 4
  Josiah P., 40
  Josiah Pearce, 4
  Rachel, 40
  Sarah, 4, 40
  Solomon S., 40
SMITH, Absalom, 103
  Amanda, 103
  Ann Eliza, 7
  Ann Rebecca, 103
  Augustus, 79
  Caroline S., 61
  Daniel W., 104
  David, 61
  Elizabeth, 34, 127
  Emma I., 76
  Ezra, 79
  Francis, 76
  Francis M., 103
  Henry T., 103
  Hester A., 126
  James, 7
  Jeremiah H., 94
  Joel, 79
  John E., 136
  Joshua, 14, 22, 50, 51, 59, 102
  Julia A., 104
  Julian, 79
  Louisa Adeliza, 103
  Lucinda, 76
  Martha, 79
  Martha Elizabeth, 76
  Mary, 79
  Mary E., 103
  Mary Henrietta, 103
  Missouri, 79
  Nimrod, 127
  Peter B., 94

Philip, 103
Rebecca, 103, 104
Richard, 104
Robert T., 126
Samuel H., 103
Stephen, 103
Washington, 104
William, 79, 103
William J., 103
SMITHS FIELD, 77
SNADER, David W., 96
  Elizabeth, 108
  Evan T., 108
  Ezra L., 108
  Jacob W., 108
  Jesse W., 108
  Levi W., 57
  Lucretia, 57
  Martha C., 108
  Philip, 108
  Sophia, 96
  William H. H., 108
SNAKE DENN, 89
SNEERINGER, Eliza, 26
  Samuel G., 26
SNIDER, Catherine, 7, 110
  Daniel, 7
  David A., 7
  George, 7
  George Washington, 7
  Jacob, 43
  Levi, 110
  Mary Ann Rebecca, 85
  Mary Magdalena, 7
  Michael, 85
  Rebecca, 43
  Susannah, 7
  William, 7
SNYDER, Catherine, 35
  Christian, 34

INDEX

Daniel, 34, 35, 133
David A., 35, 112
George, 35
George W., 35
Henry, 34
Jacob, 34
Julian, 89
Magdalana, 34
Mary, 35
Mary C., 133
Michael, 11, 34
Peter, Jr., 19
Rachel, 11
Sarah, 112
Solomon, 89
SO FAR SO GOOD, 47, 71
SOMETHING, 89
SOPER, Violette E., 28
  Wilson L., 28
SOUDER, Joshua, 46
SPALDING, Cecelia M., 61
  Edward F., 61
  George, 61
  Josephine, 61
  Mary, 61
SPANGLER, Alexander R., 33, 36
  Andrew M., 33, 36
  Augustus G., 33
  Barbara Ann, 29
  Benjamin F., 33, 36
  David, 29
  Edward, 97
  Elizabeth, 29
  Isabella, 29
  Jacob, 29
  Jesse, 29
  John, 29
  Jonas, 29
  Joseph, 29
  Josephine M., 33, 36

Lydia, 29
Margaret M, 36
Margaret M., 33
Mary C., 97
Matilda, 33, 36
William H., 33, 36
SPARKS, Airetta, 7
  Cecilia, 7
  Laban, 7
  Mathilda, 7
  Sarah, 7
SPECULATION, 78
SPIKE, The, 59
SPILTERS INCLOSURE, 53
SPORTSMAN'S HALL, 98
SPRINKLE, Elizabeth, 22
  Harriett, 103
  Henry, 103
  Ida Mary, 103
  Sarah, 103
  Simon Peter, 103
  Theodore, 103
STAIN'S NEGLECT, 73, 107, 140
STALEY, Alfred, 92
  Lydia, 92
STAMP, Clarinda J., 116
  William W., 116
STANSBURY, John S., 97
  William, 25
STANSBURY GROVE, 122
STANSBURY PLAINS, 110
STANSBURY'S GROVE, 108
STANSBURY'S PROSPECT, 7, 112
STARBOARD, 124

STARNER, George D., 138
  John, 81
  Lucy Ann, 138
  Sevilla, 81
STAUFER'S ADDITION TO MIDDLEBURGH, 63
STEAR, Lydia, 138
STEELE, Ann A., 119
  Charlotte A., 119
  Dr. J. W., 119
  Emma Kate, 119
  James E., 119
  James H., 69, 119
  John T., 119
  John William, 119
  Joseph Henry, 119
STEFFEY, Cecelia, 75
  Eliza, 75
  Eve, 75
  John, 75
  Michael, 75
STEFFY, Henry W., 86
STEGNER, Amelia, 112
  Ephraim, 112
STEIGER, Ann Maria, 32
  Anna Maria, 36
  Augustus F., 32, 36
  Benjamin F., 36
  Benjamin T., 32
  Catherine B., 32, 36
  Emma Maria, 32
  Maria, 36
STEIGERS, Barbara, 26
  Elizabeth, 26
  George, 26
  John, 26
  Margaret, 26
STEIN, Anna M., 104

INDEX

George, 104
STEINER, James, 14
Matilda, 14
STEM, Charles Wesley, 90
David E., 90
Deborah J., 90
Jacob, 90
Jesse E., 90
John Henry, 90
Joseph T., 90
Leanna V., 90
Lucinda, 90
Mary Ann, 90
William L., 90
STEPHEN'S DEFENSE, 130
STEPHEN'S FOLLY RESURVEYED, 4
STEPHENSONS GARDEN, 136
STEPNEY CAUSEWAY, 110
STEPNEY'S CAUSEWAY, 30, 136
STEVENS, Clemson, 40, 101
David, 101
George, 101
Henry, 101
John, 101
Margaret A., 40
Mary, 101
Rezin, 101
Samuel, 101
Sarah, 40
William, 101
STEVEN'S DEFENSE, 47
STEVENSON GARDEN, 115
STEVENSON'S CONCLUSION, 72, 79

STEVENSON'S DEER PARK AND TROUTING STREAM, 82
STEVENSON'S GARDEN, 4, 40, 44, 61, 66, 110, 120, 139
STEVENSON'S LOT, 4, 64
STEVENSON'S MANOR, 16, 75
STEVENSON'S MANOR CORRECTED, 75
STEVER, Mary, 21
STIER, Anna, 111
Barbara, 111
Caroline, 111
Elias, 111
Jacob, 111
John, 111
Jonas, 111
Lydia, 111
Michael, 111
Rebecca, 111
STINCHCOMBS RESERVE, 22
STOCKSDALE, Cornelius, 5
Cornelius H., 6
Dolly, 6
Edmund H., 6
Edward, 64
Elias C., 96
Eliza, 6
John, 64
Julia H., 6
Keziah Van Julia, 106
Martha, 96
Martha A., 106
Mary Jane, 106
Mathilda, 6
Nathan, 6
Noah, 64

Noah B., 106
Rebecca Jane, 96
Solomon, 6, 64
Susanna, 96
Thomas E., 5, 6
William Nelson, 106
STOCKSDALE'S HILL, 36
STOFFER'S ADDITION TO MIDDLEBURG, 73
STOFFLE, Polly, 80
Sebastian, 80
STONE, James, 30
Julia A., 30
STONEBREAKER, Henry, 111
John, 111
Joseph, 111
Lydia, 111
Mary, 111
STONER, Abraham, 126
Belinda, 125, 139
Clarissa Ann, 126
Ephraim, 125, 139
Ezra, 126
George W., 58
Jesse C., 139
Jesse L., 126
Mary C., 58
Priscilla, 91
William, 91
STONESIFER, Abraham, 31
Barbara, 31
Catherine, 31, 37
Christina, 31
Daniel, 31
Elizabeth, 31
Emily, 26
Eva, 76
Hannah, 31
Henry, 31

INDEX

Isaac, 31
Jacob, 31, 37
John, 31
Joshua, 77
Levi, 76
Marie Elizabeth, 31
Martin, 31
Peter, 31
Rachel, 31
Sarah, 77
Uriah, 26
STONEY HILLS, 57, 117
STONEY POINT, 11, 45
STONEY RIDGE, 29
STOPHELS MEADOW, 121
STORB, Eve, 60
John, 60
STORM, Anthony, 84
Christoper, 84
Elizabeth, 84
Mary A., 84
Mary Ann, 84
STORMS, Amon Jesse, 51, 86
Aretta, 85
Aritta, 93
Catherine, 41, 51, 86, 115
Christiana, 51, 85, 93
Elizabeth, 51, 86
George, 86, 93
George W., 51, 85
George W. G., 51
George Washington Gilmore, 93
Henry, 51, 86
Jacob, 51, 86, 118
Jacob D., 85
Jacob J., 51
Jacob L., 51, 93
James F., 85
Josephine, 85
Margaret, 51, 86, 115
Mary, 86
Mary Ann, 51, 86
Naomi, 51, 86, 93
Noah Webster, 51, 86
Onetta, 51
Sarah, 86
Sarah Ann, 51, 85, 93
Sarah Jane, 51, 86
Thomas, 51, 86
William, 51, 93
William J., 85
William Jesse, 51, 93
William P., 85
William W., 86
STOUFFER, Ann, 14
Catherine, 14
Christian, 14
David, 14
Henry, 14
Jacob, 14
John, 14
Josiah, 14
Louisa F., 14
STRAWBERRY MEAD, 110, 136
STREVIG, Edward, 77
Ephraim, 76
Henry B., 76
John, 77
John, Jr., 76
Lydia, 76, 77
Maria, 77
Mary A., 76
Sophia, 77
William, 77
STRICKER, 105
STRONG, Charles, 8
Tabitha, 8
STUDY, Eliza, 112
John, 112
STUFFER'S ADDITION TO MIDDLEBURG, 70
STULLER, Ann R., 75
John, 75
STULTZ, Abraham, 23
Caroline, 54
Catherine, 53
David, 53
Eliza Ann, 53
Henry, 54
Mary, 53
Mary Ann, 23, 53
Nicholas, 53
Samuel Franklin, 53
Sarah Jane, 53
William, 53
STUMP'S LOT, 77
STYNER, Peter, 119
Polly, 119
SUGAR VALLEY, 99
SULLIVAN, Augustus F., 58
Catherine, 58
Daniel, 52
George W., 58
Jeremiah, 86
Jesse, 58
John, 86
John H., 58
Julia Ann, 52
Levi Reese, 52
Lydia, 15
Margaret E., 58
Mary M., 52
Michael, 31
William, 5, 15, 52, 58
SWARTZBAUGH, John W., Jr., 65
Mary, 65
SWITZER, Elizabeth, 115
John, 115

INDEX

Sarah Ann, 25
SYKES, Catherine, 15
George, 15
James, 64
John, 15, 31
John T., 15
Lewis, 15
Nathaniel, 15
William, 15

-T-

TAGG, Mary, 112
William, 112
TAILOR, Adam, 9
Elizabeth, 9
Jacob, 9
Susannah, 9
TANEY, Ann Missouri, 97
Charles Calvin, 97
Elmira, 97
Elmira Alice, 97
Frederick, 97, 134
Nancy, 134
Solomon Frederick, 97
TASTO, Henry, 24
Sally, 24
TAYLOR, Benjamin, 87
Charles W., 65
Deborah, 87
Elizabeth, 73
Elizabeth A., 100
Francis A., 87
Mary A., 87
Matilda, 65
Noah W., 87
Samuel, 73
Sarah Ann, 65
William H., 100
Tennessee (State), 8
TERRA RUBRA, 14, 38, 47, 93, 114

TERRA RUBRA RESURVEYED, 22
TEVIS'S ADVENTURE, 84
THIRD ADDITION TO ACORN HILL, 55
THIRD ADDITION TO NEW LONDON, 93
THIS OR NOTHING, 26
THOMAS, Amelia C., 66
Ann, 50
Braxton D., 50
Daniel W., 50
Henry, 66, 76
Jane, 38
Joseph, 38
Juliet, 77
Lacy, 38
Martha Griselda, 50
Mary Levinia, 50
Moses S., 50
Rachel J., 66
Samuel, 38
Susan A., 76
Susan Ann, 66
William B., 139
THOMAS'S RESURVEY ON THE DEEPS, 111
THOMPSON, Abel, 128
Charles R., 117
Frances, 127, 128
Margaret E., 127
Susan, 117
THOMSON, John, 26, 40
Louisa, 40
THORNBACK'S ADDITION, 88

THREE BROTHERS, 80, 117
THREE SPRINGS, 42
TIMBER HILLS, 113
TIMBER RIDGE, 18
TIMBER RIDGE RESURVEY, 108
TIME ENOUGH YET, 81
TIPTON, Dianna, 106, 107
Thomas, 106, 107
TODD, Mary, 15
TOMEY, Catherine, 86
Daniel, 86
Jeremiah, 86
Mary, 86
TOOP, Amanda, 107
Mary E., 107
Samuel J., 107
TOWNSEND, Annie M., 126
Charles B., 77
Evan T., 77
Frederick, 134
Isaac W., 77
Jesse O., 77
John, 134
John R., 77
Joseph C., 77
Lydia E., 77
Mary, 77
Rachel, 134
Susan, 134
Thomas, 77, 134
William F., 77
TRANSYLVANIA, 15, 22, 32, 38, 52, 105
TRANSYLVANIA RESURVEYED, 101, 105
TRIMBLE, Elizabeth, 1
William, 1
TRINE, David W., 116

INDEX

Emanuel, 92, 116
Martha, 116
Mary Dorothy, 116
Samuel, 116
Susannah, 116
TROUBLESOME JOB, 84, 121
TROUTING STREAM, The, 47
TROUTING STREAMS CORRECTED (The), 87, 103
TROXALL, Jacob, 1
Rachel, 1
TROXEL, John, 27
Lydia, 27
TROY, 75, 114
TROY MEADOW, 134
TRUMBO, George, 122, 127, 139
TUNIOUS, Charles, 6
Sarah, 6
TURKEY THICKET, 33

-U-

UHL, Louie, 29
Mary, 29
UHLER, Catherine Ann, 83
Clara, 78
John H., 83
William, 78
ULRICH, David, 74
Elizabeth, 74
Samuel, 74
UNITED FRIENDSHIP, 10
UNITY, 43, 70
UPPER MARLBOROUGH, 56, 84, 137
UPPERCO, Benjamin, 109

George, 78
Isaac, 78
John, 78
John Thomas, 78
Mary, 78
Naomi, 109
UTZ, Daniel, 24
David, 20, 24
Eliza, 24
Elizabeth, 24
Frederick, 20, 25
George, 20
John, 20
Joseph, 24
Lydia, 24
Magdalena, 20
Michael, 11
Peter, 24
Polly, 25
Rachel, 20
Rebecca, 24
Sarah, 20
Susanna, 11
UTZ'S INHERITANCE, 20, 24, 122

-V-

VALENTINE, Ann, 111
Ezra, 86
Jacob, 86
Josiah, 86
Levi, 86
Milton, 86
Rebecca, 86
Thomas, 111
William, 86
VALLEY OF JEHOSEPHAT, The, 53
VALLEY OF STRIFE, The, 116

VAUGHN, Caleb, 8
Christopher, 1
Elizabeth, 1
Joshua, 8
Mary, 8
Richard, 8
Thomas, 8
VENUS'S ARBOUR, 39
VENUS'S HARBOR, 86
VICTORY, 8
VINE YARD, 89
Virginia (State), 3, 19, 28, 52, 70, 89
Alexandria, 136
Fink's Fork, 15
Wheeling, Ohio County, 18
VITTER, Barbara, 35
Samuel, 35

-W-

WADDLE'S DELIGHT, 14
WADE, Benedict, 37
Emanuel, 37
Larkin, 37
Rachel, 37
WAGGONER, Elizabeth, 69, 79
John, 69
William, 79
WAGNER, Catherine, 94
Charles, 102
Edward, 34
Henry, 102
Lavina J., 34
Philip, 94
Rachel R., 102
Sarah L., 102
William H., 102

INDEX

WAGONER,
  Catherine, 94
John, 108, 109
Mary E., 109
Philip, 94
WAGONER'S
  FANCY, 43
WAGUS, John, 45
Nancy, 45
Richard, 45
William, 45
WALKER, Elizabeth, 125
Stephen A., 125
WALKER'S
  PARADICE, 10
WALKER'S
  PARADISE
  RESURVEYED, 7
WALTMAN, Charles W., 125
Helen, 125
John E., 125
John Thomas, 125
Margaret Catherine, 125
Martha Ann, 125
Mary Elizabeth, 125
Richard Franklin, 125
William Josiah, 125
WAMPLER,
  Abraham, 18, 19, 41
Catherine, 9, 18, 19, 102
Elizabeth, 9
Emily Jane, 9, 19
George E., 9, 19
Henry H., 9, 19
James L., 19
James S., 9
John, 9, 18, 19
Lewis, 24
Lydia, 24
Maria L., 9, 19

Philip, 18
Samuel, 9, 18, 19
William A., 9, 19
WANTZ, David, 76
Rachel, 37, 76
Valentine, 37
WARE, Charles A., 136
E. Anna Maria, 136
Elizabeth, 43
John, 43
WAREHAME,
  Conrad, 10
George, 10
Henry, 10
WAREHIME,
  Catherine, 81
Conrad, 81
Ephraim, 81
Henry, 81
John S., 81
Manassa, 81
Nelson, 81
Noah, 81
Seranda, 81
Susannah, 81
Thomas, 81
WARFIELD, Aletha, 65
Ann Regina, 61, 65
Benjamin, 61, 65
Caroline, 61
Charles A., 65
Charles W., 65
Eliza Ann, 61
Elizabeth, 61
Ella S., 63
Evan T., 61
Gustavus, 61
Josephine E., 63
Lorenzo E., 61
Marcellus W., 63
Margaretta E., 65
Mary J. T., 63

Milton W., 109
Sarah, 18
Seth, 61
Seth H., 61
Seth N., 65
WARFIELD'S
  FOREST, 39
WARFIELD'S
  INHERITANCE, 59
WARNER, David, 69
Deborah, 69
Elias, 69, 109
Elizabeth, 69
Emanuel, 69
Francis, 44
George, 35, 69
Hannah, 125
Henry, 125
Jacob, 44, 69
Jane, 69
John, 69
Magdalena, 44
Mary, 44, 48, 69, 109
Mary E., 79
Rachel, 44
Rebecca, 69
Samuel E., 44
Sarah, 44, 69
Uriah, 69
William, 69
William H., 79, 80
WASHINGTON
  (Tract), 76, 118
Washington, D.C., 20, 36, 100, 124
Washington Territory, 130
WATERS, Ann Eliza, 70
Eliza Ann, 71
Elizabeth, 71
Jacob, 3
Maria, 3
Virginia, 70, 71

INDEX

Zadock M., 70
Zadok, 71
WATSON'S DELIGHT, 71, 78
WATSON'S TRUST, 67
WATT, Nancy, 18
Robert, 18
WAYBRIGHT, Ann, 18
John, 18
WAYS, Harriet, 118
John T., 118
WE FOUND THE BEGINNING, 22
WEAKLEY, Henry, 51
Mary, 51
Nancy, 15
Thomas, 15
William, 51
WEAKLY, Mary, 86
William, 86
WEANT, Jacob, 42
John Washington, 42
WEAVER, Anne, 10
Catherine, 10
Daniel, 2, 28
David, 2, 29, 62, 67
Elizabeth, 49, 54, 59
George, 2, 10
George E., 28
Greenburg, 29
Helen M., 72
John, 10, 91
Louis H. P., 72
Margaret, 62
Mary Elizabeth, 29
Philip, 28
Ruth, 2
Samuel, 10, 49, 54, 59
William, 28
WEBB, Hanson T., 85
William A., 109

WEBSTER, C. W., 23
WEE BIT ENLARGED (The), 47, 129, 130
WEEKLY, Emily J., 118
Mary, 118
Sarah, 118
William Michael, 118
William, Sr., 118
WELLS, Julia Ann, 22
Thomas, 22
WELL'S CARE, 10
WELL'S CARE ENLARGED, 11, 81
WELL'S INHERITANCE, 106
WELSH, Ferdinand, 3
Jane, 3
John, 3
Lydia, 3
Mary, 3
Mary Ann, 3
Robert, 3
Sarah Elizabeth, 3
Susanna, 3
William, 3
WENTZ, Ann E., 83
Ann Eliza, 50
Ann M., 67
Charles V., 83
David, 83
Eliza J., 83
Emanuel, 80
George, 35
Jacob, 83
John, 80, 83
John Valentine, 83
Mary, 80
Philip, 67
Rachel, 80, 83
Samuel, 83
Valentine, 50, 83

WERNER, Anna May, 112
Thomas, 112
WEYBRIGHT, Anna, 102
Rebecca, 102
Samuel, 102
WHALEN, Ann Rebecca, 6
Martha, 6
Sarah, 6
Susan, 96
William, 32, 96
WHAT YOU PLEASE, 44
WHEELER, Ellen V., 120
William B., 120
WHITE GRAVEL SPRING, 64
WHITE OAK BOTTOM, 22, 57, 64, 91
WHITELEATHER, Andrew, 35
Anna Maria, 35
David, 35
Jacob, 35
Martin, 35
Rebecca, 35
WHITE'S LEVEL, 18, 48, 86, 93
WHITMORE, Benjamin, 38
George, 38
Greenberry, 38
Jacob, 38
Mary, 38
William, 38
WHITMYER, Barbara, 35
Daniel, 35
Lydia, 35
Mary Elizabeth, 36
Rebecca, 35

INDEX

Sarah Ellen, 36
Simon, 35
William Ezra, 36
WIDDER, George, 59
Mary, 59
WILHELM, Elizabeth, 127
George, 127
WILHIDE, Catherine R., 114
WILKES AND LIBERTY, 61, 66
WILL RESTORED, The, 118
WILLIAMS, Abraham, 93
Absolum, 30
Amos, 55
Benjamin, 29, 109
Esther, 93
James, 29, 30
John, 29, 51, 86
Lovelace, 30
Maria, 55
Mary, 109
Mary L.B., 132
Nathan, 30
Rebecca, 51, 86
Thomas, 29
WILLIAM'S DEFENSE, 96
WILLIAM'S DELIGHT, 102
WILLIAM'S LUCK, 1, 77, 134
WILL'S FOREST, 125
WILMOT'S MANOR RESURVEYED, 75
WILMOT'S PURCHASE, 119
WILMOT'S WILDERNESS, 32, 96
WILMOTT'S MEADOWS, 82

WILMOTT'S PURCHASE, 89
WILSON, Anna E., 89
Cornelius, 74
Elizabeth, 18, 53, 87
Emily Jane, 100
Ephraim, 23
Franklin H., 89
George, 75, 87, 89
Henry, 62, 67
Isabella, 18
Jacob, 87
Jane, 18
John, 74, 83
John W., 89
Joseph, 74, 87
Joshua, 74
Levi L., 74, 100
Martha, 18
Mary Ellen, 74
Mary Jane, 18
Nathan, 74
Nicholas, 74
Penelope, 74
Robert, 18, 75
Robert W., 74
Susannah, 62, 67
Thomas, 53
William, 18, 53, 87, 101
William, Sr., 87
WILSON'S INHERITANCE, 87
WILSON'S INTENT, 123
WILT, Elizabeth, 15
Jacob, 15
WIMER, Joseph, 74
WINCHESTER'S ADDITION, 48
WINDSOR FOREST, 45, 74
WINDSOR FOREST CORRECTED, 132
WINE, Jacob, 135

WINEBRENNER, Hannah, 122, 127, 139
John, 122, 127, 139
WINFALL, 13
WINK, George, 13
Susan, 13
WINRODE, Catherine, 98
WINTERODE, Levi S., 90, 94
Maria, 94
Mary Ann, 82
Rufus J., 82
WINTERS, David, 127
Ephraim, 127
Frederick, 38
George, 127
Isaac, 127
Joseph, 30, 127
Levi, 48
Mary, 38
Mary E., 127
Reuben, 127
Stephen, 127
WINTER'S ADDITION TO WESTMINSTER, 2, 18
WINTER'S RANGE, 130
WISNER, Andrew, 42
Barbara, 42
Joshua, 41
Joshua, Jr., 42
Mary, 41
Richard, 42
Samuel, 48
Sarah Jane, 42
WIVEL, Anthony, 84
Margaret, 84
WOLF, Abigal, 5
Agatha, 5
Hester A., 108

INDEX

Hollis A., 108
Laura, 108
Mary C., 108
Samuel, 108
William, 108
WOLFE, Abraham, 115
  Charles, 115
  Daniel, 115
  John, 114
  John Martin, 115
  Joseph, 115
  Margaret, 115
  Samuel, 115
  Sarah, 114, 115
  Upton F., 65
WOLFE HILL, 129
WOODROW,
  Benjamin F., 94
  George W., 94
  Granville, 94
  John D., 94
  Margaret Ellen, 94
  Mary E., 94
WOODRUFF,
  Hamilton W., 120
  Olivia, 120
WOODS, Jesse, 68
  Mary, 68
WOOLERY, Calvin, 63
  Catherine, 73
  Christiana Virginia, 63
  Elijah, 17, 48, 63, 107
  Elizabeth Frances, 63
  Ellsworth, 107
  Eveline E., 107
  George, 63
  Martha Ann, 63
  Mary Jane, 63
  Nimrod, 73
  Noah, 63
  Rachel, 48
  Sarah, 63
WORLEY, Ann, 99

Jacob, 99
Martha A., 99
William, 99
WORMS, 10
WORTH SOMETHING, 47
WORTHINGTON,
  Benjamin, 100
  Harriet A., 100
  John, 4
WRIGHT, Isaac, 115
  Mary, 115
  Nancy, 50
WYANS, James, 62, 67
  Susannah, 62, 67
WYMERT, Lovice, 31
  Peter, 31

-Y-

YEAGERLINE, John, 111
  Susannah, 111
YEAGLE, Andrew, 86
  Anna, 86
  Anna E., 86
  Caroline, 86
  George, 86
  John, 86
  Mary, 86
  Nicholas, 86
YINGLING, Adam, 66
  Catherine, 35
  Catherine Snyder, 11
  Christian, 11, 90
  Clara, 112
  David, 11
  Edward, 40
  Ellen, 50
  George, 11
  Jacob, 11, 35, 112
  John, 11, 35
  Lydia Shaffer, 11
  Magdalena, 34
  Magdalena Snyder, 11

Margaret, 66
Mary, 38, 90
Molly, 11
Polly, 11
Sarah, 40
Sarah Hinkle, 11
William H., 50
YIPER, Elizabeth, 54
YOOST, John of
  William, 31
  Rachel, 31
YORK COMPANY
  DEFENSE, 6, 12, 19, 79, 102, 131
YOUNG, Abijah, 45
  Benjamin, 45
  David, 19
  Elhanan, 45
  Elizabeth, 19
  Hardress, 45
  Henry A., 125
  Jacob, 37, 79
  John S., 45
  Manoah, 45
  Mary, 37
  Micajah, 45
  Respeah, 45
  Samuel, 45
  Thomas E., 45
YOUNGBLOOD'S
  CHOICE, 27
YOUNG'S
  PURCHASE, 59

-Z-

ZACHARIAH'S
  CONCLUSION, 119
ZEBULON'S FANCY, 81
ZECHARIAS, Conrad, 1
  Daniel, 1
  Elizabeth, 1
  George, 1

INDEX

George Daniel, 1
Jacob, 1
Mary, 1
Savilla, 1
Susan, 1
ZECHARIAS LOT, 1
ZENTZ, Abraham, 19
  Catherine, 21
  Daniel, 111
  David, 92
  Eliza, 92
  Louisa, 111
  Philip, 20, 21
  Rachel, 20, 21
ZEPP, Abdiel, 33
  Ann Maria, 33
  Anna Lee, 109
  Artimus R., 109
  Catharine, 35
  Catherine, 20, 33
  David, 33
  Elizabeth, 33
  George, 20, 25, 33
  Henry, 33
  John J., 109
  Laura F., 109
  Margaret E. V., 109
  Mary, 33
  Noah, 33
  Peter, 35
  Presley, 109
  Rebecca, 35
  Rebecca M., 77
  Solomon, 35
  William Presley, 109
ZILE, Abraham, 113
  Charles F., 113
  Conrad, 19
  Jane R., 132
  Jesse N., 132
  John T., 113
  Lewis C., 113

  Mary A. H., 113
  Molly, 19
  Penelope, 113
  Theresa Ann, 113
  William Henry, 113
ZIMMERMAN, Ann, 8
  Ann Maria, 33, 36
  Benjamin F., 33, 36
  Catherine, 13
  Elizabeth, 25
  Frederick, 13
  George, 60
  Hannah, 60
  Jacob, 8
ZOUCK, Barbary, 41
  George, 41
  Henry, 41
  John, 41

www.ingramcontent.com/pod-product-compliance
Lightning Source LLC
Chambersburg PA
CBHW050758160426
43192CB00010B/1565